Shalom Kay,
May you be blessed as you read
Tony Robinson

The Scroll of the Gospel of David

Discovering a prophecy of the death, burial and resurrection of Yeshua (Jesus) in II Samuel 15:10 – 20:2

by
Tony Robinson

Copyright © 2008 by Tony Robinson

The Scroll of the Gospel of David
Discovering a prophecy of the death, burial and resurrection
of Yeshua (Jesus) in II Samuel 15:10 – 20:2
by Tony Robinson

Printed in the United States of America

ISBN 978-1-60647-161-6

All rights reserved solely by the author. The author guarantees all contents are original and do not infringe upon the legal rights of any other person or work. No part of this book may be reproduced in any form without the permission of the author. The views expressed in this book are not necessarily those of the publisher.

Unless otherwise indicated, Bible quotations are taken from The New King James Version of the Bible. Copyright © 1982 by Thomas Nelson, Inc. Used by permission.

www.xulonpress.com

To Ginga (AKA Mom), Dad, Tina, Sean, Evan, AJ and Erica
May Adonai richly bless you and fill you with
mercy, grace, peace and wisdom

Table of Contents

Introduction		ix
1.	The Special Significance of II Samuel 15:10 – 20:2	13
2.	In the Beginning	27
3.	The Betrayal	49
4.	Beyond the Sign of the Messiah	69
5.	Death, Burial, Resurrection and Salvation!	97
6.	The Resurrection in Its Proper Chronological Position	125
7.	What Is the Good News?	145
8.	The Complete Picture	169
Endnotes		193

Introduction

Although Jews and Christians both agree in the promise of a Messiah, they are at odds concerning the authenticity of Yeshua's (Jesus') claims of being the Messiah. Both religions have well-developed Messianic theology, but their conclusions are dissimilar. Christians claim that Yeshua is the fulfillment of ancient Jewish hopes for a Messianic deliverer and the New Testament contains many references to passages in the Tanakh (Old Testament) to help bolster the belief that He fulfilled the prophetic utterances of Messianic hope. Nonetheless, Jewish thought concerning the Messiah remains at odds with the Christian belief.

Jewish expectations concerning the identity and work of the Messiah are based primarily on the Tanakh and other Jewish sources including the Talmud and other Rabbinic writings. For example, although Jewish Messianic beliefs are not monolithic, one of the most ancient and prevalent views of the Messianic hope is that there will be two Messiahs. These two Messiahs are identified as Messiah ben Joseph (son of Joseph) and Messiah ben David (son of David). It is believed that Messiah ben Joseph will come to deliver the nation of Israel from its enemies; however, he will be killed in the process. Afterward, Messiah ben David will come, triumphantly overthrow Israel's enemies, and raise Messiah ben Joseph from the dead![1] This line of thought arose because of what the sages of Israel saw as two separate streams of Messianic prophecy. They believe one stream of prophecy presents the Messiah as a suffering servant. Joseph is the Messianic figure who represents the Messiah as a suffering servant. However, they also saw a line of Messianic prophecy that represented the Messiah as a ruling, conquering king. In their minds, this stream of thought was represented by King David. Thus, having rejected Yeshua as the Messiah, many Jewish people await the coming of Messiah(s).

On the other hand, Christians believe there is one Messiah who will come two times. Based on their understanding of the Tanakh and New Testament, they believe that Yeshua appeared the first time as a suffering servant, fulfilling the prophecies of Messiah ben Joseph. His purpose was to die a horrible death on the tree in order to pay the penalty for the sins of the world and secure forgiveness and salvation to all who would believe upon Him. They also believe He will come a second time as a ruling, conquering king to overthrow His enemies and set up His rule and reign upon the earth.

In many ways the Jewish and Christian views are actually not that far apart. However, when looking at passages claimed by both groups to be Messianic in scope, differences in interpretation are numerous. For example, Christians claim that Isaiah 53 is a prophetic picture of the Messiah who would suffer and die on behalf of the nation of Israel; whereas, Jews assert that

Isaiah 53 is a prophecy of the Jewish nation suffering at the hands of a cruel, gentile-dominated world. It is understandable how both groups can come to divergent interpretations since Isaiah 53 occurs on the heels of a series of prophecies (Isaiah 40 – 53) that seem to be applicable to both the nation of Israel and the Messiah. How is one to know the proper interpretation(s) of Isaiah 53? Furthermore, how does one know for certain that Joseph's and David's lives contain Messianic themes? It seems both Jews and Christians realize that the lives of certain people in the Tanakh are to be interpreted Messianically. Yet, what is the basis for such a notion? For example, could Samson and Daniel be Messianic figures also? What about people who may not be as important as a Joseph, David, Samson or Daniel? How about the two spies sent to spy the land of Jericho – could they possibly be Messianic figures? Without some type of clear-cut methodology, it is not clear how to determine whether or not various characters in the Tanakh are Messianic figures – as a matter of point, this book will clearly prove how and why the two spies sent to Jericho are actually Messianic figures!

The subject of Messianic prophecy is particularly troublesome when Christians and anti-missionaries argue their points. Anti-missionaries are not convinced by most Christian arguments concerning Messianic prophecy. They feel that Christians simply leap-frog through the Scriptures willy-nilly, quoting passages here and there and applying them to Yeshua's life. Also, most Christians barely have any objective evidence from the Tanakh to prove that Yeshua is the Messiah *without a constant reliance upon the New Testament*. This should not be the case, especially since Yeshua Himself stated numerous times that the prophets prophesied concerning His life. He even stated that Moses prophesied of Him (John 5:39 and 46)! Even though Yeshua made these bold statements, it is unfortunate that most Christians can point to only a very limited number of passages in the Tanakh that reveal prophetic information about the Messiah. Also, if it weren't for the New Testament passages that refer back to Messianic prophecy in the Tanakh, the vast majority of Christians would be at a total loss to demonstrate from Scripture (Tanakh only) the basis for Yeshua's claims to be the Messiah. Worst, most can hardly find more than one or two Messianic passages in the books written by Moses. Nonetheless, although most people are hard pressed to show how the Tanakh teaches the gospel (the death, burial and resurrection of the Messiah), and although most Jewish people reject the notion that Yeshua is the promised Messiah, I would like to assert the following:

First, there is a plethora of easily understood evidence in the Tanakh that clearly teaches how to know for sure whether or not a passage is Messianic in scope. In fact, the evidence is so abundant that it is staggering. Secondly, the death, burial and resurrection of the Messiah in three days is *the most prophesied event* in the entirety of the Tanakh concerning the work of the Messiah! This book will clearly demonstrate the veracity of the two assertions above. Not only will you learn 1) how to know if a passage is Messianic or not and 2) how to see the numerous prophecies of the death, burial and resurrection of the Messiah, you will see how *many other events recorded in the gospels were clearly prophesied in the Tanakh*. The following is just a small sampling of events recorded in the New Testament that were foretold in the pages of the Torah, Prophets and Writings:

- Herod would kill male babies in an attempt to kill Yeshua
- Yeshua was incarcerated with two criminals
- One of the criminals executed with Yeshua would receive eternal life while the other would die in his sins

- Bread and wine would be the symbols of the body and blood of the Messiah
- Yeshua would wear a crown of thorns
- Yeshua would be hung on a tree
- Peter would outrun John to the tomb
- Judas would betray the Messiah and hang himself

Believe it or not, the first six of the events listed above are prophesied as early as the book of Genesis! These and many other prophecies concerning the mission of the Messiah will be presented along with the prophetic picture that was recorded centuries before the actual events occurred. One may be tempted to wonder how it is possible to see such events in the Tanakh. These events can only be seen when one applies what are traditionally thought of as "Jewish" interpretation techniques. The greatest sages of Israel elucidated the mysteries of the Scripture thematically. They analyzed the Scriptures by noting and organizing recurring themes. For example, they noted that the prophets of Scripture organized their narratives in thematic patterns – the most important of these being chiastic structures and parallelisms.[2] While most people view chiastic structures and parallelisms as literary techniques used to beautify the text and/or as simply a style or mode of communication, I will show that these literary devices are primarily used by the LORD to convey theology, particularly Messianic theology. Numerous chiastic structures and parallelisms will be analyzed to discover how they converge to convey Messianic theology. I purposefully does not make use of extensive footnotes from non-Biblical works because one of the secondary purposes of the book is to demonstrate how much reference information is already contained in the Bible itself! These self-contained Bible references have gone largely unnoticed because most people do not study the Scriptures thematically. The art of connecting passages that share the same words, phrases, themes, events, concepts or circumstances was used extensively by the sages of Israel to plumb the depths of the wisdom of Scripture and to elucidate problematic texts that baffled the most astute Torah commentators. It is my assertion that the numerous themes, chiastic structures and parallelisms which appear in the Bible were placed there for a reason, primarily to teach Messianic truths. Else, why go through the trouble of arranging passages so meticulously? The Scriptures are woven in a grand design with a compelling purpose – the heralding of the supreme work of the Messiah!

By utilizing a thematic approach to Scripture interpretation, the reader will be able to discover a world of Messianic prophecy that potentially has remained hidden for centuries. Instead of finding an isolated Scripture reference here and there (in the Tanakh) and then inferring that it is Messianic because it matches a New Testament reference, the thematic approach that I take will allow the reader to see how extensively Messianic theology is developed in the Tanakh. Furthermore, the thematic approach will allow the reader to see how II Samuel 15:10 – 20:2 actually presents a thematic picture of the suffering, death, burial and resurrection of the Messiah in three days that chronologically follows the gospel accounts! This discovery is a testimony to the inspiration of the Tanakh and the New Testament writings. Furthermore, it is a witness to the sovereignty of the God of Abraham, Isaac and Jacob, the One and only One who can tell the end from the beginning. It is my hope and prayer that this book will 1) open the eyes of its readers to be able to see and understand how extensively the Bible is connected by themes and literary patterns, 2) lay the foundation for understanding that the death, burial and resurrection of the Messiah in three days is the most prophesied event in the entirety of the Tanakh concerning the Messiah, 3) provide irrefutable evidence that Yeshua of Nazareth is the promised Messiah who died and was resurrected in three days and 4) be a witness to an unbelieving world of the glory and majesty of the One and only true God who created the heavens and the earth, is able to tell the end from the beginning and Who demands that all men everywhere repent and believe the gospel concerning His One and only begotten Son, Yeshua of Nazareth.

Tony Robinson

Chapter 1

The Special Significance of II Samuel 15:10 – 20:2

Introduction

During my thematic studies of the book of II Samuel, Adonai[1] opened my understanding to one of the most profound presentations of the Gospel I have ever seen. Yes, a presentation of the Gospel in II Samuel, traditionally thought of as an "historical" book! And how is it possible that a presentation of the gospel (the death, burial and resurrection of the Messiah) could be found in one of these books? Well, Yeshua[2] was very emphatic that the Gospel was clearly described in the Tanakh.[3] Note Luke's account of Yeshua's words to the two disciples traveling on the road to Emmaus:

> [27]And beginning at Moses and all the Prophets, He expounded to them *in all the Scriptures the things concerning Himself* . . . .[44]Then He said to them, "These are the words which I spoke to you while I was still with you, that *all things must be fulfilled which were written in the Law of Moses and the Prophets and the Psalms concerning Me*." [45]And He opened their understanding, that they might comprehend the Scriptures (Luke 24:27, 44-45).

In the above passage, we are told that Yeshua taught them concerning Himself from the Torah (Law of Moses), the prophets (e.g., II Samuel) and the Psalms (writings). Therefore, we can be sure that this information is indeed located in the Tanakh. Yeshua went on to state the following:

> [46]Then He said to them, "Thus it is written, and *thus it was necessary for the Christ to suffer and to rise from the dead the third day,* [47]*and that repentance and remission of sins should be preached in His* name to all nations, beginning at Jerusalem (Luke 24:46-47).

In this passage, Yeshua presented the basics of the Gospel: 1) the Messiah would suffer and die, 2) He would rise from the dead and 3) repentance and remission of sins would be preached in His name. Believe it or not, this same Gospel message can actually be found in various places throughout the Tanakh. This book will focus on one particular passage, II Samuel 15:10 through II Samuel 20:2, the story of David's flight from his rebellious son Absalom.

This book is entitled, *The Scroll of the Gospel of David,* for the following reasons: 1) I chose the phrase, "The Scroll," because as many of you are aware, books of the Tanakh were written in Hebrew on scrolls of animal skins. In other words, II Samuel 15 – 20 would have been found within the context of a larger scroll containing the entirety of II Samuel. Thus, the passage we are about to study would have been found on a scroll. 2) I chose the phrase, "of the Gospel of David," because of the four Gospel accounts that have been handed down to us (Matthew, Mark, Luke and John). Each Gospel writer penned his own version of the Good News in order that we might believe and be saved. I am endeavoring to demonstrate that II Samuel 15:10 – 20:2 contains a thematic presentation of the Gospel which chronologically follows the four "New Testament" Gospel accounts. Hence, *The Scroll of the Gospel of David.* For within this passage, we will clearly see a thematic presentation of the Gospel and one of many compelling examples of what Yeshua referred to in Luke 24:46-47.

The Importance of II Samuel 15:10 – 20:2

Why and how is II Samuel 15:10 – 20:2 relevant to a study of the Gospel? First of all, it is very unique in its literary presentation. The flow of events found in this passage is incredibly well ordered. If you have not yet done so, please, take the time to read II Samuel 15:10 – 20:2 using the following outline as a guide so that you will be better equipped to see its thematic flow.

- ♦ II Samuel 15:10-12—Absalom's rebellion
- ♦ II Samuel 15:13-37—David's escape from Jerusalem
- ♦ II Samuel 16:1-4—David's encounter with Ziba, Mephibosheth's servant
- ♦ II Samuel 16:5-14—David's encounter with Shimei
- ♦ II Samuel 16:15-23—Absalom violated David's concubines
- ♦ II Samuel 17:1-14—The advice of Ahithophel and Hushai
- ♦ II Samuel 17:15-29—David's escape across the Jordan
- ♦ II Samuel 18:1-18—The battle and Absalom's death
- ♦ II Samuel 18:19-32—David was informed of Absalom's death
- ♦ II Samuel 19:1-15—David's return across the Jordan
- ♦ II Samuel 19:16-23—David's encounter with Shimei
- ♦ II Samuel 19:24-30—David's encounter with Mephibosheth
- ♦ II Samuel 19:31-39—David's encounter with Barzillai
- ♦ II Samuel 19:40-43—The men of Judah and Israel's quarrel over David
- ♦ II Samuel 20:1-2—The rebellion of Sheba

On the surface, this outline may not look too significant. However, have you noticed that certain events seem to have been repeated? For example, the opening verses (II Samuel 15:10-12) convey the story of Absalom's rebellion against David, whereas the last couple of verses in the outline (II Samuel 20:1-2) concern a rebellion against David by a man named Sheba. Note how David encounters Shimei and someone associated with the house of Saul (Ziba, then Mephibosheth) towards the beginning (II Samuel 16:1-4 and 16:5-14) and end (II Samuel 19:16-23 and 19:24-30) of the outline above. Lastly, note how David crossed the Jordan two times: once as he fled from Jerusalem (II Samuel 17:15-29) and again when he returned (II Samuel 19:1-15). These "double takes" are the subtle clues of one of the Tanakh's most often-used and fascinating literary constructions—a chiastic structure! A chiastic structure is a literary technique wherein a story is divided into two halves and the themes of the first half of the story are repeated in the second half of the story *in reverse order*. Furthermore, the two halves of the chiastic structure "point" to the most important element of the structure, the central axis. This is illustrated in the diagram below.

      Theme1
          Theme2
              Theme3
                  Theme4
                      Central Axis
                  Theme4
              Theme3
          Theme2
      Theme1

A chiastic structure is essentially ***thematic method of organizing a narrative***. They are so extensive that you can barely read a chapter without moving into or out of one. They are literally everywhere. Some are as small as a few verses, while others span entire books! Chiastic structures represent one of the Holy One's ways of demonstrating which Scriptures have *thematic relevance* to each other. As we progress through this study, we will see many more chiastic structures and how this literary device can be used as an extraordinary hermeneutic tool. For now, let's gain some basic understanding of chiastic structures by analyzing the one hidden within II Samuel 15:10 – 20:2.

The Chiastic Structure of II Samuel 15:10 – II Samuel 20:2

A) II Samuel 15:10-12—Absalom *rebelled against the king*; "When you hear the *sound of the shofar*"; Absalom *stole the hearts of the men of Israel*; "There's *no one before the king to understand you*"

  B) II Samuel 15:13-24—The kings servants said, "Whatever my lord the king decides, *your servants are ready*"; Ittai said, "In whatever place my lord the king will be – *whether for death or life – there your servant will be*;" David and his servants *pass through the Kidron valley*

    C) II Samuel 15:32-37—Hushai *came to meet the king*; the king stated "*You will be a burden to me*"; "You will *defeat Ahithophel's council* for me; *stay behind*"

      D) II Samuel 16:1-4—Ziba *came to meet the king*; the king *asked a question about Mephibosheth*; the king *gave Mephibosheth's property to Ziba*

        E) II Samuel 16:5-13—*David came to Bahurim*; Shimei *came out to meet David*; *Abishai wanted to kill Shimei*; *David forgave Shimei*

          F) II Samuel 16:15-19—*Hushai won Absalom's trust*; "Whom shall I serve, is it not *my friend's son?*"

            G) II Samuel 16:20-23—Ahithophel *advised Absalom how to win the trust of Israel*; consort with *your father's concubines*; *pitched a tent on the roof for Absalom*

              H) II Samuel 17:1-14—Ahithophel wanted to *chase after David*; Ahithophel stated, "The people will be at *peace*"; Ahithophel really *desired to kill David*; Absalom had to *choose between which two people* he would send against David; *Ahithophel*, who suggested that he kill David *was rejected*; Hushai stated "And if he is brought *into a city*"

                I) II Samuel 17:18-19—Jonathan and Ahimaaz *descend into a well*; a woman *spread a curtain over the well*

                  J) II Samuel 17:23—*Ahithophel's suicide by hanging*

                    K) II Samuel 17:24-25—Absalom *appointed Amasa* over his army in place of Joab; *David's position in Mahanaim*

                      L) II Samuel 17:27-29—Three men brought David and his servants all sorts of provisions because they were hungry, exhausted and thirsty in the desert

                    K`) II Samuel 18:1-5—David *appointed officers* and divided his camp into thirds; *David's position near the city gate*

                  J`) II Samuel 18:9-15—Absalom *hanging in the elm tree*; David's servant refusing to accept bribery of silver; *Absalom's death*

                I`) II Samuel 18:17—Joab's men throw *Absalom's body into a large pit* and erected a *mound of stones over him*

              H`) II Samuel 18:19-32—Ahimaaz wanted to *run to David*; Ahimaaz called out to the king "*Peace!*"; Ahimaaz really *desired to bring David news*; Joab *chose between sending two people to David*; *Ahimaaz*, who suggested that he carry the message *was rejected*; David was sitting *between the two gates of the city*

G`) II Samuel 19:5-11—Joab *advised David how to win the trust of his servants*; "Save the lives of *your concubines*"; David *sat at the city gate*

F`) II Samuel 19:12-15—*David won the hearts of the men of Judah*; "You are bone of my bone and flesh of my flesh"

E`) II Samuel 19:16-23—*Shimei was from Bahurim*; he *hastened to meet the king*; *Abishai wanted to kill Shimei*; Shimei *begged David for forgiveness*

D`) II Samuel 19:24-30—Mephibosheth *came to meet the king*; the king *asked Mephibosheth a question*; *Mephibosheth and Ziba must divide the property*

C`) II Samuel 19:31-39—Barzillai *came to meet the king*; "*I will be a burden to you*"; Barzillai states that he has no discernment; Let me *stay back*

B`) II Samuel 19:40-43—The men of Israel and Judah argue over who is *more loyal to the king*; David and his servants *pass over the Jordan*

A`) II Samuel 20:1-2—*Sheba rebelled against the king*; he *sounded the shofars*; the men of *Israel followed Sheba*; "*we have no part in David*"

Chiastic structures are extremely valuable because they teach numerous thematic lessons that sometimes are not readily apparent. The important words in each point of the structure are in bold and italicized print so you can easily see how they are thematically connected. Chiastic structures are analyzed by comparing and contrasting the points that are thematically related in the opposite sides of the structure (compare A to A`, B to B`, etc.). Please take the time to study it so that you can appreciate its beauty. As you can see, II Samuel 15:10 - 20:2 was deliberately written so that the themes in the first half of the story were repeated in the second half of the story in reverse order. Isn't it amazing? Note the central axis, point L, where three of David's friends brought food and provisions for him and his servants. The central axis is always a focal point of a chiastic structure; however, it usually functions in one of two ways:

- Sometimes, the central axis is the most important point in the chiastic structure. In other words, when the Holy One wants to make something stand out and grab your attention He may accomplish this by making it the central axis of a chiastic structure. This is His way of saying, "Hey! This is a very important piece of information!"

- Other times, it functions as the turning point or point of contrast between the two halves of the chiastic structure. When the central axis functions in this manner, you will usually see contrasts between elements in the two halves of the story. Or, the events that occur in the second half of the story are in reverse of the direction of events that occurred in the first half. This is the case here. Before the central axis, David is on the run, fleeing for his life. Immediately after the central axis, David, seemingly strengthened and encouraged from the provisions of his three friends, began to formulate a battle plan and then went on to defeat his enemy.

This chiastic structure is truly a work of art. Only Adonai could have inspired such beauty. How blessed are our eyes to be able to behold His wisdom in action! Personally, I think chiastic structures are one of the highest forms of prophecy. Why? It's one thing for a person to tell a story and make the themes of the first half match the themes in the second half in reverse order. However, we must remember that these stories are not fanciful make-believe, made up in the minds of the authors. These are real events that happened to real people! It's one thing to tell a story in a thematic pattern equivalent to a chiastic structure. It's quite another to be able to orchestrate this within the context of real people and actual events. Only an all-wise, all-knowing, Almighty God could do such things!

At its most literal level, this story is simply the account of how David successfully thwarted an attempted coup by his own son. However, is that the only significance of this story? David is one of the many people the Tanakh uses to teach about the mission and ministry of Messiah Yeshua. Judaism teaches that both David and Joseph are Messianic figures. They know that when one studies the events in the lives of David and Joseph that one is actually learning about the promised Messiah. How do they know this? There are many reasons why; however, I'd like to share with you how Adonai taught me to recognize Messianic prophecy. There is more behind the story of II Samuel 15:10 – 20:2 than just a failed coup attempt. But before we uncover this hidden message, let us prove that David truly is a Messianic figure.

The Sign of the Messiah

The primary purpose of the Tanakh is to reveal the Messiah. We have already seen how Yeshua taught the two disciples on the road to Emmaus concerning Himself from the Tanakh. Now let's view other scriptures which verify that the Tanakh is all about the Messiah.

*[46]For if you believed Moses, you would believe Me; for **he wrote about Me** (John 5:46).*

*[39]You search the Scriptures, for in them you think you have eternal life; **and these are they which testify of Me** (John 5:39).*

In these statements, Yeshua boldly stated that the Torah of Moses was written to inform us about Him! His statement is consistent with Psalm 40, which states that the Scriptures are written about the Messiah.

*[6]Sacrifice and offering You did not desire; My ears You have opened. Burnt offering and sin offering You did not require. [7]Then I said, "Behold, I come; **In the scroll of the book it is written of me**. [8]I delight to do Your will, O my God, And Your law is within my heart (Psalm 40:6-8)."*

What source did the New Covenant writers use for the gospel?

*[1] Paul, a bondservant of Jesus Christ, called to be an apostle, separated **to the gospel of God** [2]**which He promised before through His prophets in the Holy Scriptures**... (Romans 1:1-2)*

*[1] Therefore, since a promise remains of entering His rest, let us fear lest any of you seem to have come short of it. [2]For indeed **the gospel was preached to us as well as to***

them; but the word which they heard did not profit them, not being mixed with faith in those who heard it (Hebrews 4:1-2).

There are many more Scriptures that clearly show we should believe Yeshua is the Messiah, not because of the testimony of the New Covenant Scriptures, but because the Torah, Prophets and Writings tell us so! The New Covenant Scriptures are essentially a commentary *confirming* the message of the Torah, Prophets and Writings! It is wrong to think that they establish Messianic truth.

We know the Tanakh teaches about the Messiah, but how? Our most important clue comes from something Yeshua stated in Matthew 12:38-40.

Matthew 12:38-40—Then some of the scribes and Pharisees answered, saying, "Teacher, *we want to see a sign from You.*" But He answered and said to them, "An evil and adulterous generation seeks after *a <u>sign</u>*, and *no <u>sign</u> will be given to it except the sign of the prophet Jonah. For as Jonah was three days and three nights in the belly of the great fish, so will the Son of Man be three days and three nights in the heart of the earth.*"

Note how Yeshua connected His death, burial and resurrection with the story of Jonah and the big fish! In other words, Yeshua stated that the story of Jonah was actually the story of His resurrection. How so? What should have happened to Jonah when he was swallowed by the big fish? Obviously, he should have died. But instead of dying, he came forth alive in three days. The significance? It's a picture of death, burial and resurrection. Please note the following thematic connections between the events in Jonah's life and Messiah Yeshua's life.

Events in Jonah's Life	*Messianic Significance*
Jonah was swallowed by a large fish	A picture of death
Jonah was in the fish's belly for three days	A picture of burial in the earth for three days
Jonah was spewed forth from the fish's belly	A picture of resurrection

Remember, Yeshua stated the story of Jonah was a sign. A sign is a marker telling you, "Here is what you're looking for." In other words, the story of Jonah and the big fish is a sign telling us, "Look in this story for a picture of the work of the Messiah." So, what is the sign of Jonah? It's the sign of resurrection! Now here's what's most exciting—this sign is not unique to Jonah! The sign of resurrection is found in the life of every Messianic figure in the Tanakh. There are many people who were confronted with death, their lives were then spared, and the number three is visible. This thematic formula (life, death and the number three) is a sign indicating when a passage has Messianic significance. The number three is important because it is the number of resurrection.

From Yeshua's own words we learn that His resurrection from the dead is the *sign* that verifies He is the promised Messiah. Note that it is His *resurrection* that brings together the powerful themes of *Life and Death*! I submit to you that it is this theme of *The Resurrection* that is the *sign* of the Messiah also given throughout the Tanakh! If we want to see the Messiah in the Tanakh, we need to look for the theme of *Life from the Dead, or Resurrection*!

As you read the Tanakh, anytime you see 1) pictures of *resurrection* or 2) pictures of renewed *life* as a result of deliverance from impending *death*, the Tanakh is about to present a teaching concerning the Messiah. I call these themes, *The Resurrection and the Life,* and they are especially strengthened when coupled in some manner with the number *three* (3, 30, 300, 3000, etc.). Coupled together, the theme of *Resurrection* and the *Number Three* constitute *The Sign of the Messiah*!

Although I could give multiple examples, please note how the following passages present veiled Messianic teachings.

- The first LIVING things (plants, grass, etc.) were created on day THREE! This is not strictly life from the dead; however, the principle of life coming from a state where there is no life is clear.
- The Torah's picture of the RESURRECTION of the Messiah is found in the Holy Days. The Holy Day that is a shadow of Yeshua's RESURRECTION is the THIRD Holy Day, the Early First Fruits (the Day of the Omer Wave Offering found in Leviticus 23)! The offering of the barley sheaves on the day after the Sabbath that occurs during the week of unleavened bread is a prophetic picture of the resurrection of the Messiah.
- Jonah, who was in the belly of a great fish, should have been dead. But on the THIRD day he came forth ALIVE! Truly, death was swallowed up in victory![4]
- The Akeida (binding of Isaac) found in Genesis 22—Abraham was supposed to offer Isaac as an olah (whole burnt offering). Although Adonai prevented him from actually sacrificing Isaac on the THIRD day, the manner in which the Torah relates the story hints that Isaac died and was RESURRECTED. That's why Hebrews 11:17-19 records that Abraham received Isaac from the dead through RESURRECTION figuratively!

Most of you are probably already familiar with Joseph and Moses as pictures or types of the Messiah. Let's look at the Sign of the Messiah in their lives and the life of David to see what we can learn from them. How do we know for sure that Joseph and Moses were types of the Messiah? We can see the Sign of the Messiah (i.e., the sign of resurrection) in their lives.

The Sign of the Messiah in Moses' Life

Am Yisrael (the people of Israel) were proliferating abundantly in the land of Egypt before the birth of Moses. Their birth rate was so fast that Pharaoh decreed every male baby was to be thrown into the Nile River (Exodus 1:22 - 2:10). Therefore, when Moses was born *he should have been thrown into the Nile River to his death*. However, his mother, seeing something special about him, hid him for *three* months. After she could no longer hide him, she put him into a basket and set him afloat in the Nile River; whereupon Pharaoh's daughter drew him forth, thus *saving his life*. This story is the Sign of the Messiah in Moses' life because it has the theme of resurrection.

Events in Moses' Life	Messianic Significance
Moses was supposed to be thrown into the Nile River at his birth	A picture of death
Moses' mother put him in a basket and set him afloat in the Nile River after three months	A picture of burial in the earth for three days
Pharaoh's daughter drew Moses from the Nile River	A picture of resurrection

Notice that when Moses' mother threw him into the Nile she was completing the picture of his death, because she put him where Pharaoh said male babies were supposed to be placed for their death – in the Nile River! Her placement of Moses in the basket in the Nile River is a powerful allusion to his death and burial. By taking Moses out of the river, the daughter of Pharaoh "resurrected" him, because he surely would have died were it not for her deliverance.

Thus, the Torah has painted a picture of a child, Moses, who was supposed to *die*. His mother hid him for **THREE** months, then she obeyed Pharaoh's command by casting him into the water (in the basket). But Pharaoh's *death* sentence was cancelled when his daughter took Moses out of the river, and he was given **LIFE**! This is the Sign of the Messiah – The Sign of Resurrection! Whenever you chance upon the sign of the Messiah as you read the scriptures, three things will be evident.

- ♦ The Sign of the Messiah is a sign. Just like a hotel sign alerts you to the fact that you have found your hotel, likewise, a story that conveys the Sign of the Messiah alerts you that the passage contains Messianic prophecy. In other words, pay attention because Messianic prophecy is at hand.
- ♦ Secondly, whenever you see the Sign of the Messiah in a passage, it is a veiled prophecy of the death, burial and resurrection of the Messiah. For example, the story at hand concerning the circumstances of Moses' birth contains all of the thematic elements of Yeshua's death, burial and resurrection in three days. Thus, the death, burial and resurrection of Yeshua in three days is the most prophesied event concerning the Messiah in the entirety of the Tanakh!
- ♦ Lastly, when you happen upon the Sign of the Messiah it means that the story you are reading has Messianic significance. In other words, as you read the story, you can be assured that it will contain information about the life, work, and ministry of Messiah Yeshua.

Now that we know the story of Moses' birth is 1) a sign alerting us to Messianic prophecy, and 2) a veiled prophecy of Yeshua's death, burial and resurrection in three days, let's go on to see what it can teach us about the life, work and ministry of Yeshua. This story teaches us a couple of things. It teaches us about the death, burial and resurrection of the Messiah and that

Moses' life will be a shadow of the Messiah. How so? Well, since this story is about the birth of Moses, we should first guess that perhaps it is teaching us about the birth of the Messiah. And that's exactly the point. This story in the book of Exodus is the story about the birth of Am Yisrael's future deliverer! Now think of the events surrounding the birth of Moses, the deliverer of Israel, and Yeshua, the deliverer of mankind. Do you see any connections? Yes! At the time of Moses' birth, the enemy of Am Yisrael tried to destroy him by killing all male babies. Now, fast forward to the birth of the Messiah. After His birth, wise men from the East came to worship him. In Jerusalem, they inquired about the birth place of the King of the Jews (Messiah), whereupon the scribes stated that He would be born in Bethlehem of Judea (Matthew 2:1-18). King Herod asked the wise men to report back to him concerning the location of the Messiah's birth place so that he, too, could worship Him. However, this was simply a ploy by Herod to discover the Messiah so that he could kill him. After worshipping the child, the wise men were warned in a dream not to return to Herod. Herod, realizing that he had been tricked, slew all of the male children within Bethlehem and its environment who were two years old and younger.

Could the prophecy be any clearer? The story of the circumstances of Moses' birth was actually a veiled prophecy of the circumstances surrounding Yeshua's birth! The death of male children at the birth of Moses was actually a prophetic picture of future events, specifically that male children would be innocently killed in association with the birth of the Messiah. Yes, the death of male children in Bethlehem was actually a sign and a fulfillment of prophecy given in the Torah! And how were we supposed to figure out that the story of Moses' birth was actually the story of the Messiah's birth? There is only one way. We must understand the Sign of the Messiah, i.e., the sign of resurrection. Once we see the sign of resurrection in the life of a character in the Tanakh, we know for sure that his life will teach us about the Messiah. Let's discover this sign in the life of Joseph.

The Sign of the Messiah in Joseph's Life

While in jail (Genesis 40), Joseph interpreted the dreams of two of Pharaoh's servants, the chief baker and butler. In Joseph's interpretation of the dream, one of them was promised *life* in *three days*, while the other was promised *death* in *three days*. Although more primitive in form, this is the sign of the Messiah, the sign of resurrection, because it incorporates the themes of life, death and the number three. At this point, let me add that there are many nuances and twists concerning the basic teaching on the Sign of the Messiah. For example, sometimes the Sign of the Messiah doesn't occur in the life of the primary Messianic figure (Joseph, in this example). Sometimes the Sign of the Messiah occurs in the life/lives of someone/people intimately associated with the Messianic figure (the cupbearer and the baker). These nuances represent different permutations of the foundation teaching on the Sign of the Messiah. At this point, I realize that these nuances may be a little confusing. However, as you continue through the book I will cover these issues in more details with pertinent examples. For now, if you think the Sign of the Messiah should exclusively occur in the life of the primary Messianic figure or if you aren't convinced that the Sign of the Messiah can occur in the lives of others associated with the Messianic figure, then note the following amazing parallels between the lives of the baker and cupbearer and Yeshua's life!

Events Associated With Joseph's Life	Messianic Significance
The cupbearer and baker both had *exalted positions* in the very presence of Pharaoh	Yeshua was highly *exalted at the right hand* of the Father
This is a story about Joseph's *incarceration with two other "criminals"*	The gospels tell of how Yeshua was *incarcerated with two criminals*
One of the those incarcerated with Joseph received *life* and the other received *death*	One of the thieves incarcerated with Yeshua received *eternal life,* while the other *died in his sins*
The cupbearer retained his *life in three days*, whereas the baker *died*	Yeshua was raised to *life from the dead in three days*
The baker was killed by being *hanged on a tree*	Yeshua was killed by being *hanged on a tree*
The cupbearer mainly bears *wine*. The baker primarily bakes *bread*	*Bread* and *wine* are the Passover emblems of the Messiah's death
Joseph asked the cupbearer to *"remember him"* when he went before Pharaoh	The criminal asked Yeshua to *"remember"* him when He came into His kingdom
As a result of his exaltation, the cupbearer was *restored to his original position* of glory in Pharaoh's presence	As a result of his exaltation, Yeshua was *restored to his original position* of glory in the Father's presence
In the symbolism of his death, the baker had a *basket (vegetation) upon his head*	When Yeshua was executed He had a *crown of thorns (vegetation) upon His head*

As you can see, we have hit the nail on the head! What a goldmine of treasures the story of Joseph's incarceration has been! Once again, all we've done is noted the powerful themes of life, death and the number three. Truly, it is the Sign of the Messiah, or the sign of resurrection, which points us to Messianic prophecy in the making.

There was one slight difference between the stories of Moses and Joseph. In the case of Moses, the sign of the Messiah occurred *in the life of the Messianic figure (Moses)*. In the case of Joseph, the sign of the Messiah occurred *in the lives of those closely associated with the Messianic figure (the cupbearer and the baker)*. As you can see, it was the baker's life who actually provided us with a prophecy of the Messiah's death via hanging on a tree! Remember this. As I stated earlier, sometimes the Sign of the Messiah occurs in the life of someone associated with the Messianic figure instead of the Messianic figure himself. Also, sometimes the Messianic figure will actually be more than one person. It's the nature of Messianic prophecy.

Thus, whenever we see the sign of resurrection, we should pay attention, knowing that Messianic prophecy is at hand. Furthermore, we now know that the sign of the Messiah may be found in the life of the Messianic figure or in the life of someone closely associated with him. With this as a foundation, let us now go on to see the sign of the Messiah in David's life.

The Sign of the Messiah in David's Life

I Samuel 30:1-31 is an account of how David and his men rescued their families and possessions from the Amalekites who had stolen them while David and his men were away with the Philistines. As David and his men pursued the Amalekites, they came upon an Egyptian youth in the field (I Samuel 30:11-13).

> And they found an Egyptian in the field, and brought him to David, and gave him bread, and he did eat; and they made him drink water; And they gave him a piece of a cake of figs, and two clusters of raisins: and when he had eaten, *his spirit came again to him: for he had eaten no bread, nor drunk any water, three days and three nights.* And David said unto him, To whom belongest thou? and whence art thou? And he said, I am a young man of Egypt, servant to an Amalekite; and my master left me, because three days ago I fell sick (I Samuel 30:11-13, KJV).

What is the significance of these verses? Did you get it? These two verses contain the Sign of the Messiah! Notice the phrase *three days and three nights*. Does it sound familiar? It should. The Messiah was dead for three days and three nights in the grave before His resurrection. This picture is painted by the story of the Egyptian youth who had neither bread nor water for three days and three nights. Anyone can live on bread and water. By stating that the Egyptian hadn't eaten bread nor drank water for *three days and three nights* the Tanakh is hinting at death. It's painting a picture of the death of the Egyptian youth. Also, note the wording of verse twelve where it states, "his spirit came again to him." Now I know that the Egyptian didn't actually die; however, the passage is written in such a manner as to hint at his "death." Therefore, let's follow through on the picture of death painted by the wording. In order for his *spirit to come to him again*, it had to have left him. What has happened if your spirit has left you? You have died! Note what event occurred when the breath/spirit of God entered the two witnesses of the book of Revelation:

> ¹¹Now after the three-and-a-half days the breath (spirit) of life from God entered them, and they stood on their feet, and great fear fell on those who saw them (Revelation 11:11).

When the breath/spirit entered them, they rose from the dead! This is the picture being painted of the Egyptian youth when it states that his spirit came to him again. It's painting a picture of his resurrection!

Events Associated With David's Life	Messianic Significance
The Egyptian had neither bread nor water for three days	A picture of death
His spirit came again to him	A picture of resurrection

Once again, we have discovered the Sign of the Messiah in the life of someone associated with the Messianic figure. Furthermore, this story is clearly another allusion to the death, burial and resurrection of the Messiah! Think of this folks. If it's true that the gospel is the death, burial and resurrection of the Messiah in three days, then shouldn't it be the focal point of prophecy concerning the Messiah? If it's true that salvation for mankind is only possible because of the awesome act of self-sacrifice exhibited by Yeshua our Messiah, then shouldn't prophecies of that act be predominant in the Tanakh? The death, burial and resurrection of the Messiah is the most prophesied event concerning the Messiah in all the Tanakh! Adonai has not left us guessing about the primary work of the Messiah. It fills the pages of the Tanakh and this book will introduce you to a few of these prophecies.

Now that we have seen the Sign of the Messiah in David's life, we can rest assured that his life will teach us about the work of the Messiah. This story in I Samuel 30:1-31 is the proof we needed to understand this fact.

In Summary

This chapter has shown us the following things:

- ◆ The purpose of the Tanakh is to inform us about the person and ministry of the Messiah.
- ◆ II Samuel 15:10 – 20:2 was written as a chiastic structure, a very highly organized literary technique used by the Holy One to thematically organize narratives found in the Tanakh.
- ◆ The Sign of the Messiah is a teaching/understanding that helps us understand when a person's life will teach us about the person and ministry of the Messiah. Whenever we see a person who should have died, but lives, and the number three (3, 30, 300, 3,000 etc.), we know beyond a shadow of a doubt we are into Messianic prophecy.
- ◆ David has the Sign of the Messiah in his life and is therefore a Messianic figure.
- ◆ As we progress through our study of II Samuel 15:10 – 20:2, we should do so with the understanding that David is a Messianic figure, and that some events in his life are Messianic in significance.

In the next chapter, we will begin to analyze II Samuel 15:10 – 20:2 with the understanding that David is a Messianic figure and that the events in his life will teach us about the Messiah.

Chapter 2

In the Beginning

Introduction

In the first chapter, I stated that the story of Absalom's rebellion began in II Samuel 15:1-9. But why did he rebel against his father? I believe the event that catalyzed Absalom's rebellion was the rape of his sister Tamar by their half brother Amnon (II Samuel 13 - 14). There is ample thematic evidence to support such a notion. Before looking at that evidence, let's review a brief summary of events leading up to Absalom's rebellion.

After Amnon raped his half-sister Tamar, Absalom had him murdered and fled to Geshur for three years. Initially, David mourned daily for Amnon. However, after time, he was comforted over his loss and began to long for Absalom's return. Joab, the commander of David's army, noticed that the king wanted to be reconciled with his son Absalom, so he asked a wise woman from Tekoa to go before the king and tell him a fabricated story of how one of her sons had killed his brother and how the family wanted her to deliver the son to them so they could avenge his brother's death by killing him. She also told David she was a widow and that the remaining son was the only heir to her husband. Therefore, if he was to be killed, her husband's name would perish in the earth. Joab did this hoping that David would render a judgment in favor of the son who had murdered his brother. This would then pave the way for Absalom to be forgiven and restored to King David. The ploy worked. After David judged in favor of the son who had murdered his brother, the woman revealed her true intentions to him and he had Joab return Absalom to Jerusalem under the stipulation that Absalom could not see his face. Absalom grew impatient after living in Jerusalem for two years without being able to see the king's face, but was eventually restored to good favor with David through the intercession of Joab. Now let's see what we can glean from a closer look at II Samuel 13 – 14. First we will examine II Samuel 13, the story of Amnon's rape of Tamar, then II Samuel 14, the story of the wise woman who pleaded to David to have her son protected. Remember, our goal is to prove that Amnon's rape of Tamar catalyzed events leading to Absalom's rebellion.

Amnon's Rape of Tamar (II Samuel 13:1-39)

Read II Samuel 13:1-6. As you read, pay particular attention to verses two to three. Does this passage sound familiar? Have you read another passage in Scripture that is similar to this one? It should remind you of hasatan (Satan) in the garden. Please notice the following thematic connections between II Samuel 13:3-4a and Genesis 3:1.

- In both passages, someone is referred to as subtle, crafty or cunning.
- In both passages, after the Scripture notes that someone is subtle, the subtle one goes on to tempt someone else by asking a question.
  - Genesis 3:1 — Now *the serpent was more cunning* than any beast of the field which the LORD God had made. And he said to the woman, "*Has God indeed said, 'You shall not eat of every tree of the garden'?*"
  - II Samuel 13:3-4a — But Amnon had a friend whose name was Jonadab the son of Shimeah, David's brother. Now *Jonadab was a very crafty man*.[4] And he said to him, "*Why are you, the king's son, becoming thinner day after day? Will you not tell me?*"

We have just made what I call a thematic connection – two passages that share the same words, themes, circumstances, etc. Personally, I believe Adonai has arranged His eternal, holy words thematically. Hopefully, as we progress through this study, you also will realize this truth. It's a very important concept to grasp. In fact, I can boldly state that making thematic connections is perhaps the fundamental tool Adonai has given to help us interpret His words. Have you noticed how often the Scriptures present a story in seemingly less detail than you desire? How often have you read a passage and then thought, "I have more questions about this passage than when I began reading it?" Although this happens often, it's by design! Adonai is only interested in sharing His wisdom with those who will submit to His way of thinking and His program of understanding. Instead of putting all of the information you need to interpret a passage in one place, He has dispersed relevant information throughout the Scriptures and you can only gain access to that extra information by making thematic connections as we have in the present example of Amnon and the serpent. At first glance, this first connection may not seem so important. However, whenever you make one thematic connection between two passages you should always look for others. In those cases where you find multiple thematic connections, you can rest assured that Adonai planned their occurrence. If you're not convinced that our thematic connection between Genesis 3:1 and II Samuel 13:3-4a is significant, then please note the many other ways these two passages are thematically connected!

- Genesis 2:16-17 states that the Tree of the Knowledge of Good and Evil was forbidden fruit for Adam and Chavah (Eve). II Samuel 13:2b states "It was improper for Amnon to do anything to her (Tamar)." Thus, Tamar was "forbidden fruit" for Amnon!
- In Genesis 3:6, Chavah gave Adam food (presumably from her hand). In II Samuel 13:5b, 6b and 10a, note how often the phrase, "Eat from her hand," appears!
- In Genesis 3:7-8, Adam and Chavah sewed fig leaves to cover themselves and hid from Adonai because they were ashamed of their naked bodies. In II Samuel 13:13, Tamar stated "Where can I take my shame?"

- After Adam and Chavah sinned, the Scripture mentions Chavah's clothes (covering) twice. II Samuel 13:18-19 mentions Tamar's robe of many colors!
- After Adam and Chavah sinned, Adonai came and asked a question designed to tell Him why they were so distraught (Genesis 3:11). When Absalom saw Tamar weeping bitterly, he asked her if she had been with Amnon (II Samuel 13:20)!
- After sinning, Chavah was banished from the garden. Furthermore, an angel was posted to prevent her from returning to the Tree of Life. In II Samuel 13:17-18, Amnon had his servant put Tamar out of his house. He then bolted the door so she could not return.

There is still another connection we can make between Genesis 3 and II Samuel 13. After Absalom had Amnon murdered, a rumor was told David that <u>all</u> his sons had been murdered. Jonadab appeared on the scene and told David that the rumor wasn't true, that only Amnon had been killed. In other words, Jonadab was telling David that *he hadn't been told the entire truth, only part of the truth.* Well, in Genesis 3:4-5, that's exactly how hasatan convinced Chavah to eat the forbidden fruit! Essentially, he convinced her that Adonai had not told her the whole truth about the trees – that she could in fact eat from the Tree of the Knowledge of Good and Evil without dying.

By now it should be very obvious that these two passages are *thematically connected.* As I stated earlier, Adonai is the One Who inspired these connections. When you study thematically, your first job is to make thematic connections. Next, you need to discover the reason why Adonai intended for you to make these connections. Usually, there is information in one of the thematically connected passages that will help shed light on the other. In other words, if two passages, A and B, are thematically connected, then usually there is information in one – let's say A –that is not in passage B. Furthermore, by making the thematic connection between A and B we will be able to better interpret B in light of the information gained from passage A. In the case at hand, let us consider what has been connected. Clearly Jonadab has been thematically connected to the serpent! He is doing everything the serpent did in Genesis 3. Therefore, the Holy One wants us to connect Jonadab to the serpent. But why? Well, what was really happening with the serpent in Genesis 3? The serpent was simply an agent of hasatan. Hasatan entered the serpent and tempted Chavah in order to get her to sin. So likewise, by connecting Jonadab to the serpent, the Holy One intends for us to see that just as hasatan had entered the serpent to tempt Chavah into sin, so likewise, hasatan entered Jonadab in order that he tempt Amnon into sinning against Tamar! This extra piece of information (the satanically inspired temptation of Amnon) was not readily evident until we were able to connect Jonadab to the serpent. We can be assured that this was Adonai's intent because of all of the incredibly "coincidental" similarities (thematic connections) between these two passages. Thus, the story of Amnon's rape of Tamar takes on a new dimension that was not readily evident when reading it apart from the story of Chavah's temptation.

This is a beautiful example of how to make thematic connections and understand why they exist. The Scriptures are laden with thematic connections. Each one has been given to help you connect people, places and events so that you can gain extra information to help you more fully interpret one of the thematically connected passages. Apart from the clear thematic connections between events in II Samuel 13 and Genesis 3, we would never have known *hasatan was working through Jonadab* to tempt Amnon. However, the thematic connections have clearly shown this to be the case. For now, the main point I want you to remember is that *Amnon's rape of Tamar was satanically inspired.*

Thematic Reinforcements

Believe it or not, II Samuel 13 is also thematically connected to another passage! How is the fact that Amnon had relations with his half sister (a forbidden sexual union) thematically connected to another event in II Samuel? This is thematically connected to David's sin with Bathsheba (another forbidden sexual union since she was married to another man). II Samuel 11 – 12 records the events surrounding David's sin with Bathsheba. His sin is thematically connected to Amnon's because 1) both of them allowed themselves to be tempted by a beautiful woman, 2) they both gave in to the temptation, and 3) they both sinned by having relations with the woman they desired. As I stated earlier, whenever you see one connection between two passages you should endeavor to uncover more. It turns out that there are many connections between II Samuel 11 – 12 (the story of David's sin with Bathsheba) and II Samuel 13 – 14 (the story of Amnon's sin with Tamar). In order to help you see them, I will present a side by side comparison of these chapters. And, just for the fun of it, I'll include Genesis 3-4 also.[5]

Genesis 3 – 4	*II Samuel 11 – 12*	*II Samuel 13 - 14*
Genesis 3:1-5—Chavah was *tempted* to sin by eating the forbidden fruit	II Samuel 11:1-2—David was *tempted* when he saw Bathsheba bathing	II Samuel 13:1-5—Amnon was *tempted* to sin by desiring Tamar
Genesis 3:6-7—Adam and Chavah *sinned*	II Samuel 11:3-5—David *sinned*	II Samuel 13:6-14—Amnon *sinned*
Genesis 3:8-19—Adonai *pronounced judgment* on Adam & Chavah	II Samuel 12:11-23—Adonai *pronounced judgment* on David[6]	II Samuel 13:32-33—Absalom *issued Amnon's death sentence* after the rape
Genesis 3:22-24—Chavah was *banished* from the garden; an angel posted to *prevent re-entry*	II Samuel 12:15-23—David is *separated* from his son because Adonai took the child[7]	II Samuel 13:15-18—Tamar was *banished* from Amnon's house; servant locked the door to *prevent re-entry*
Genesis 4:1-8—Cain *slew* Abel (brothers)	II Samuel 11:14-25—David has Uriah *murdered*	II Samuel 13:23-36—Absalom has Amnon *murdered* (brothers)[8]
Genesis 4:9-15—Cain is *driven (banished)* from the earth's produce		II Samuel 13:37—Absalom is *banished* from King David's presence

As you can see, our initial connection of Amnon's sin with David's sin was right on the mark! Adonai definitely wants us to see that these two stories are thematically connected. But there is one other connection that I haven't mentioned yet, the icing on the cake, so to speak.

More Chiastic Revelations

While reading II Samuel 14, the story of the woman sent to David by Joab to secure forgiveness for Absalom, I noted that the story contained a chiastic structure. It appears below:

A) II Samuel 13:37-14:1—*Absalom fled*, he went to Geshur; Joab <u>perceived</u> *that David's heart was set on Absalom*
  B) II Samuel 14:1-4—Joab sent to Tekoa and brought *a wise woman* from there; and Joab *put the words into her mouth*; she *fell on her face to the ground and prostrated herself*
    C) II Samuel 14:5-7—David said, "*What* problem do you have?;" the *woman related her story*
      D) II Samuel 14:8—David *issued a command concerning the woman*
        E) II Samuel 14:11a—"Please let the king remember the LORD your God, and *do not permit the avenger of blood to destroy anymore*, lest they destroy my son."
          F) II Samuel 14:11b—"*Not one hair of your son shall fall to the ground*"
            G) II Samuel 14:13—"Why then have you schemed such a thing against the people of God? *For the king speaks this thing as one who is guilty, in that the king does not bring his banished one (Absalom) home again.*"
          F') II Samuel 14:14—For *we will surely die* and become *like water spilled on the ground*, which *cannot be gathered up again*
        E') II Samuel 14:16—For the king will hear and *deliver his maidservant from the hand of the man who would destroy me and my son* together
      D') II Samuel 14:17—The woman *refers to David's command concerning her*
    C') II Samuel 14:18-19a—David said, "*Is* Joab's hand with you in all this?;" the *woman related the ploy*
  B') II Samuel 14:19b-22—and he *put all these words into the mouth* of your maidservant; my lord is *wise like the wisdom* of an angel of God; Joab then *fell upon his face to the ground, and he prostrated himself*
A') II Samuel 14:22-23—go and *bring back the lad*, Absalom; "Today your *servant (Joab)* <u>realizes</u> *I have found favor in your eyes*"

Although this chiastic structure has a few things to teach us, let's just concentrate on the central axis. Do you understand the significance of what's being said here? The wise woman from Tekoa is pointing the finger at David! Basically, she's stating, "Look, everything I've said about my son was just a ploy to get you to see that I'm actually talking about you and how you've treated Absalom." It wasn't until I saw the central axis that I made the following connection. After David sinned with Bathsheba, Adonai sent Nathan the prophet to him with a story about a rich man who had taken a poor man's only ewe and sacrificed it for a friend. After David pronounced judgment on the rich man, Nathan pointed the finger at David and essentially said, "The rich man is actually you!" This is what has happened in our central axis! Just as Nathan the prophet pointed the finger at David, so likewise, this woman is pointing the finger at David. The connections look like this:

- After David had Uriah killed, Adonai sent Nathan the prophet to David with a story about a poor man and his ewe. After Absalom had Amnon killed, Joab sent the wise woman from Tekoa to David with a story about a son who had killed his brother.
- Both Nathan and the woman told David a fabricated story in order to see what David's judgment on the matter would be.
- After David rendered his judgments concerning the stories of Nathan and the woman, they both turned the tables on David and accused him of being the guilty party in their stories.

Now isn't that an awesome manner that Adonai has chosen to help us see the connection between these two stories? Could He have possibly been more obvious? After seeing the connections above, shouldn't we know beyond a shadow of doubt that the stories of II Samuel 11-12 (David's sins and Nathan's accusation) and II Samuel 13-14 (Amnon's sin and the woman's accusation of David) are thematically connected! So what have we discovered? We've discovered that just as Amnon's rape of Tamar (II Samuel 13) was thematically connected to David's sin with Bathsheba, so likewise, the story of the woman confronting David (II Samuel 14) is thematically connected to Nathan confronting David concerning his sin with Bathsheba and the commanded murder of Uriah. We've made the connections. That's our first task. However, as I've stated before, our job now is to determine why the Holy One wants us to make these connections.

Putting it All Together

Why are the stories concerning the rape of Tamar and the murder of Amnon (II Samuel 13-14) thematically connected to David's adultery with Bathsheba and murder of Uriah (II Samuel 11-12)? The clue we need is found in II Samuel 12:7-12.

⁷Then Nathan said to David, "You are the man! Thus says the LORD God of Israel: 'I anointed you king over Israel, and I delivered you from the hand of Saul. ⁸I gave you your master's house and your master's wives into your keeping, and gave you the house of Israel and Judah. And if that had been too little, I also would have given you much more! ⁹Why have you despised the commandment of the LORD, to do evil in His sight? You have killed Uriah the Hittite with the sword; you have taken his wife to be your wife, and have killed him with the sword of the people of Ammon. *¹⁰Now therefore, the sword shall never depart from your house*, because you have despised Me, and have taken the wife of Uriah the Hittite to be your wife.' ¹¹Thus says the LORD: '*Behold, I will raise up adversity against you from your own house*; and I will take your wives before your eyes and give them to your neighbor, and he shall lie with your wives in the sight of this sun. ¹²*For you did it secretly, but I will do this thing before all Israel, before the sun.*'"

II Samuel 12:10-12 is our key passage. Nathan prophesied that because of David's sins, *the sword would not depart from his house* and that he would raise up *adversity against David from his own house*! The reason why Amnon's sexual sin against Tamar is thematically connected to David's sexual sin against Bathsheba is because, as Nathan said, David is going to suffer *measure for measure* Divine judgment. David sinned by having a forbidden sexual relationship and his own son committed a sexual sin against David's own daughter (another forbidden sexual relationship)! Like father, like son. Uriah was killed by David's command, and in like manner, Amnon, David's son, was murdered at Absalom's command. Like father, like son. In other words, Adonai wants us to understand that the story of Amnon's lust for Tamar is directly connected to David's lust for and sin with Bathsheba. The process of raising up adversity in David's own house has begun now! Furthermore, this adversity has begun in the same manner that David sinned – sexual misconduct and murder (measure for measure judgment)!

This is also the reason why the story of the woman accusing David is a thematic mirror image of the story of Nathan accusing David—to get us to see that the event concerning Absalom's murder of Amnon and his flight from David is directly connected to David's murder of Uriah! The judgment has begun in the same manner it was initiated! It's the Holy One's way of telling us, "Remember the prophecy that Nathan delivered to David concerning the sword not departing from his house, and that adversity will arise from within his own household? It has begun now!"

This brings us to II Samuel 14:28-33. Joab had won David's approval for Absalom to return to Jerusalem; however, David would not allow Absalom to see his face for two years! Absalom finally had enough, and through Joab, was able to force a reunion with David. The very next event concerns Absalom's rebellion in II Samuel 15. Why did Absalom rebel? I'm not sure. There are a number of reasons. Maybe he was upset with David for not punishing Amnon after he had raped Tamar. Was he upset that David had not wanted to see his face because he had killed Amnon? Could he have detected weakness in David who really never disciplined him properly for killing his brother? I'm not sure. But one question we can certainly answer is this. What events started the fulfillment of the prophecy of Nathan that the sword would not depart from David's house? It was the rape of Tamar by Amnon, which then led to his murder by Absalom, which then led to Absalom's rebellion. *But the key event that catalyzed the entire process culminating in Absalom's rebellion was Amnon's rape of Tamar.*

Why Was the Rape of Tamar Such an Important Event?

The rape of Tamar by Amnon was important for the following reason. Remember what we learned about the tempting of Amnon by Jonadab? Jonadab was clearly thematically connected to the serpent and the serpent was simply an agent of hasatan. Hasatan entered the serpent and tempted Chavah in order to get her to sin, and in like manner, he entered Jonadab in order that he tempt Amnon into sinning against Tamar! Thus we can now make a final statement concerning the rape of Tamar by Amnon.

The key event which started the process of bringing the sword to David's house was the **_satanically-inspired_** temptation of Amnon to rape his half-sister Tamar.

Since the overall goal of this book is to show that David's *flight* from Absalom is actually a veiled thematic presentation of the Gospel, let's connect these events to the suffering of the Messiah.

What Event Catalyzed the Suffering of Messiah Yeshua?

At this point, we need to answer a question. What event started the process of the Messiah's suffering? I believe the event that catalyzed the start of Yeshua's suffering occurred just before the Passover meal. According to Matthew 26:1-5, 14-16 and Mark 14:1-2, 10 and 11, Judas went to the chief priests and offered to betray the Messiah into their hands for thirty pieces of silver. The Scripture goes on to state in Matthew 26:16, "From that time he (Judas) sought opportunity to betray him." This is the event that began the process of Messiah's suffering. Judas began searching for the right moment to betray the Master. But the Gospel of Luke adds one more important detail concerning Judas' betrayal.

Luke 22:3—Then *hasatan entered Judas*, surnamed Iscariot, who was numbered among the twelve.

Just before Judas went to the chief priests and scribes to betray the Messiah, we are informed that hasatan entered him! In other words, Judas' agreement to betray the Messiah was ***satanically inspired***.

Thus, II Samuel 13-15:9 contains many details of events that led up to David's flight from his renegade son Absalom. The main event catalyzing his flight was the *satanically-inspired* temptation of his son Amnon to rape his half-sister Tamar. "Coincidentally," the Gospel of Luke informs us that the event catalyzing the suffering of the Messiah was the *satanically-inspired* temptation of Judas to betray the Messiah. Now at first glance, this may not seem to be such a big connection between David's flight from Absalom and Yeshua's sufferings; however, we're about to travel down a long road of amazing thematic parallels that are too numerous to be coincidental, too intentional to be chance. In order to aid your memory and thought processes, refer to the running chart of the connections we make between the story of David's flight from Absalom and Yeshua's sufferings. This chart will be found at the end of each chapter. This first connection is the only one that exists outside of II Samuel 15:10-20:2. From this point on, we will work our way *chronologically* through II Samuel 15:10-20:2 and the Gospels, at times using our original chiastic structure to help with our thematic analysis.

David's Response to Absalom's Rebellion

David's Prophetic Picture

In II Samuel 15:13, David was informed that Absalom had rebelled and that "The heart of every man of Israel had turned towards Absalom." In response, he said the following:

¹⁴So David said to all his servants who were with him at Jerusalem, "***Arise, and let us flee, or we shall not escape from Absalom. Make haste to depart, lest he overtake us suddenly and bring disaster upon us***, and strike the city with the edge of the sword (II Samuel 15:14)."

Notice how ***David informed his servants of Absalom's evil intentions and the potential that they would suffer if he caught them.*** He did this so the servants would be prepared for the coming ordeal.

Yeshua's Prophetic Fulfillment

In the Gospel accounts of the last supper (Matthew 26:20-25, Mark 14:17-21, Luke 22:21-23 and John 13:21-35), ***Yeshua informed His disciples of the evil intentions of the one*** who would betray him! Furthermore, at this time Yeshua informed His disciples of ***the coming persecution*** (John 15:18-27 and John 16:1-4). Thus, in both stories, the servants/disciples of the Messianic figure/Messiah were warned about the troubles that would soon be visited upon them.

David's Servants' Response to Him

David's Prophetic Picture

In response to David's warning, his servants declared their loyalty to him (II Samuel 15:15 and 19-21.

¹⁵And the king's servants said to the king, "*We are your servants, ready to do whatever my lord the king commands.*"

¹⁹Then the king said to Ittai the Gittite, "Why are you also going with us? Return and remain with the king. For you are a foreigner and also an exile from your own place. ²⁰In fact, you came only yesterday. Should I make you wander up and down with us today, since I go I know not where? Return, and take your brethren back. Mercy and truth be with you." ²¹*But Ittai answered the king and said, "As the LORD lives, and as my lord the king lives, surely in whatever place my lord the king shall be, **whether in death or life, even there also your servant will be.**"*

Notice how this loyalty is expressed in two ways:

♦ II Samuel 15:15 shows how <u>all</u> of David's servants collectively ***declared their loyalty to him***.
♦ II Samuel 15:19-21 is a passage relating how Ittai the Gittite, one of David's many servants, personally expressed his devotion to the king. In fact, notice how resolute Ittai the Gittite was, stating that ***he would even die for King David***.

Also, note David's response to Ittai the Gittite. Ittai was already an exile who had just fled to Israel. David was concerned that Ittai would have to flee for his life again, so soon after arriving. Therefore, David suggested that Ittai stay behind so that he would not have to endure another exile. As you can see, David is expressing extra concern for Ittai and trying to lessen his burden.

The Scroll of the Gospel of David

The passages noted above (II Samuel 15:15-21) are also part of our major chiastic structure (II Samuel 15:10-20:2). II Samuel 15:15-21 (element B) is thematically connected to II Samuel 19:40-44 (element B') through the chiastic structure. A shortened form of the chiastic structure has been reproduced for you below.

A)

    B) II Samuel 15:13-24—The kings servants said, "Whatever my lord the king decides, *your servants are ready*"; Ittai said, "In whatever place my lord the king will be – *whether for death or life – there your servant will be*

    B') II Samuel 19:40-44—The men of Israel and Judah argue over who is *more closely related to King David.*

A')

If you read II Samuel 19:40-44, you will notice that the main theme is how the men of Judah and Israel argued over King David. This argument, which was very severe, occurred because of the jealousy that existed between the men of Judah and the men of Israel. Both groups tried to state why they were more worthy to be closer to the king. The argument was very similar to the argument of two siblings over the affections of one of their parents. As you can see, I have made use of a thematic connection again to help give further insight to the proper interpretation of events in II Samuel 15:15-21. II Samuel 19:40-44 provides more thematic evidence that loyalty to David is the primary theme associated with II Samuel 15:15-21.

Yeshua's Prophetic Fulfillment

The next event in the Gospels occurs in Luke 22:24-34. There are two main themes developed in this passage.

- In Luke 22:24-30, the disciples got into an argument over which of them would be considered the greatest in the kingdom.
- In Luke 22:31-34, Peter confessed his loyalty to Yeshua, stating that he would go to prison and death with Him if he needed to.

Concerning Peter's statement that he would die for the Messiah, let us also note the parallel passages in Matthew 26:30-35 (especially verse 35) and Mark 14:26-31 (especially verse 31) which record that the other disciples also stated they would die for Yeshua. The thematic parallels between the Gospel accounts and II Samuel 15 are so strong they are virtually irresistible.

Earlier we saw that all of David's servants confessed their loyalty to David. All of Yeshua's disciples confessed their loyalty to Him. Then, we read how Ittai the Gittite went a step further, stating that he would die for David. Surely, we can see the prophetic parallel in Peter who stated the same! We also noted how David was concerned for Ittai's well being, giving him the option of staying behind so that he wouldn't be burdened any longer. Should we be surprised that Yeshua was concerned for Peter? Remember how Yeshua tried to lessen Peter's burden by praying that he would be able to stand in the moment of temptation.

³¹And the Lord said, "Simon, Simon! Indeed, Satan has asked for you, that he may sift you as wheat. ³²But I have prayed for you, that your faith should not fail; and when you have returned to Me, strengthen your brethren." ***³³But he said to Him, "Lord, I am ready to go with You, both to prison and to death."*** ³⁴Then He said, "I tell you, Peter, the rooster shall not crow this day before you will deny three times that you know Me (Luke 22:31-34)."

Lastly, we cannot possibly miss the prophetic connection between the argument of the men of Judah with the men of Israel and the rivalry amongst the disciples! The men of Judah and Israel argued over which group deserved to be closest to King David. Yeshua's disciples argued over who would be greatest in the kingdom. Would not those greatest in the kingdom be closest to the King?

As you can see, the thematic/prophetic parallels are right on the mark. What's even more miraculous is the usefulness of our chiastic structure. Although the story of David's servants confessing their loyalty to David (II Samuel 15:15-21) occurred in the correct chronological timeline to be a prophetic picture of Yeshua's disciples confessing their loyalty to Him at the beginning of His suffering, the argument between the men of Judah and Israel occurs chapters later, near the end of David's flight from Absalom. However, the chiastic structure thematically connects these two events! Thus, the information concerning the rivalry between the men of Judah and Israel, which occurred chronologically later in the story, has been brought to its proper prophetic timeline (i.e., concomitant with the expression of loyalty to David by his servants) through the chiastic structure. Thus, all of the information recorded in the Gospels concerning 1) the rivalry of Yeshua's disciples, 2) their willingness to die for him and 3) Peter's explicit confession that he would die for the Messiah, all have a prophetic parallel at the correct chronological placement in the story of David's flight from Absalom! O, the depth of the riches of the wisdom of Adonai!

David's Movements

David's Prophetic Picture

Once David and his servants then began their escape in earnest they crossed the Kidron Brook (II Samuel 15:22-23).

²²So David said to Ittai, "Go, and cross over." Then Ittai the Gittite and all his men and all the little ones who were with him crossed over. ²³And all the country wept with a loud voice, and all the people crossed over. ***The king himself also crossed over the Brook Kidron***, and all the people crossed over toward the way of the wilderness.

Yeshua's Prophetic Fulfillment

After the Passover meal, Yeshua and His disciples crossed the Kidron Brook as they left for a new destination (John 18:1a).

When Jesus had spoken these words, He went out with His disciples *over the Brook Kidron* . . .

Once again, our chiastic structure helps us see that David's crossing of the Kidron was an important event by thematically connecting it to when David crossed the Jordan River on his return to Jerusalem after Absalom's defeat.

A)
    B) II Samuel 15:13-24 — David and his servants ***pass through the Kidron Valley***

    B') II Samuel 19:40-44 — David and his servants ***pass over the Jordan Brook***
A')

David's First Stop

David's Prophetic Picture

After David crossed the Kidron Brook, he approached the Mount of Olives. The prophet Samuel definitely wanted us to understand the importance of this. Note how carefully he documented David's steps with respect to the Mount of Olives.

[30] So ***David went up by the Ascent of the Mount of Olives***, and wept as he went up; and he had his head covered and went barefoot. And all the people who were with him covered their heads and went up, weeping as they went up (II Samuel 15:30).

[32] Now it happened ***when David had come to the top of the mountain***, where he worshiped God — there was Hushai the Archite coming to meet him with his robe torn and dust on his head (II Samuel 15:32).

[1] ***When David was a little past the top of the mountain***, there was Ziba the servant of Mephibosheth, who met him with a couple of saddled donkeys, and on them two hundred *loaves* of bread, one hundred clusters of raisins, one hundred summer fruits, and a skin of wine (II Samuel 16:1).

Clearly, the Mount of Olives was Samuel's focal point as he used its location to gauge David's earliest steps as he fled from Absalom. Let's focus on II Samuel 15:32. The Scripture reference to II Samuel 15:32 noted above is from the New King James Version (NKJV). I'd like to give you the translation from the Stone Edition of the Artscroll Tanakh, a Jewish translation.

David was approaching the summit ***where he would prostrate himself to God*** . . . (II Samuel 15:32)[9]

When I read from my Artscroll Tanakh, I make it a point to read the commentary because quite often it is very informative. The commentary on this verse states the following:

The summit of the Mount of Olives overlooked the Tent of the Ark in Jerusalem. ***Whenever he approached Jerusalem, David would prostrate himself*** as soon as the Tent came into view (Rashi).

This was a very important note because it gave more meaning to II Samuel 15:32. Without the note, it's hard to understand what was meant by, "he would prostrate himself to God." There are two important themes in the passages above. First, the fact that David traveled to the Mount of Olives is important. Secondly, associated with his trip, the Scripture notes that David engaged in an activity that was a habit. He habitually prostrated himself to God when he reached the summit of the Mount of Olives.

Yeshua's Prophetic Fulfillment

Do you know where Yeshua was going after He crossed the Kidron Brook? Well, by now you should probably be able to guess. Yes, He was on his way to the Mount of Olives where the Garden of Gethsemane was located. This is confirmed for us in Matthew 26:36-46, Mark 14:32-42, Luke 22:39-46 and John 18:1.

³⁹Coming out, ***He went to the Mount of Olives, as He was accustomed***, and His disciples also followed Him (Luke 22:39).

Furthermore, did you notice how Luke noted that Yeshua was accustomed to going to the Mount of Olives? In other words, just as David was accustomed to prostrating himself as he approached the summit of the Mount of Olives (a habit), so likewise, Yeshua was accustomed to going to the Garden of Gethsemane on the Mount of Olives (a habit).

David's Distress

David's Prophetic Picture

The writer of II Samuel recorded David's emotional state of being as he approached the Mount of Olives in II Samuel 15:30.

³⁰So David went up by the Ascent of the Mount of Olives, and ***wept as he went up***; and he had ***his head covered and went barefoot***. And all the people who were with him ***covered their heads and went up, weeping*** as they went up.

The people were weeping because they were so upset concerning Absalom's rebellion and their need to escape for their lives. Notice how the Scripture describes David and the people with him. Their heads were covered and David went barefoot. What do these signs (covering the head and walking barefoot) mean? One of the easiest ways to study thematically is to simply see how a particular word, phrase or theme is used throughout the Scriptures. The phrase "covered their heads" is used in Jeremiah 14:1-4.

¹ The word of the LORD that came to Jeremiah concerning the droughts. ²"Judah mourns, and her gates languish; they mourn for the land, and the cry of Jerusalem has gone up. ³Their nobles have sent their lads for water; they went to the cisterns and found no water. They returned with their vessels empty; ***they were <u>ashamed</u> and confounded and covered their heads***. ⁴Because the ground is parched, for there was no rain in the land, ***the plowmen were <u>ashamed</u>; they covered their heads***.

Notice the phrase "covered their heads," has been thematically connected to the concept of *shame* two times in these verses! In other words, it seems that *covering the head* was a sign of shame. In fact, we can make another case for this interpretation based on what we read concerning Tamar's rape. Please note II Samuel 13:12-19.

¹²But she answered him, "No, my brother, do not force me, for no such thing should be done in Israel. Do not do this disgraceful thing! ¹³And I, ***where could I take my shame***? And as for you, you would be like one of the fools in Israel. Now therefore, please speak to the king; for he will not withhold me from you." ¹⁴However, he would not heed her voice; and being stronger than she, he forced her and lay with her. ¹⁵Then Amnon hated her exceedingly, so that the hatred with which he hated her was greater than the love with which he had loved her. And Amnon said to her, "Arise, be gone!" ¹⁶So she said to him, "No, indeed! This evil of sending me away is worse than the other that you did to me." But he would not listen to her. ¹⁷Then he called his servant who attended him, and said, "Here! Put this woman out, away from me, and bolt the door behind her." ¹⁸Now she had on a robe of many colors, for the king's virgin daughters wore such apparel. And his servant put her out and bolted the door behind her. ¹⁹Then Tamar put ashes on her head, and tore her robe of many colors that was on her, and ***laid her hand on her head*** and went away ***crying bitterly***.

In II Samuel 13:13, before Amnon raped Tamar, she asked, "And where could I take my shame?" She knew that if he did such a despicable thing it would bring shame upon her. Later, after Amnon raped her, she "Laid her hand on her head." Did she not *cover her head* by laying her hand on her head? Yes, she did. Furthermore, she left weeping. Therefore, I'm suggesting that David and the people wept and covered their heads because of the *shame* of the situation they found themselves in, fleeing from the King's rebellious son. Let us now see how the word *barefoot* is used elsewhere in Scripture.

¹ In the year that Tartan came to Ashdod, when Sargon the king of Assyria sent him, and he fought against Ashdod and took it, ²at the same time the LORD spoke by Isaiah the son of Amoz, saying, "Go, and remove the sackcloth from your body, and ***take your sandals off your feet***." And he did so, ***walking naked and barefoot***. ³Then the LORD said, "Just as My servant Isaiah has walked ***naked and barefoot*** three years for a sign and a wonder against Egypt and Ethiopia, ⁴so shall the king of Assyria lead away the Egyptians as prisoners and the Ethiopians as captives, young and old, ***naked and barefoot, with their buttocks uncovered, to the <u>shame</u> of Egypt*** (Isaiah 20:1-4).

Now, we see that the concept of walking barefooted is *also* associated with *shame* as Isaiah walked naked and barefoot to symbolize how Egypt would soon be taken captive by the king of Assyria, walking naked and barefoot with their buttocks uncovered. This short thematic excursion has taught us why David and his servants were weeping. They were weeping specifically over the shame of their situation.

Yeshua's Prophetic Fulfillment

After Yeshua reached the Garden of Gethsemane, He began to agonize in prayer. In fact, the Scripture records that during His prayer time in the Garden, He sweated as it were, drops of blood! Yeshua's agony is recorded for us in Matthew 26:36-46, Mark 14:32-42 and Luke 22:39-46.

And He was withdrawn from them about a stone's throw, and He knelt down and prayed, [42]saying, "Father, if it is Your will, take this cup away from Me; nevertheless not My will, but Yours, be done." [43]Then an angel appeared to Him from heaven, strengthening Him. [44]And ***being in agony, He prayed more earnestly. Then His sweat became like great drops of blood falling down to the ground*** (Luke 22:41-44).

Not only was Yeshua in mental anguish, He, like David, was overwhelmed with sorrow and grief as He contemplated what lay ahead of Him.

[32]They went to a place called Gethsemane, and Jesus said to his disciples, "Sit here while I pray." [33]He took Peter, James and John along with him, and he began to be deeply distressed and troubled. [34]"***My soul is overwhelmed with sorrow to the point of death***," he said to them. "Stay here and keep watch (Mark 14:32-34)."

Tears flowed from David; however Yeshua's agony was so much worse that He shed blood during His anguishing. And why was Yeshua agonizing to the point of sweating drops of blood? He was agonizing so desperately because He knew what awaited Him—suffering and death. This *suffering and death* which He contemplated as He struggled to remain faithful to His Father's will, was soon to be the source of *shame* that awaited Him.

[1] Therefore we also, since we are surrounded by so great a cloud of witnesses, let us lay aside every weight, and the sin which so easily ensnares us, and let us run with endurance the race that is set before us, [2]looking unto Jesus, the author and finisher of our faith, who for the joy that was set before Him ***endured the cross, despising the shame***, and has sat down at the right hand of the throne of God (Hebrews 12:1-2).

Provisions for David

David's Prophetic Picture

Our next portion of Scripture, II Samuel 16:1-4, relates how Ziba brought donkeys, bread, raisins, figs and wine for David and his servants. Ziba was the servant of Mephibosheth, the son of Jonathan, son of Saul, the former king of Israel. To understand the importance of this act, we simply need to understand the *purpose for these gifts*. Ziba brought them food to eat for physical strength. So likewise, he brought them the donkeys because donkeys were used as beasts of burden to carry loads. Furthermore, people would ride them. In other words, the donkeys were given to help David and his servants preserve their physical strength.

Yeshua's Prophetic Fulfillment

As Yeshua prayed, agonizing over His impending death, Luke 22:43 records that an angel appeared! Why did the angel appear?

⁴³Then an angel appeared to Him from heaven, ***strengthening Him***.

As you can see, the physical provisions provided by Ziba for David (the Messianic figure) are prophetic pictures thematically connected to the spiritual strength Yeshua would receive from angels! In case you doubt that II Samuel 16:1-4 refers thematically/prophetically to Yeshua's strengthening by an ***angel***, let me remind you that this passage is also part of our chiastic structure, thematically connected to II Samuel 19:25-31. That portion of the chiastic structure is reproduced below.

A)

  B)

    C)

      D) II Samuel 16:1-4—Ziba ***came to meet the king***; the king ***asked a question about Mephibosheth***; the king ***gave Mephibosheth's property to Ziba***

      D') II Samuel 19:25-31—Mephibosheth ***came to meet the king***; the king ***asked Mephibosheth a question***; ***Mephibosheth and Ziba must divide the property***

    C')

  B')

A')

The chiastic structure clearly connects II Samuel 19:25-31 to II Samuel 16:1-4. Now I have made the thematic case that II Samuel 16:1-4 is actually a prophetic passage thematically connected to the spiritual strengthening of the Messiah by angels, yet II Samuel 16:1-4 does not mention angels. Well, guess what? Let's look at II Samuel 19:27, which occurs within the verses thematically connected to II Samuel 16:1-4.

²⁷And he has slandered your servant to my lord the king, but my lord the king is like the ***angel of God***. Therefore do what is good in your eyes.

Mephibosheth stated that David was like the angel of God! This reference to an angel strengthens my assertion that II Samuel 16:1-4 pertains to angelic strength for Yeshua. Once again, we see that information needed to interpret one passage of Scripture is found in another passage of Scripture thematically connected to the original Scripture. This time, the thematic connection was found in passages thematically connected through our primary chiastic structure.

Summary

From this point on, I will let the *Running Chart of the Thematic Connections Between II Samuel 15:10 – 20:2 and the Gospels* summarize what we have learned. It will be the last bit of information in each chapter. The last chapter will contain the entire running chart of thematic connections. The next chapter will begin right here where we left off in II Samuel 16:1-4. We will use this Scripture one more time to make one huge thematic connection to the events surrounding the arrest of Yeshua. It is almost miraculous in scope and simply beautiful to behold.

Running Chart of the Thematic Connections Between II Samuel 15:10 – 20:2 and the Gospels

II Samuel	*The Gospels*
II Samuel 13-14—Amnon, under satanic influence from hasatan, raped Tamar, initiated events leading to David's flight from Absalom	**Luke 22:1-6**—Judas, under satanic influence from hasatan, agreed to betray the Messiah, thus initiating events leading to Yeshua's sufferings
II Samuel 15:13-14— David informed his servants of Absalom's evil intentions and the potential that they would suffer if he caught them	**Matthew 26:20-25, Mark 14:17-21, Luke 22:21-23, John 13:21-35, John 15:18-27 and John 16:1-4**—Yeshua informed His disciples of the evil intentions of the one who would betray him and of the coming persecution
II Samuel 15:15 and 19-21—II Samuel 19:40-44 is thematically connected to II Samuel 15:15 and 19-21 through the chiastic structure and shows us how the men of Judah and Israel argue over who is closest to King David. David's servants declare their loyalty to David and Ittai the Gittite declared his willingness to die for King David	**Matthew 26:31-35, Mark 14:27-31, Luke 22:24-34 and John 13:36-38**—The disciples argue over who will be greatest in the kingdom; then they declare their willingness to die for Yeshua; and Peter declared his loyalty to Yeshua and willingness to die for Him.
II Samuel 15:22-23—David crossed the Kidron Valley	**John 18:1a**—Yeshua crossed the Kidron Brook

II Samuel 15:32—David approached the summit of the Mount of Olives where he would prostrate himself as a matter of habit	Matthew 26:36-46, Mark 14:32-42, Luke 22:39-46 and John 18:1—Yeshua went to the Garden of Gethsemane on the Mount of Olives to pray as was His habit
II Samuel 15:30—David and his servants approached the Mount of Olives weeping, with their heads covered and barefoot (bearing signs of shame)	Matthew 26:36-46, Mark 14:32-42 and Luke 22:39-46—Yeshua agonized in prayer on the Mount of Olives as He contemplated His impending suffering and death, His source of shame
II Samuel 16:1-4—Ziba, Mephibosheth's servant, brought David provisions for physical strength	Luke 22:43—Yeshua was given spiritual strength by an angel

Thematic Moments

I'm sure that some readers of this book may initially flinch at my usage of thematic connections, especially if this is a new paradigm of Bible interpretation for you. With that in mind, I'd like to use every opportunity to win you over to the thematic approach of Scripture interpretation. In order to do so, I'd like to use this section of each chapter entitled, *Thematic Moments*, to present some additional thematic support for some of the main assertions made in each chapter.

The greatest testimony to the truth and efficacy of a thematic approach to Scripture analysis primarily lies in chiastic structures and parallelisms[10] and secondarily in the plethora of thematically connected passages that seem to always lead one to the same conclusions.

As I stated in Chapter 1, chiastic structures and parallelisms are so prevalent that it is virtually impossible to read one page of the Bible and not move into or out of one! Some are only a few verses long . . .

Joshua 6:15-20b

A) Joshua 6:15—Am Yisrael *went around* the city…seven times
  B) Joshua 6:16—Kohanim were *blowing shofars*; Joshua said *"Cry out!"*; Adonai has **given you the city**
    C) Joshua 6:17a—Everything in the city is *consecrated* to Adonai
      D) Joshua 6:17b—Rachav the harlot and all her family shall live because she hid the spies
    C') Joshua 6:18-19—Beware of the *consecrated stuff*; don't bring destruction upon yourself; the silver, gold and the copper and iron vessels **belong to Adonai, in His treasury**
  B') Joshua 6:20a—the *sound of the shofar*; the people *cried out*; the wall fell and Am Yisrael *went into the city*
A') Joshua 6:20b—Am Yisrael *went straight* ahead and they conquered the city

Joshua 8:9a-14c

A) Joshua 8:9a—Joshua sent ambushers out to lie in wait between Ai and Bethel
  B) Joshua 8:9b—Joshua lodged that night *amongst the people*
    C) Joshua 8:10-11a—Joshua arose early, mustered his people and they approached Ai
      D) Joshua 8:11b—A *valley* lay between them at Ai
        E) Joshua 8:12—They set 5,000 men in an *ambush between Bethel and Ai (i.e., behind the city)*

A') Joshua 8:12-13a— They set 5,000 men in an *ambush between Bethel and Ai*
  B') Joshua 8:13b—Joshua went *into the midst of the valley* that night
    C') Joshua 8:14a—The men of Ai, hurried, *arose early, and approached Am Yisrael*
      D') Joshua 8:14b—The men of Ai gathered at an appointed place before the *plain*
        E') Joshua 8:14c—They didn't know there was an *ambush behind the city*

Some chiastic structures are fairly long, such as the one that has become the basis for this book (II Samuel 15:10 – 20:2), while others span entire books of the Bible! One group of chiastic structures and parallelisms I find particularly interesting are those where the first half is in one book, and the second half is in another book . . .

Joshua 3:9-5:12—Exodus 14:13-16:4

A) Exodus 14:13-14—Moses said, "Don't fear…stand still *and see the salvation of YHVH…* He will *destroy the Egyptians*; He will fight for you"
  B) Exodus 14:15-20—Adonai told Moshe ahead of time what would happen; *the angel of God and pillar of cloud that went before them*, went behind them
    C) Exodus 14:21-22—Moses stretched out his *hand over the sea*; Adonai turned the sea into dry land; the waters were *divided*; Am Yisrael went into the *midst of the Red Sea on dry ground*; the water was a heap on the left and right
      D) Exodus 14:26—*Adonai commanded Moses what to do so that the water would return*
        E) Exodus 14:27-28—Moses stretched his *hand over the sea* and the water returned
          F) Exodus 15:8 and 19—The waters heaped up; *the deep congealed*; Am Yisrael *walked on dry ground*
            G) Exodus 15:14-15—The people *heard and feared*; may they fear the greatness of Your mighty arm
              H) Exodus 16:4—The manna began coming down

A`) Joshua 3:9-10—Joshua said, "He shall *destroy the inhabitants*; you shall *know the living God is among you*"
  B`) Joshua 3:11-14—Joshua told the people ahead of time what would happen; the *ark of the covenant went before the people*

C`) Joshua 3:15-17—The priests *feet dipped into the edge of the Jordan*; the *water split*; the people crossed *on dry ground*; the priests stood on dry ground in the *midst of the Jordan*

D`) Joshua 4:15-17—*Adonai commanded Joshua what to do so that the water would return*

E`) Joshua 4:18—As the priests *feet touched the dry ground* the water returned

F`) Joshua 4:19-24—Tell your children Israel *crossed on dry ground*; Adonai *dried up the water* of the Jordan

G`) Joshua 5:1—The Amorite and Canaanite kings *heard* how Adonai dried up the Jordan's waters *and feared*

H`) Joshua 5:12—The manna ceased

So what shall we make of these literary jewels? I think the answer is obvious. When you consider that every story of the Bible is probably part of some chiastic structure or parallelism and/or thematically connected to some other passage in the Bible, it becomes abundantly clear that the Divine hand of inspiration was as work when holy men of God were moved to pen the words of Scripture. In fact, the odds of producing such a literary design are simply astronomical! Therefore, I conclude that Adonai placed all of these chiastic structures, parallelisms and thematic connections in Scripture for a reason. Why else go to such astronomical odds to so order Scripture? If He chose to extend to such lengths to place these literary gems in Scripture, then I think it behooves us to search them out and seek Him as to their importance. What I have found is that these multitudinous thematic connections, parallelisms and thematic connections contain the wisdom of our Great God! He did not "exert" such an effort just to beautify the text. There is a purpose behind each chiastic structure, each parallelism and every thematic connection. And I think this book will clearly demonstrate the fruit of seeking out such wisdom in the manner which He has presented it.

As for thematic connections, they appear everywhere, and taken together, they always present a unified picture. For example, let's look at Absalom. How does the Scripture represent him? First, let me say that the Scripture has volumes to speak concerning his character. Let's do a quick thematic survey of Absalom's character. Adonai is very interested in helping us understand the motivations behind the major characters of the Bible's stories.

Note how Absalom is thematically connected to Adonijah, another of David's sons who tried to take David's kingdom.

- Both Absalom and Adonijah tried to take the kingdom from David, and prepared chariots and horsemen to go before them.
    - I Kings 1:5—Then Adonijah the son of Haggith exalted himself, saying, "*I will be king*"; and *he prepared for himself chariots and horsemen*, and fifty men to run before him.
    - II Samuel 15:1, 10—In the course of time, *Absalom provided himself with a chariot and horses and with fifty men to run ahead of him* . . . Then Absalom sent secret messengers throughout the tribes of Israel to say, "As soon as you hear the sound of the trumpets, then say, '*Absalom is king in Hebron.*'"

- Absalom and Adonijah are thematically connected through the hair upon their heads.

- o I Kings 1:52—Solomon said, "If he will be a loyal man, **not a single hair of his will fall to the ground.**"
- o II Samuel 18:10-15—Absalom's death occurred while he hung by his hair from a tree. Thus, when he died not one hair fell to the ground.

♦ Both Absalom and Adonijah were handsome.
- o I Kings 1:6—(Speaking of Adonijah, the prophet noted) "... Moreover, *he was very handsome* ..."
- o II Samuel 14:25-26—*There was no one in all of Israel as praiseworthy for his beauty as Absalom*; from the bottom of his foot to the top of his head there was no blemish in him.

♦ Both Absalom and Adonijah desired David's concubines.
- o I Kings 2:17—Adonijah requested that Abishag, King David's concubine, be given to him.
- o II Samuel 16:20-22—Absalom consorted with David's ten concubines he had left to keep the house.

Once one is made aware of these glaring similarities, the obvious question is, "Why has Adonai given us so many thematic connections between Absalom and Adonijah?" It seems easy for me to conclude (thematically) that Absalom = Adonijah in some manner. But, how?

Well, it turns out that Absalom is thematically connected to someone else too. Can you think of someone else who murdered their brother? Yes, Cain murdered Abel! We can also thematically connect Absalom to Cain through the story told by the wise woman from Tekoa in II Samuel 14!

⁵ Then the king said to her, "What troubles you?" And she answered, "Indeed I am a widow, my husband is dead. ⁶ Now your maidservant had *two sons; and the two fought with each other in the field, and there was no one to part them, but the one struck the other and killed him* (II Samuel 14:5-6).

Does this story of a man who murdered his brother in a field sound familiar to you?

Now Cain talked with Abel his brother; and it came to pass, *when they were in the field*, that *Cain* rose up against Abel his brother and *killed him* (Genesis 4:8).

It should. It's the story of Cain and Abel. Remember, the wise woman from Tekoa told this story to King David in order to get him to spare Absalom's life (the one responsible for the murder of his brother Amnon).
Can you think of someone else who desired to kill their brother? Yes, Esau!
Lastly, since we know that Absalom is thematically equivalent to Adonijah, please note how Absalom and Adonijah are both thematically connected to hasatan!

♦ Of hasatan, the Scripture states, *You were the seal of perfection, full of wisdom and perfect in beauty* (Ezekiel 28:12b). Of Absalom, the Scripture states, *There was no one*

in all of Israel as praiseworthy for his beauty as Absalom; from the bottom of his foot to the top of his head there was no blemish in him (II Samuel 14:25-26).
- ♦ Of hasatan, the Scripture states, '*<u>I will ascend</u> into heaven, <u>I will exalt</u> my throne above the stars of God; <u>I will</u> also sit on the mount of the congregation on the farthest sides of the north; <u>I will ascend</u> above the heights of the clouds, <u>I will</u> be like the Most High (Isaiah 14:13-14).*' Of Adonijah, the Scripture states, *Then Adonijah the son of Haggith <u>exalted himself</u>, saying, "<u>I will</u> be king (I Kings 1:5)."* Of Absalom, the Scripture states, *Then Absalom sent secret messengers throughout the tribes of Israel to say, "As soon as you hear the sound of the trumpets, then say, '<u>Absalom is king</u> in Hebron (II Samuel 15:10).'*' Thus, both Absalom and Adonijah, like hasatan, exalted themselves and tried to usurp a kingdom that was not theirs by setting themselves up as king.
- ♦ Notice how king Solomon spoke to Adonijah compared to how Adonai spoke to hasatan.
  - o Then Solomon said, "If he proves himself a worthy man, not one hair of him shall fall to the earth;[11] ***but if wickedness is found in him***, he shall die (I Kings 1:52)."
  - o You *were* perfect in your ways from the day you were created, ***till iniquity was found in you*** (Ezekiel 28:15).

So, we see that Absalom has been clearly thematically connected to Adonijah, Cain, Esau and last but not least, hasatan! Not exactly the best cast of characters. In light of the people Absalom is clearly thematically connected to, do you think that perhaps Adonai is diligently teaching us about Absalom's character? I rest my case.

Chapter 3

The Betrayal

Introduction

The last section of Chapter 2 brought us to II Samuel 16:1-4, the story of Ziba, who brought provisions for David. If you will recall, Ziba was the servant of Mephibosheth, son of Jonathan, son of Saul, former king of Israel. We thematically connected II Samuel 16:1-4 to the strengthening of Yeshua by an angel. Furthermore, I mentioned that the story of Ziba's generosity would be used again to make another very significant thematic connection to the events surrounding the arrest of Yeshua. Thus, we will begin in II Samuel 16:1-4.

The Kiss of Betrayal Part I

David's Prophetic Picture

II Samuel 16:1-4 reads as follows:

> ¹ When David was a little past the top of the mountain, there was Ziba the servant of Mephibosheth, who met him with a couple of saddled donkeys, and on them two hundred loaves of bread, one hundred clusters of raisins, one hundred summer fruits, and a skin of wine. ²And the king said to Ziba, "What do you mean to do with these?" So Ziba said, "The donkeys are for the king's household to ride on, the bread and summer fruit for the young men to eat, and the wine for those who are faint in the wilderness to drink." ³Then the king said, "And where is your master's son?" And Ziba said to the king, "Indeed he is staying in Jerusalem, for he said, 'Today the house of Israel will restore the kingdom of my father to me.'" ⁴So the king said to Ziba, "Here, all that belongs to Mephibosheth is yours." And Ziba said, "I humbly bow before you, that I may find favor in your sight, my lord, O king!"

As you can see, it seems that Ziba came to show support for David. We have already seen how David's servants showed their support for him. Furthermore, we also saw how Ittai the Gittite confessed that he was willing to die with David (II Samuel 15:15 and 19-21). Therefore, it would seem natural, from the context, that Ziba would also be showing his support. However, let's take notice of something. II Samuel 16:1-4 is part of our chiastic structure. It's thematically connected to II Samuel 19:24-30.

> ²⁴Now Mephibosheth the son of Saul came down to meet the king. And he had not cared for his feet, nor trimmed his mustache, nor washed his clothes, from the day the king departed until the day he returned in peace. ²⁵So it was, when he had come to Jerusalem to meet the king, that the king said to him, "Why did you not go with me, Mephibosheth?" ²⁶And he answered, "My lord, O king, my servant deceived me. For your servant said, 'I will saddle a donkey for myself, that I may ride on it and go to the king,' because your servant is lame. ²⁷And he has slandered your servant to my lord the king, but my lord the king is like the angel of God. Therefore do what is good in your eyes. ²⁸For all my father's house were but dead men before my lord the king. Yet you set your servant among those who eat at your own table. Therefore what right have I still to cry out anymore to the king?" ²⁹So the king said to him, "Why do you speak anymore of your matters? I have said, "You and Ziba divide the land."' ³⁰Then Mephibosheth said to the king, "Rather, let him take it all, inasmuch as my lord the king has come back in peace to his own house."

Whenever you have passages that are thematically connected through a chiastic structure, you should compare and contrast them to determine why they are thematically connected. I have reproduced a portion of the chiastic structure showing you how the passages are thematically connected.

A)

  B)

    C)

      D) II Samuel 16:1-4—Ziba *came to meet the king*; the king *asked a question about Mephibosheth (where is Mephibosheth)*; the king *gave Mephibosheth's property to Ziba*

      D') II Samuel 19:25-31—Mephibosheth *came to meet the king*; the king *asked Mephibosheth a question (why didn't Mephibosheth come to flee with the king)*; *Mephibosheth and Ziba must divide the property*

    C')

  B')

A')

The chiastic structure clearly connects II Samuel 19:25-31 to II Samuel 16:1-4. Both passages refer to someone associated with Saul, the former king of Israel, coming to meet King David. In II Samuel 16:1-4 it was Ziba, Mephibosheth's servant; while in II Samuel 19:25-31 it was Mephibosheth. In both passages, David asks a question concerning Mephibosheth, and questions his loyalty since David has bestowed so much kindness and grace upon him. Even though these two passages are clearly thematically connected, have you noticed any problems concerning what Ziba and Mephibosheth said? It seems that someone is lying! In II Samuel

16:1-4, Ziba stated that Mephibosheth had stayed behind hoping to be crowned king of Israel in his grandfather's place. However, in II Samuel 19:25-31, Mephibosheth stated that Ziba had deceived and slandered him and left him behind! So, who's telling the truth? Based on the text, can you tell whom David believed? The key to understanding David's judgment is his decision concerning Mephibosheth's estate. Remember, he had originally given it to Ziba after he stated that Mephibosheth stayed behind, thus showing disloyalty to David. After Mephibosheth's testimony, David simply said they should split the estate. It seems that David did not know whom to believe! After all, had he believed Mephibosheth, why should Ziba retain any of the property after lying? Thus, David doesn't know whom to believe. Has the Scripture left us in the dark concerning who was telling the truth?

No! In fact, we can be certain who was telling the truth. But, in order to do so, we must make a critical thematic connection to another story found elsewhere in Scripture. Before I give you any clues, read the two passages concerning Ziba and Mephibosheth again and try to make a connection between this story and another. Need some help? Okay, here's a hint:

Where else in Scripture can we read a story about two people who came before a king of Israel with opposing testimony?

Did you make a connection this time? If not, I'll give you one more clue.

Where else in Scripture can we read a story about two people who came before the king of Israel with opposing testimony, where one person essentially said, "The other person can have it?"

The story of Ziba and Mephibosheth before King David is thematically connected to the two harlots who argued before King Solomon about the living and dead baby. Here are the thematic connections.

Ziba & Mephibosheth—II Samuel 16 and 19	*The Two Harlots—I Kings 3:16-28*
Ziba and Mephibosheth both appeared before King David	The two harlots both appeared before King Solomon
Ziba and Mephibosheth were both from the same house—Ziba was Mephibosheth's servant	The two harlots lived in the same house
Ziba and Mephibosheth gave contradictory testimony	The two harlots gave contradictory testimony
David said, "Split the property between the two of you."	King Solomon said, "Split the child between the two of you."
Mephibosheth stated, "Let him (Ziba) take it all."	The true mother of the child stated, "Give her the newborn and do not put it to death."

As you can see, these two stories share many connections; this is definitely by Divine design. Making the connection is your first job. Your second task is to understand why two passages are thematically related. Thematically, both stories are essentially mirror images of each other. However, there's one detail present in the story about the harlots that's missing in the story of Ziba and Mephibosheth. In the story of the two harlots, we know who was telling the truth. In the story of Ziba and Mephibosheth, we don't know. However, the woman who told the truth made a statement that is thematically equivalent to Mephibosheth's. They both stated that they would rather not see something split in half! Therefore, since the woman who stated, "Give her the newborn and do not put it to death (by splitting it in half)," was telling the truth, we surmise that Mephibosheth, who stated, "Let him (Ziba) take it all," was also telling the truth! Once again, information lacking in one passage (who was telling the truth between Ziba and Mephibosheth) is present in another passage (the story of the two harlots appearing before King Solomon) thematically connected to it.

There is one more connection we didn't mention. I Kings 3:26 states it was the true mother's compassion that motivated her decision not to want to see the child split in half and killed. Similarly, in II Samuel 19:30, Mephibosheth's heartfelt *concern for David's safety* is what motivated his decision to give up his own estate! Beloved, this has been a classic usage of a thematic connection. I cannot overemphasize to you the importance of this technique. Adonai intended for us to make the connection between Ziba and Mephibosheth and the two harlots so we could know that Ziba was lying and Mephibosheth was telling the truth. This is how your Bible works. As we progress, you will see more and more of this type of analysis. Even though it may seem new, you'll grow to understand how thematic analysis works. As you become more comfortable with this technique you will grow to appreciate its beauty. Furthermore, you will learn to trust that your conclusions—based on thematic connections—are correct. Adonai arranged His Holy Words thematically, and He intends that we study them thematically.

There is another piece of information that points to Mephibosheth's integrity. II Samuel 19:25 states that Mephibosheth "Had not bathed his feet and had not trimmed his mustache, he had not laundered his clothing from the day the king left until the day that he returned in peace." These signs of grief are further proof that Mephibosheth had actually remained loyal to David and that Ziba had slandered him before David.

This information now sheds new light on what was actually occurring in II Samuel 16:1-4. Now we know that when Ziba said, "Indeed he (Mephibosheth) is staying in Jerusalem, for he said, 'Today the house of Israel will restore the kingdom of my father to me,'" that he was lying, slandering Mephibosheth! But why did he slander him? Again, the answer is found in the story of the two harlots. Why did the one harlot lie and say that the baby was hers? She wanted the other harlot's baby because her child died. In other words, she *coveted the possession* of the other harlot. Ziba coveted Mephibosheth's estate. He wanted it, and he got what he wanted by slandering Mephibosheth. Notice what Ziba stated to David. After slandering Mephibosheth and receiving his estate, he said, "I humbly bow before you, that I may find favor in your sight, my lord, O king!" Well, isn't that a nice thing to say after you have slandered your master and wrongfully taken his estate! Do you see what Ziba was doing? Basically, he was buttering up David—you know, fawning and groveling. He's not being truthful. He doesn't give a hoot about David. He simply wanted Mephibosheth's property and now he's slobbering all over David because he's gotten what he wanted. Ziba approached David with ulterior motives—he was greedy. He had a secret agenda that was veiled behind an outward show of respect for David.

Furthermore, hasn't Ziba slandered Mephibosheth, *implying that he has betrayed David*? That is exactly the situation. This is a story about one man who had a secret agenda. Because of his covetousness, he wanted to get his hands on Mephibosheth's property. In order to do so, he had to slander Mephibosheth and make David believe that he had betrayed him.

Yeshua's Prophetic Fulfillment

If you will remember, the next event to occur in the Gospels was the betrayal of the Messiah by Judas (Matthew 26:47-50, Mark 14:43-46, Luke 22:47-48 and John 18:2-9). How was this accomplished?

⁴⁸Now he that betrayed him gave them a sign, saying, "Whomsoever I shall kiss, that same is he: hold him fast." ⁴⁹And forthwith he came to Jesus, and said, "Hail, master" and kissed him (Matthew 26:48-49).

Judas walked up to the Messiah and kissed Him, but it wasn't sincere. It was the kiss of betrayal. Just like Ziba, Judas approached Yeshua and acted towards Him in a deceptive manner. Ziba buttered up David and groveled before him. Judas kissed the Messiah. You see the picture? Ziba was prophetically acting in the place of Judas who also had ulterior motives when he approached the Messiah. Furthermore, why did Ziba sweet talk David—for Mephibosheth's possessions? And why did Judas betray the Messiah—for thirty pieces of silver? Lastly, remember what we learned about Ziba, the person who prophetically acted out the role of Yeshua's betrayer, Judas? Ziba was greedy and tried to steal his master's possessions, taking advantage of the fact that Mephibosheth was lame in his feet. Well, it just so happens that we have another amazing thematic connection between Ziba and Judas. According to the Gospel of John, Judas was a thief!

⁴But one of His disciples, Judas Iscariot, Simon's son, who would betray Him, said, ⁵"Why was this fragrant oil not sold for three hundred denari and given to the poor?" ⁶*This he said, not that he cared for the poor, but **because he was a thief**, and had the money box; and **he used to take what was put in it*** (John 12:4-6).

We've seen a prophetic picture of one aspect of the betrayal of the Messiah. Ziba approached David with insincere groveling just as Judas approached Yeshua with an insincere kiss. The other part of the prophetic picture is that of betrayal. The Messiah was betrayed by a close confidant. This is pictured in Ziba's accusation that Mephibosheth had stayed behind in order to be crowned king in his grandfather's place. In other words, instead of remaining faithful to David, Ziba has implied that Mephibosheth betrayed David by staying behind. As you can see, the prophetic picture of the Messiah's betrayal, although a shadow, is very clear indeed.

The Kiss of Betrayal Part II

David's Prophetic Picture

This brings us to II Samuel 16:5-23, which concerns David's confrontation with a man named Shimei and the advice given to Absalom by Ahithophel, David's former advisor. However, before examining this passage, let's review some information about chiastic structures. In Chapter 1, we presented a framework for understanding chiastic structures. We noted how the themes of the first half of a story are repeated in the second half of the story in reverse order. Furthermore, we saw how both halves of the chiastic structure pointed to the central axis, the most important point of the structure. Using this framework, we were able to see that II Samuel 15:10 – 20:2 was a large chiastic structure. As is so often the case, large chiastic structures have many smaller chiastic structures "nested" within them! It's not unusual to find many smaller chiastic structures within a larger one! Furthermore, some of the elements of one chiastic structure may be part of the elements of another chiastic structure. I want to examine two chiastic structures that are both part of each other. The first is found in II Samuel 15:25-37. The second is found in II Samuel 15:27-16:23. Even though these are two separate chiastic structures, note how they overlap from II Samuel 15:27-37. Although the second chiastic structure (II Samuel 15:27-16:23) is the next section of Scripture in our chronological trek through the story of David's flight from Absalom, the first chiastic structure (II Samuel 15:25-37) contains information that will help us in our study of one of the important characters in this portion of our study.

The Chiastic Structure of II Samuel 15:25-37

A) II Samuel 15:25-29—David makes an *"if, then"* statement followed by a *"but if, then"* statement; Zadok and Abiathar are to *return to the city (of Jerusalem)*; David *mentioned the two sons of the priests*; Zadok and Abiathar *carried the ark of God back to Jerusalem*; David said he would *wait until "word comes from" Zadok*

  B) II Samuel 15:30—David *went up by the ascent of the Mount of Olives*; all the people who were with him *covered their heads*

    C) II Samuel 15:31—Someone told David, saying, "Ahithophel is among the conspirators with Absalom." And David said, "O LORD, I pray, turn the counsel of Ahithophel into foolishness!"

  B') II Samuel 15:32—David had *come to the top of the mountain*; Hushai met David with *dust on his head*

A') II Samuel 15:33-36— David makes an *"if, then"* statement followed by a *"but if, then" statement*; David said, "Do you not have Zadok and Abiathar *the priests with you there (i.e., in Jerusalem)*"; David mentions *the two sons of the priests*; Hushai, David's friend *returned to Jerusalem*; "By them (Jonathan and Ahimaaz) *you shall send me everything you hear*"

This chiastic structure is a short one. However, it is still important. As I've mentioned before, the central axis is always a focal point of a chiastic structure. It usually functions in one of two ways:

- Sometimes, the central axis is the most important point in the chiastic structure. In other words, when the Holy One wants to make something stand out and grab your attention He may accomplish this by making it the central axis of a chiastic structure. This is His way of saying, "Hey! This is a very important piece of information!"
- Other times, it functions as the turning point, or point of contrast between the two halves of the chiastic structure. When the central axis functions as the turning point, you will usually see contrasts between elements in the two halves of the story. Or, the events that occur in the second half of the story reverse the direction of events that occurred in the first half of the story. We have already seen this once with our primary chiastic structure, II Samuel 15:10-20:2. If you remember, in the central axis (point L), three of David's friends brought food and provisions for him and his servants. Before the central axis, David was on the run, fleeing for his life. Immediately after the central axis, David, seemingly strengthened and encouraged from the provisions of his three friends, began to formulate a battle plan and then went on to defeat his enemy.

In the present structure, the themes of the second half of the story are essentially the same themes of the first half. In other words, there is no reversal in direction when one compares the first and second halves. Therefore, we should understand that the primary purpose of this chiastic structure pertains to the importance of its central axis. Through the central axis of the chiastic structure, The Holy One has personally hinted to us to *watch this person Ahithophel*. He's an important person in this narrative.[12]

The Chiastic Structure of II Samuel 15:27-16:23

A) II Samuel 15:27-28— *Are you not a seer*? See, I will wait in the plains of the wilderness until *word comes from you to inform me*[13]

  B) II Samuel 15:30—David was on his way to the *top of the Mount of Olives*; David and the people with them *covered their heads* and David went *barefoot*[14]

    C) II Samuel 15:31—Then someone told David, saying, "*Ahithophel is* among the conspirators *with Absalom*." And David said, "O LORD, I pray, *turn the counsel of Ahithophel into foolishness!*"

      D) II Samuel 15:32-34—*Hushai expressed loyalty and solidarity to David by approaching him* with his robe torn and dust on his head; David told Hushai to return to the city *and say to Absalom, "I will be your servant, O king; as I was your father's servant previously, so I will now also be your servant."*

        E) II Samuel 15:37—So David's friend *Hushai arrived at Jerusalem as Absalom was entering the city.*

          F) II Samuel 16:2b—Ziba brought donkeys for the king's household to ride on, *food* for the young men to eat and wine "*For those who are faint in the wilderness to drink*"

            G) II Samuel 16:3a—"And where is *your master's son?*"

              H) II Samuel 16:4a—". . . Israel will *restore the kingdom of my father to me.*"; "Here, *all that belongs to Mephibosheth is yours*"

                I) II Samuel 16:4b—"I (Ziba) *humbly bow before you*, that I may find favor in your sight, my lord, O king!"

J) *II Samuel 16:5—Now when King David came to Bahurim, there was a man from the family of the house of Saul, whose name was Shimei the son of Gera, coming from there.*

I') II Samuel 16:5b-6—He (Shimei) came out, *cursing continuously* as he came. And *he threw stones at David* and at all the servants of King David.

H') II Samuel 16:8—"... the house of Saul, *in whose place you have reigned* and the LORD has *delivered the kingdom into the hand of Absalom your son.*"

G') II Samuel 16:11a—"See how *my son* who came from my own body seeks my life."

F') II Samuel 16:14—The king and all the people who were with him <u>**became weary**</u>; so they <u>**refreshed themselves**</u> there (with the provisions brought by Ziba)

E') II Samuel 16:15-16a—*Absalom and all the men of Israel came to Jerusalem;* Then *Hushai the Arkite, David's friend, went to Absalom (in Jerusalem)*

D') II Samuel 16:16b-19—*Hushai expressed loyalty and solidarity with Absalom by approaching him* and saying "Long live the king"; Hushai said to Absalom, *"Furthermore, whom should I serve? Should I not serve the son? Just as I served your father, so I will serve you."*

C') II Samuel 16:20-21—Absalom said to Ahithophel, *"Give us your advice. What should we do?"*; *Ahithophel advised Absalom* concerning how to win over the men of Israel

B') II Samuel 16:22—They pitched a tent for Absalom *on the top of the house*; Absalom went in to his father's concubines in the sight of all Israel

A') II Samuel 16:23— Now *the advice of Ahithophel*, which he gave in those days, *was as if one had inquired at the oracle of God*

As you are well aware, I am proceeding chronologically through the story of David's flight from Absalom. Therefore, chronologically we need to analyze II Samuel 16:5-23. However, we must always remember that the Scriptures aren't written solely in chronological order. As we can see from the chiastic structure above, II Samuel 16:5-23 is part of a larger thematic presentation of David's flight from Absalom, i.e., it's part of a chiastic structure. Therefore, I suggest that we allow the chiastic structure to help guide us at this juncture in our study. It is true that chronologically we have arrived at II Samuel 16:5-23. But as you can see from the chiastic structure, there is important information preceding these verses that is part of the thematic presentation of II Samuel 16:5-23, namely, the first part of our chiastic structure (II Samuel 15:27-16:4).

A general outline of II Samuel 15:27-16:23 is shown below.

- II Samuel 15:27-29—David sent Zadok and Abiathar back to Jerusalem as spies
- II Samuel 15:30-31—David heard about Ahithophel's treachery
- II Samuel 15:32-37—David sent his friend Hushai back to Jerusalem as a spy
- II Samuel 16:1-4—Ziba brought David provisions

- II Samuel 16:5-14 — Shimei confronted David
- II Samuel 16:15-19 — Hushai befriended Absalom
- II Samuel 16:20-23 — Ahithophel's advice to Absalom

At this point, I want to examine the actions of two people — Hushai and Shimei. Let's first look at Hushai. We read about Hushai in two parts of our chiastic structure (II Samuel 15:32-37 and II Samuel 16:15-19). In II Samuel 15:32-37 we learn that Hushai is David's loyal friend. Hushai wanted to flee with David; however, David asked him to return to Jerusalem as a double agent who could befriend Absalom and then send information concerning Absalom's plans via Ahimaaz and Jonathan, Zadok's and Abiathar's sons.

This brings us to II Samuel 16:15-19, where Hushai approaches Absalom. Please read these few verses. What is Hushai doing when he stated the following to Absalom?

- Hushai approached Absalom and said, *"Long live the king! Long live the king!"*
- When Absalom questioned Hushai concerning his lack of loyalty to David, Hushai said, "No, but whom the LORD and this people and all the men of Israel choose, his I will be, and with him I will remain. Furthermore, whom should I serve? Should I not serve in the presence of his son? *As I have served in your father's presence, so will I be in your presence.*"

What was Hushai doing? I'll tell you what he was doing. He was "betraying David!" I put *betraying* in quotes because we know that he wasn't actually betraying David. He was simply doing what David asked him to do. But as you can see, he was playing his role perfectly. *He made Absalom believe that he had betrayed his friend David!*

II Samuel 16:15-19 should also remind you of another scene in our story. Note how Hushai approached Absalom. We know he was not being truthful when he said, "Long live the king! Long live the king!" What scene does this remind you of? It reminds me of Ziba approaching David! Remember Ziba, the greedy servant of Mephibosheth, who has already presented us with a picture of Judas the betrayer? Please note the following parallels between II Samuel 16:1-4 (the story of Ziba approaching David) and 15-19 (the story of Hushai approaching Absalom).

- *Ziba approached* David with provisions and stated, "I humbly bow before you, that I may find favor in your sight, my lord, O king," *groveling and fawning before David. Hushai approached Absalom* saying, "Long live the king! Long live the king," *groveling and fawning over Absalom* to win his trust.
- *David asked Ziba, "And where is your master's son (Mephibosheth)?"* because he wondered why Mephibosheth was not *showing loyalty* to him (by fleeing with David), even though David had showered him with grace and kindness. *Absalom asked Hushai, "Is this your loyalty to your friend? Why did you not go with your friend?"* because he wondered why Hushai was turning on David.

As you can see, Hushai is "betraying" David just as Ziba stated that Mephibosheth had been disloyal to David. By connecting Hushai's betrayal of David before Absalom to Ziba's actions before David, we have made yet another thematic connection proving that we properly interpreted Ziba's actions. Clearly, Ziba has been thematically connected to Hushai, someone engaged in the act of "betrayal." Do you see what is happening? First, we were presented with the story of Mephibosheth's "betrayal," now we've been presented with the story of Hushai's "betrayal." Do you think perhaps Adonai wants us to focus on the theme of *betrayal*?

Lastly, I'd like to comment once more on Ziba's bad character. I believe we've already seen enough thematic support that he lied to David and slandered his master. However, please note to whom Ziba is thematically connected in our chiastic structure above (elements I and I'). He is thematically connected to Shimei a true traitor! Once again, a chiastic structure has helped us by making a key thematic connection. By the way, this is another function of chiastic structures and parallelisms. They connect people, places and things that we may not have connected on our own.

Yeshua's Prophetic Fulfillment

Once again, the Tanakh is presenting us with a picture of the betrayal of the Messiah! Remember, David is our Messianic figure whose life is a picture of the Messiah's life. In the first part of this chapter (The Kiss of Betrayal Part I), we saw how Ziba made David believe that Mephibosheth had betrayed him. We also saw how Ziba approached David with an insincere show of groveling. These were prophetic shadows of how Judas betrayed the Messiah with a kiss. But remember how many thematic connections we had to make in order to see the picture? Now, the Tanakh is giving us yet another picture of betrayal! This is a second witness, so to speak, of the betrayal of the Messiah. And it doesn't need half the explanation as did the example of Ziba approaching David. Hushai, a friend of David, was clearly "betraying" him before Absalom. This is another clear snapshot of the betrayal of Messiah Yeshua by Judas, His close friend. Hushai is a picture of Judas betraying the Master.

You may ask why the Tanakh has given us two pictures of the betrayal. The answer is simple. It's the nature of Messianic prophecy. This is why there are so many Messianic figures (Adam, Enoch, Abel, Joseph, David, Samson and the list goes on and on). The Ruach (Spirit) uses multiple personalities to teach us different aspects of the Messiah's life and mission. I call them snapshots of salvation. For example, the Ruach used Mephibosheth and Hushai to teach us that the Messiah would be betrayed by a close friend. However, He used Ziba to give us a prophetic picture of the kiss of betrayal. And guess what? There is yet another personality in the account of David's flight from Absalom who will play the role of Judas! Yes, another—three witnesses to the truth of the betrayal of the Messiah. Do you believe I can find a fourth? Well, could we not state that Ziba betrayed Mephibosheth? Yes, we can. Ziba, a slave of Saul's family, should have remained loyal to his master, Mephibosheth. Instead, because of his greed, he falsely slandered his master, taking advantage of Mephibosheth's lame feet. Yes, he betrayed his master just as Judas betrayed his master, Yeshua!

Let's take a closer look at some verses we've glossed over. According to II Samuel 15:12, Ahithophel was David's counselor!

While Absalom was offering sacrifices, he also sent for **Ahithophel the Gilonite, David's counselor**, to come from Giloh, his hometown. And so the conspiracy gained strength, and Absalom's following kept on increasing.

According to II Samuel 15:31, Ahithophel was one of the conspirators.

³¹ Then someone told David, saying, "**Ahithophel is among the conspirators with Absalom.**" And David said, "O LORD, I pray, turn the counsel of Ahithophel into foolishness!"

Lastly, according to II Samuel 16:23, Ahithophel was a very important advisor to David, then to Absalom.

Now in those days the advice Ahithophel gave was like that of one who inquires of God. That was how both David and Absalom regarded all of Ahithophel's advice.

These verses clearly teach us that Ahithophel betrayed David! Ahithophel used to be David's trusted advisor and confidant. However, he betrayed David and joined forces with Absalom. Now our picture is complete. We have been given three pictures of the betrayal of the Messiah. Remember, in the Chiastic Structure of II Samuel 15:25-37, the central axis concerned the fact that Ahithophel was one of the conspirators! During analysis of that chiastic structure I showed you that the main purpose of its central axis was to emphasize the importance of the fact that Ahithophel was one of the conspirators. Of the three examples of betrayal that we've seen, Ahithophel is the most important. Although all three people involved in the pictures of the betrayal—Mephibosheth, Hushai and Ahithophel—are prophetic pictures of Judas Iscariot, you must remember that only Ahithophel actually betrayed David! Ziba slandered Mephibosheth to make it seem to David as if he'd betrayed him. Hushai "betrayed" David as part of a plan for him to be a double agent on David's behalf. Thus, neither of them actually betrayed David. Ahithophel is quite another story. He actually betrayed David. Thus, it seems that Ahithophel has emerged as a very prominent person in this story. Have you noticed that Ahithophel is the only co-conspirator mentioned by name? Truly, he is very important to our study. In fact, as we continue our story, once more you will see Ahithophel fulfill his prophetic role as Judas Iscariot. The picture will be clear and there will be no doubt that he is a prophetic shadow of Judas. For now, let us turn our attention to the second important story in the chiastic structure of II Samuel 15:27-16:23, the story of Shimei's confrontation with David.

The Confrontation

David's Prophetic Picture

Basically, II Samuel 16:5-14 describes how a man named Shimei came throwing rocks at David and his servants. Furthermore, he cursed David.

⁵Now when King David came to Bahurim, there was a man from the family of the house of Saul, whose name was Shimei the son of Gera, coming from there. *He came out, cursing continuously as he came. ⁶And he threw stones at David and at all the servants of King David.* And all the people and all the mighty men were on his right hand and on his left. ⁷Also *Shimei said thus when he cursed: "Come out! Come out! You bloodthirsty man, you rogue! ⁸The LORD has brought upon you all the blood of*

the house of Saul, in whose place you have reigned; and the LORD has delivered the kingdom into the hand of Absalom your son. So now you are caught in your own evil, because you are a bloodthirsty man (II Samuel 16:5-8)!"

As you can guess, Shimei is one deceived man! How could he make those statements? Did he have access to any of the facts concerning David and Saul? Notice how he stated that David was a bloodthirsty man and a rogue! In case you don't remember, let's take inventory of a few facts concerning David and Saul.

- ♦ I Samuel 14:41-45—Saul was actually about to slay his own son Jonathan because of a rash oath he'd taken. If it weren't for the people, Saul would have killed his own son!
- ♦ I Samuel 16:14-23—Saul was tormented by a spirit of melancholy; however, David would play his harp and minister to Saul and cause the spirit to depart from him.
- ♦ I Samuel 18:1-16—Saul became morbidly jealous of David and twice tried to impale him with a spear.
- ♦ I Samuel 18:17-29—Saul tried to have David killed by the Philistines.
- ♦ I Samuel 19:9-10—Saul tried to impale David with a spear again.
- ♦ I Samuel 19:11-24—David was forced to flee for his life after Saul sent men to kill him in his sleep.
- ♦ I Samuel 20:33—Saul hurled his spear at his own son Jonathan, intending to kill him but missed.
- ♦ I Samuel 21-26—A collection of stories detailing how Saul tried to kill David but failed. Numerous times, David could have easily killed Saul, but refused to do so.

Please read the following account and ask yourself, "Who was the bloodthirsty man?"

¹⁶And the king said, "You shall surely die, Ahimelech, you and all your father's house!" ¹⁷Then the king said to the guards who stood about him, "Turn and kill the priests of the LORD, because their hand also is with David, and because they knew when he fled and did not tell it to me." But the servants of the king would not lift their hands to strike the priests of the LORD. *¹⁸And the king said to Doeg, "You turn and kill the priests!" So Doeg the Edomite turned and struck the priests, and killed on that day eighty-five men who wore a linen ephod. ¹⁹Also Nob, the city of the priests, he struck with the edge of the sword, both men and women, children and nursing infants, oxen and donkeys and sheep—with the edge of the sword* (I Samuel 22:16-19).

I could go on and on. There are more examples of Saul's reckless behavior. One wonders if Shimei was in his right mind as he leveled these baseless charges against David!

In response to Shimei's unbecoming behavior, Abishai the son of Zeruiah said to the king, "Why should this dead dog curse my lord the king? Please, *let me go over and take off his head*!" However, please note David's response to Abishai concerning his suggestion and Shimei's accusations!

¹⁰But the king said, "What have I to do with you, you sons of Zeruiah? *So let him curse, because the LORD has said to him, 'Curse David.' Who then shall say, 'Why have*

you done so?" ¹¹And David said to Abishai and all his servants, "See how my son who came from my own body seeks my life. How much more now may this Benjamite? ***Let him alone, and let him curse; for so the LORD has ordered him.*** ¹²It may be that the LORD will look on my affliction, and that the LORD will repay me with good for his cursing this day (II Samuel 16:10-12)."

Isn't that amazing? First of all, David spared Shimei's life, preventing Abishai from taking off his head. But what's more important is David's attitude. Now, if anyone knows Shimei is making false accusations it's David, and yet David didn't retaliate or deny! In fact, David stated that the LORD told Shimei to curse him! What? This is almost unbelievable. David's attitude is one of acquiescence to his fate. Instead of fighting back, David has commanded his servants to refrain from any violence. He has submitted to what he perceived was the Father's will.

Yeshua's Prophetic Fulfillment

After Judas' kiss of betrayal, the soldiers confronted the Messiah and arrested Him (Matthew 26:47-56, Mark 14:43-50, Luke 22:47-53 and John 18:2-11). This was His confrontation with His accusers just as David was confronted by Shimei. And true to the prophetic picture, Peter drew his sword, striking at the high priest's servant's ***head***, wanting to take off his head like Abishai had prophetically suggested! Instead, he was only able to cut off his right ear.

Next, Yeshua spoke to His disciples just as David spoke to Abishai, telling them to refrain from violence.

⁵² But Jesus said to him, ***"Put your sword in its place***, for all who take the sword will perish by the sword. ⁵³ Or do you think that I cannot now pray to My Father, and He will provide Me with more than twelve legions of angels? ⁵⁴ ***How then could the Scriptures be fulfilled, that it must happen thus?"*** ⁵⁵ In that hour Jesus said to the multitudes, "Have you come out, as against a robber, with swords and clubs to take Me? I sat daily with you, teaching in the temple, and you did not seize Me. ⁵⁶ ***But all this was done that the Scriptures of the prophets might be fulfilled."*** Then all the disciples forsook Him and fled (Matthew 26:52-56).

In this passage, Yeshua rebuked Peter just as David rebuked Abishai, not wanting His disciples to kill those confronting Him. Did you notice how Yeshua stated twice that these events were occurring to fulfill the prophetic writings? Now, we know of at least one place that prophetically spoke of this particular event, II Samuel 16:5-14!

Lastly, note Yeshua's attitude towards those who came to arrest Him even though He had done no wrong and compare them to the words David spoke.

⁵⁰And one of them struck the servant of the high priest and cut off his right ear. ⁵¹But ***Jesus answered and said, "Permit even this."*** And He touched his ear and healed him (Luke 22:50-51).

¹¹So Jesus said to Peter, "Put your sword into the sheath. ***Shall I not drink the cup which My Father has given Me*** (John 18:11)?"

¹⁰But the king said, "What have I to do with you, you sons of Zeruiah? ***So let him curse, because the LORD has said to him, "Curse David.' Who then shall say, "Why have you done so?***"'¹¹And David said to Abishai and all his servants, "See how my son who came from my own body seeks my life. How much more now may this Benjamite? ***Let him alone, and let him curse; for so the LORD has ordered him.*** ¹²It may be that the LORD will look on my affliction, and that the LORD will repay me with good for his cursing this day (II Samuel 16:10-12)."

As you can see, the Messiah is conveying the same message David did, i.e., "Let these events occur and do not interfere. I am totally submitted to what the Father is doing in this situation and I dare not resist His will." Yes, beloved, when David spoke to Abishai asking him to allow Shimei to curse him, and when he stated that the LORD had commanded Shimei to curse him, he was actually giving us a prophetic glimpse of the Messiah who would one day submit to the heavenly Father's will, allowing himself to be captured by His accusers, not wanting harm to come upon them. This, my friends, is an amazing story, all foretold centuries ago by the prophets of Israel. Each piece is in its correct order, being brought to light by the Ruach Adonai (Spirit of the Lord). Bless His Holy Name.

Taking Counsel

David's Prophetic Picture

As of II Samuel 16:20, Absalom has two people advising him on how to defeat David—Hushai and Ahithophel. At this point, I'd like to give you a brief summary of II Samuel 16:20-17:14.

- ♦ II Samuel 16:20-23—Ahithophel advised Absalom on how to win the support of the men of Israel
- ♦ II Samuel 17:1-4—Ahithophel offered his advice on how to kill David.
- ♦ II Samuel 17:5-14—Hushai offered his advice on how to kill David.

II Samuel 16:20 is an important verse. It states that Absalom asked Ahithophel, "Give us your advice. What should we do?" Furthermore, in II Samuel 17:5-6, Absalom asked Hushai for his advice on how to kill David. We know that Ahithophel was one of David's trusted advisors (II Samuel 15:12). Furthermore, we know that David specifically sent Hushai to "defeat the advice/counsel of Ahithophel (II Samuel 15:34)." Notice how the word advice/counsel keeps coming up? In fact, the word advice occurs explicitly seven times within II Samuel 16:20-17:14! Another literary device Adonai uses to get our attention is repetition. By using the word *advice* so many times in such a short number of verses, the Holy One wants us to see that the primary focus of these verses pertains to how Absalom secured advice from those he had gathered around him. In other words, it is very plain to see that *Absalom has **gathered people** around him and is **taking counsel** from them.*

For what purpose have these people gathered together to give Absalom counsel? The answer appears in the counsel/advice of Ahithophel and Hushai.

¹ Moreover Ahithophel said to Absalom, "Now let me choose twelve thousand men, and I will arise and pursue David tonight. ² I will come upon him while he is weary and weak, and make him afraid. And all the people who are with him will flee, and *I will strike only the king*. ³ Then I will bring back all the people to you. When all return except the man whom you seek, all the people will be at peace (II Samuel 17:1-3)."

¹¹ Therefore I advise that all Israel be fully gathered to you, from Dan to Beersheba, like the sand that is by the sea for multitude, and that you go to battle in person. ¹² So we will come upon him in some place where he may be found, and *we will fall on him as the dew falls on the ground*. And of him and all the men who are with him there shall not be left so much as one. ¹³ Moreover, if he has withdrawn into a city, then all Israel shall bring ropes to that city; and we will pull it into the river, until there is not one small stone found there (II Samuel 17:11-13)."

It is plain to see that they gathered and took counsel on how they could kill David! That was the purpose for the gathering and it was the subject of the advice/counsel of Hushai and Ahithophel.

Yeshua's Prophetic Fulfillment

We have already seen 1) the prophetic betrayal by Judas, 2) the confrontation between Yeshua and those sent to arrest Him, and 3) Peter striking at the high priest's servant's ear. The next portion of the Gospel accounts (Matthew 26:56-75, Mark 14:50-72, Luke 22:54-71 and John 18:12-23) concern two major events:

- All of the disciples forsook Yeshua and fled. Later, Peter denied knowing Yeshua three times.
- The chief priests and elders took counsel on how they might kill Yeshua.

The prophetic picture of the chief priests taking counsel on how they might kill Messiah Yeshua has been provided for us by the meeting between Absalom, Ahithophel and Hushai (as well as others), as they gathered to determine how they would put David to death! Matthew 26:56-75,

Now the chief priests, the elders, and all the council sought false testimony against Jesus to put Him to death (Matthew 26:59).

As you read the Gospel accounts you will see that the prophetic picture painted by the author of II Samuel hits the mark! Once again, we are confronted with an amazing prophecy of an event in the life of Messiah Yeshua which occurs in its correct prophetic sequence!

The other event pertains to the fact that the disciples forsook Yeshua. Let's go back to a passage we've looked at briefly.

I will come upon him while he is weary and weak, and make him afraid. And all *the people who are with him will flee, and I will strike only the king* (II Samuel 17:2).

This passage contains part of Ahithophel's advice to Absalom. Read this verse carefully. It should remind you of another prophecy concerning the Messiah!

"Awake, O sword, against My Shepherd, against *the man who is my companion*," says the LORD of hosts. "*Strike the Shepherd*, and *the sheep will be scattered* (Zechariah 13:7a) . . ."

Ahithophel's advice, which prophetically occurs at the same time the disciples fled in fear, is almost a direct quote from Zechariah 13:7! Also notice the phrase "the man who is my companion." Ahithophel was David's trusted companion and confidant! The themes connecting these prophetic acts in II Samuel to Yeshua's sufferings are almost endless.

As if that wasn't enough proof, there's another reason why we can know beyond a shadow of doubt that Zechariah 13:7, and thus Ahithophel's advice, pertains directly to Yeshua's disciples fleeing from Him. Because, the Master Himself said so!

[31] Then Jesus said to them, "All of you will be made to stumble because of Me this night, for it is written: 'I will strike the Shepherd, and the sheep of the flock will be scattered (Matthew 26:31).'"

At this point, I'd like to draw your attention to one more prophetic picture concerning those who came to arrest Messiah Yeshua. Hushai's plan (II Samuel 17:11-12a) required that *all Israel be fully gathered, from Dan to Beersheba, like the sand that is by the sea for multitude*. In other words, Hushai's plan required that a multitude go forth to capture David. It just so happens that the Gospels mention that a multitude went to arrest Yeshua.

In that hour Jesus said to the *multitudes*, "Have you come out, as against a robber with swords and clubs to take Me? I sat daily with you, teaching in the temple, and you did not seize Me (Matthew 26:55).

Then Judas, having received a *detachment of troops, and officers from the chief priests and Pharisees*, came there with lanterns, torches, and weapons (John 18:3).

Thus, we see that II Samuel 16:20-17:14 is a prophecy of those who would one day take counsel on how to kill the Messiah. Through the words of Ahithophel's advice, we see that the Messiah's disciples will flee from Him because of fear of the sword. Through the words of Hushai, we learn that a multitude will go to arrest the Messiah. Absolutely amazing!

Summary

Below is the ***Running Chart of the Thematic Connections Between II Samuel 15:10 – 20:2 and the Gospels*** summarizing what we have learned in this chapter.

Running Chart of the Thematic Connections Between II Samuel 15:10 – 20:2 and the Gospels

II Samuel	The Gospels
II Samuel 16:1-4—Greedy Ziba, who tricked David into giving him Mephibosheth's estate, approached David with insincere compliments (groveling, fawning, etc.) and ulterior motives; Ziba made David think that Mephibosheth had betrayed him	**Matthew 26:47-50, Mark 14:43-46, Luke 22:47-48 and John 18:2-9**—Judas, the greedy thief, approached Yeshua with an insincere kiss of betrayal
II Samuel 15:30-37 and 16:15-19—Ahithophel betrayed David and Hushai "betrayed" David	**Matthew 26:47-50, Mark 14:43-46, Luke 22:47-48 and John 18:2-9**—Judas betrayed the Messiah
II Samuel 16:5-14—David was confronted by Shimei who accused him of many wrongdoings; Abishai, David's servant, wanted to cut Shimei's head off; David submitted to Adonai's will even stating that Shimei was sent by Adonai to curse him; David informed Abishai not to harm Shimei by retaliation	**Matthew 26:47-56, Mark 14:43-50, Luke 22:47-53 and John 18:2-11**—Yeshua was confronted by His accusers, a multitude of people who came to arrest Him; Peter cut off the ear (on the head) of the high priest's servant; Yeshua submitted to His Father's will and didn't resist being arrested; informed His disciples not to retaliate
II Samuel 16:20-17:14—Ahithophel and Hushai gather to give Absalom counsel on how to kill David; Ahithophel promised to strike David and cause his followers to flee; Hushai wanted to bring a multitude to take David	**Matthew 26:56-75, Mark 14:50-72, Luke 22:54-71 and John 18:12-23**—The chief priests and elders gathered together to take counsel on how to put Yeshua to death; in direct fulfillment of Zechariah 13:7 and Ahithophel's advice, Yeshua's disciples all forsook Him; a multitude came to arrest Yeshua

Thematic Moments

This portion of our story has seen many references to Ahithophel, David's trusted counselor, who betrayed him. I find it interesting that Hushai also finds prominence within this context. As I study thematically, I try to make myself aware of as many thematic connections as I can to the subject at hand, because I have found that often a thematic connection will contain nuggets of wisdom that would otherwise be impossible to determine. For example, the book of II Samuel is not the only place in the Scripture that mentions Hushai and Ahithophel.

> [32] Also Jehonathan, David's uncle, was a *counselor, a wise man, and a scribe*; and Jehiel the son of Hachmoni was with the king's sons. [33] *Ahithophel was the king's counselor, and Hushai the Archite was the king's companion.* [34] After *Ahithophel*

was Jehoiada the son of Benaiah, then Abiathar. And the general of the king's army was Joab (I Chronicles 27:32-34).

This passage is taken from a section where the Chronicler is recounting some of David's royal officials. Once again, we see that Ahithophel is noted as being David's counselor. We saw earlier that Ahithophel's advice was almost as good as hearing from a prophet! Thus, I'm sure that David respected Ahithophel and valued his friendship and wisdom. It is a shame that he would be so treacherous as to betray David like he did. In contrast to Ahithophel, Hushai remained faithful and loyal to David. Ten times in Scripture, Hushai is recounted as David's trusted friend! O how beautiful it is for brothers to dwell together in unity. In sum, it seems that Hushai and Ahithophel are mentioned so many times to point out the disparity between their service to King David.

One has to wonder why Ahithophel would betray David after having served him as such a close confidant. Perhaps the reason lies within the following facts:

So David sent and inquired about the woman. And someone said, "Is this not Bathsheba, the ***daughter of Eliam***, the wife of Uriah the Hittite (II Samuel 11:3)?"

Eliphelet the son of Ahasbai, the son of the Maachathite, ***Eliam the son of Ahithophel the Gilonite*** (II Samuel 23:34)

Then Absalom sent for ***Ahithophel the Gilonite***, David's counselor, from his city—from Giloh—while he offered sacrifices. And the conspiracy grew strong, for the people with Absalom continually increased in number (II Samuel 15:12).

These verses clearly demonstrate that Ahithophel was Bathsheba's grandfather! Perhaps Ahithophel turned against David because of how he treated her. It is not difficult to conceive that Ahithophel may have lost respect for David after the incident with Bathsheba and the commanded murder of Uriah the Hittite, Ahithophel's grandson-in-law.

At this point, I'd like for you to read a passage from the Gospel of John.

[18] "I do not speak concerning all of you. I know whom I have chosen; but that the Scripture may be fulfilled, '***He who eats bread with Me has lifted up his heel against Me.***' [19] Now I tell you before it comes, that when it does come to pass, you may believe that I am He. [20] Most assuredly, I say to you, he who receives whomever I send receives Me; and he who receives Me receives Him who sent Me." [21] When Jesus had said these things, He was troubled in spirit, and testified and said, "***Most assuredly, I say to you, one of you will betray Me.***" [22] Then the disciples looked at one another, perplexed about whom He spoke. [23] Now there was leaning on Jesus' bosom one of His disciples, whom Jesus loved. [24] Simon Peter therefore motioned to him to ask who it was of whom He spoke. [25] Then, leaning back on Jesus' breast, he said to Him, "Lord, who is it?"

[26] Jesus answered, "***It is he to whom I shall give a piece of bread when I have dipped it.***" ***And having dipped the bread, He gave it to Judas Iscariot, the son of Simon.*** [27]

Now after the piece of bread, Satan entered him. Then Jesus said to him, "What you do, do quickly." [28] But no one at the table knew for what reason He said this to him. [29] For some thought, because Judas had the money box, that Jesus had said to him, "Buy those things we need for the feast," or that he should give something to the poor. [30] Having received the piece of bread, he then went out immediately. And it was night (John 13:18-30).

This passage recounts how Yeshua foretold of His betrayal by Judas. In John 13:18, Yeshua quoted from Psalm 41:

Even *my own familiar friend in whom I trusted*, who ate my bread, has lifted up *his* heel against me (Psalm 41:9).

As you can see, we have done well to understand that Ahithophel is truly a picture of Judas Iscariot! Psalm 41 was written by David and he is surely talking about Ahithophel, his familiar friend whom he trusted. Yeshua is clearly informing us that Psalm 41 is a Messianic Psalm shedding light on how He would be betrayed. Our thematic connections have drawn us to the same conclusions! Ahithophel is a picture of Judas Iscariot, a close friend and confidant of Yeshua, who betrayed him for 30 pieces of silver.

Amazingly enough, Psalm 41 is not the only Messianic Psalm. So, how does one know when a psalm has Messianic content? Traditionally people look to the New Testament to determine which psalm is Messianic. This is done by simply noting which passages from the Tanakh are referenced by the New Testament writers. The only problem with this approach is this. The New Testament was not meant to be an exhaustive source of Messianic information. The New Testament only touches on Messianic prophecy. There is so much more waiting to be discovered. All we need to do is allow Adonai to point out which psalms are Messianic thematically. He is more than willing and able to teach us about the Messiah in the Tanakh if we submit ourselves to His plan of revelation.

I have found that the same thematic tools used heretofore can be used to uncover Messianic prophecy in the Psalms. We simply need to look for the following:

- Psalms with obvious Messianic content
- Psalms with thematic connections to other Messianic passages
- Psalms with thematic connections to known Messianic figures
- Psalms with thematic connections to other Messianic psalms
- Psalms with thematic connections involving pictures of death and resurrection (elements of The Sign of the Messiah)

Time does not permit me to give you an extensive list of Messianic Psalms, but I can say that there are so many that it's almost easier to list the Psalms that are not Messianic! Nevertheless, I'd like to share with you how one could know that Psalm 41 is Messianic even apart from Yeshua's reference in John 13:18!

Psalm 41 clearly presents us with shadowy images of deliverance from impending death.

¹ Blessed is he who considers the poor; *the LORD will deliver him in time of trouble.* ² The LORD *will preserve him and keep him alive*, and he will be blessed on the earth; *You will not deliver him to the will of his enemies.* ³ The LORD will strengthen him on his bed of illness; You will sustain him on his sickbed. ⁴ I said, "LORD, be merciful to me; heal my soul, for I have sinned against You." ⁵ My enemies speak evil of me: "When will he die, and his name perish (Psalm 41:1-5)?"

Verse one states that Adonai, "Will deliver him in time of trouble." Then, verse two states that Adonai will keep him alive and, "Not deliver him to the will of his enemies." And what is typically the will of one's enemies? Death! In other words, Adonai will save his live. This passage hints of deliverance from death, which is a dominant theme in the lives of all Messianic figures.

Now that we have identified Psalm 41 as a Messianic Psalm, we can identify another Messianic Psalm by making the proper thematic connection. Notice what is stated in Psalm 55!

¹² For it is not an enemy who reproaches me; then I could bear it. Nor is it one who hates me who has exalted himself against me; then I could hide from him. ¹³ *But it was you, a man my equal, my companion and my acquaintance.* ¹⁴ *We took sweet counsel together, and walked to the house of God in the throng* (Psalm 55:12-14).

Psalm 55:12-14 is thematically connected to Psalm 41:9. The common theme is that David's close companion has turned against him. Clearly, Psalm 55:12-14 is another prophesy about Ahithophel.

Chapter 4

Beyond the Sign of the Messiah

Introduction

In the last chapter, we studied II Samuel 16:1 through II Samuel 17:14. Thematically, these verses presented us with a clear picture of the betrayal of Messiah Yeshua. Significant events which occurred in the Garden of Gethsemane, including Judas' kiss of betrayal and Yeshua's arrest by a multitude, were prophesied through the events chronicled in II Samuel 16:1 – 17:14. The beauty of Adonai's wisdom is readily evident when you consider the following. The writer of II Samuel, under the unction of the Ruach HaKodesh (Holy Spirit), simply recorded the events of David's flight from Absalom in chronological order, beginning with Absalom's rebellion until his demise. At the pashat or literal level of interpretation, this story pertains to the events that occurred as a fulfillment of Nathan's prophecy (that the sword would not depart from David's house); however, by studying the scriptures thematically, we have discovered two fascinating revelations. First, we have clearly shown that another story is being told thematically! It is the Gospel, the story of Messiah Yeshua's suffering, death and resurrection. *Secondly, the thematic presentation of the Gospel told through David's flight from Absalom matches the chronological presentation of it in the four Gospel accounts!* Only the Holy One of Israel could be so clever and wise as He tells us the end from the beginning.

This chapter will continue the process of mapping the suffering of the Messiah through the story of David's flight from Absalom. However, we will soon discover a "glitch" in the chronological presentation of the Gospel. Although the story of David's flight from Absalom continues in chronological order, the second story, which presents us with a thematic presentation of the Gospel, will meander from its chronological course. At that point, we will need to make a digression in our study. The topics discussed will contain plenty of valuable information to help understand 1) the significance of the chronological departure from the thematic presentation of the Gospel, 2) why the thematic presentation of the Gospel departs from chronological order, and 3) a justification for the departure.

Finishing the Portrait of Judas

David's Prophetic Picture

The next portion of scripture we need to examine begins with II Samuel 17:15. As I began to study this passage and the first few verses after it, I noted the following chiastic structure (which includes II Samuel 17:14).

The Chiastic Structure of II Samuel 17:14-23

A) II Samuel 17:14—Absalom said, "The advice of Hushai the Archite is **better than the advice of Ahithophel**"; The Lord had purposed to defeat the good advice of Ahithophel *to bring disaster on Absalom*

  B) II Samuel 17:15—Hushai said to Zadok, "**Thus and so Ahithophel advised** Absalom and the elders of Israel."

    C) II Samuel 17:16—Hushai said, "Do not spend this night in the plains of the wilderness, *but speedily cross over...*"

      D) II Samuel 17:17—So a female servant would come and tell them, *and they would go and tell King David*

        E) II Samuel 17:18—A lad saw them and *told Absalom*. But both of them went away quickly and came to a man's house in Bahurim, who *had a well in his court, and they went down into it*

          F) II Samuel 17:20a—Absalom's servants asked, "**Where are Ahimaaz and Jonathan?**"

            G) II Samuel 17:20b—So the woman said to them, "They have gone over the water brook."

          F') II Samuel 17:20c— . . . and when *they had searched and could not find them*

        E') II Samuel 17:21a—Now it came to pass, after they had departed, *that they came up out of the well* and went and *told King David*

      D') II Samuel 17:21b— . . . and *went and told King David*

    C') II Samuel 17:21c—Ahimaaz and Jonathan told David, "Arise and *cross over the water quickly*."

  B') II Samuel 17:21d— Ahimaaz and Jonathan told David, "For *thus has Ahithophel advised* against you."

A') II Samuel 17:23—Ahithophel saw that *his advice was not followed*; *he hanged himself* and died

One of the most important hermeneutic paradigms for anyone to grasp concerning the scriptures is that of thematic connections. The Holy One has organized the scriptures thematically. Hundreds, if not thousands, of thematic connections exist within it. One of the clearest ways to determine which scriptures are thematically connected is to examine them within the context of a chiastic structure. After all, by definition, the chiastic structure exists by virtue of the pattern of common themes expressed in the two halves of the structure! In other words, once you've found a chiastic structure, you know that each element in the first half is thematically connected to another in the second half. Although this chiastic structure seems to be rather simple in complexity, in actuality, it contains a high level of prophecy and teaching. Analysis of chiastic structures requires that you compare and contrast each element that is thematically connected, e.g., compare A to A', and B to B', etc. At this time however, we will only examine element A.

From our chiastic structure, we learn that II Samuel 17:14 is thematically connected to II Samuel 17:23. There are two clear connections here. First, both passages mention the *advice* of Ahithophel. Secondly, both passages connect a character in our story to *an ominous event*. In the case of Absalom, the scripture states that Adonai had decreed disaster upon him. On the other hand, Ahithophel hanged himself. Therefore, even though the event concerning Ahithophel's death occurred towards the end of the chiastic structure, its thematic connection to II Samuel 17:14 (the beginning of the chiastic structure) places it at the chronological beginning of this section of scripture. In other words, although II Samuel 17:23 occurred after the events of II Samuel 17:14-22, its thematic connection to II Samuel 17:14 "moves it forward" in the chronological order allowing us to consider it along with II Samuel 17:14.

Remember, II Samuel 16:1 – 17:14 pertained to events that prophetically spoke of the betrayal of Messiah Yeshua by Judas Iscariot. Furthermore, we saw through numerous means that Ahithophel presented us with a clear picture of Judas. Now, through our chiastic structure, we can see that the next major event still concerns Ahithophel. Let's examine II Samuel 17:23 more closely.

> Now when *Ahithophel saw that his advice was not followed*, he saddled a donkey, and arose and *went home* to his house, to his city. Then he *put his household in order*, and *hanged himself*, and died; and *he was buried in his father's tomb* (II Samuel 17:23).

I want to draw your attention to the actions committed by Ahithophel. They are summarized as follows:

- *Ahithophel saw that his advice was not followed*—In other words, he had time to think about his advice and the fact that it was dismissed. Ahithophel's contemplation of the fact that David's assassination would not be carried out according to his plan prompted him into action.
- *He . . . went home*—Ahithophel's immediate action was to go somewhere; home.
- *He put his household in order*—After mulling over the events, Ahithophel decided to straighten out his affairs. In other words, he wanted to clear up any issues pertaining to his family.
- *He . . . hanged himself*—After clearing up issues at home, he hanged himself.
- *He was buried in his father's tomb*—The scripture goes on to give us details concerning Ahithophel's burial.

Yeshua's Prophetic Fulfillment

Now, let's look at the betrayal of Yeshua. The Gospel of Matthew records the events which occurred following Yeshua's arrest.

Then Judas, His betrayer, *seeing that He had been condemned, was remorseful and brought back the thirty pieces of silver to the chief priests and elders,* ⁴ saying, *"I have sinned by betraying innocent blood."* And they said, "What *is that* to us? You see *to it!"* ⁵ Then *he threw down the pieces of silver in the temple and departed,* and went and hanged himself. ⁶ But the chief priests took the silver pieces and said, "It is not lawful to put them into the treasury, because they are the price of blood." ⁷ And *they consulted together and bought with them the potter's field, to bury strangers in.* ⁸ Therefore that field has been called the Field of Blood to this day. ⁹ Then was fulfilled what was spoken by Jeremiah the prophet, saying, *"And they took the thirty pieces of silver, the value of Him who was priced,* whom they of the children of Israel priced, ¹⁰ *and gave them for the potter's field, as the LORD directed me* (Matthew 27:3-10)."

As you can see, Ahithophel's suicide was actually a prophetic picture of the suicide of Judas! Once again, we see that the prophetic picture hits the mark perfectly. Furthermore, the events recorded in the Gospel of Matthew are a perfect thematic match with the events recorded concerning Ahithophel.

- *Ahithophel saw that his advice was not followed* — In other words, he had time to think about his advice concerning David's assassination and the fact that it was not followed. Ahithophel's contemplation of this prompted him into action.
    - So likewise, Judas had time to *contemplate his actions*. Matthew 27:3 states, "Judas, His betrayer, *seeing that He had been condemned, was remorseful."*
- *He . . . went home* — Ahithophel's immediate action was to go somewhere; home.
    - So likewise, Judas' immediate action was to go somewhere. According to Matthew 27:3, he went to the priests and elders.
- *He put his household in order* — After mulling over the events, Ahithophel decided to straighten out his affairs. In other words, he wanted to clear up any issues pertaining to his family.
    - So likewise, Judas wanted to clear up matters concerning his actions. According to Matthew 27:4-5, Judas confessed his sin saying, *"I have sinned by betraying innocent blood."* Then *he threw down the pieces of silver in the temple and departed."* As you can see, Judas is also trying to "straighten out his affairs."
- *He . . . hanged himself* — After clearing up issues at home, he hanged himself.
    - So likewise, according to Matthew 27:5, Judas hanged himself!
- *He was buried in his father's tomb* — The scripture goes on to give us details concerning Ahithophel's burial.
    - So likewise, Matthew 27:7-10 records information concerning Judas' burial place.[15]

At this point, I'd like to make use of our main chiastic structure to provide another thematic connection linking Ahithophel with Judas. Please note element J and J' in our main chiastic structure:

F
  G
    H
      I

        J) II Samuel 17:23—*Ahithophel's suicide by hanging*
          K) II Samuel 17:24-25—Absalom appointed Amasa over his army in place of Joab; David's position in Mahanaim
            L) II Samuel 17:27-29—Three men brought David and his servants all sorts of provisions because they *were hungry, exhausted and thirsty in the desert*
          K`) II Samuel 18:1-5—David appointed officers and divided his camp into thirds; David's position near the city gate
        J`) II Samuel 18:9-15—*Absalom hanging in the elm tree*; David's servant refusing to accept bribery of silver; *Absalom's death*

      I'
    H'
  G'
F'

Elements J and J' thematically connect Ahithophel to Absalom[16] in that both of their deaths involved "hanging!" One other significant point concerns the conversation between Joab and a certain man who saw Absalom hanging from the tree. Joab asked him why he didn't kill Absalom. To which the man replied that David had said not to touch him. He went on to state the following:

"Though I were to receive a thousand shekels of silver in my hand, I would not raise my hand against the king's son. For in our hearing the king commanded you and Abishai and Ittai, saying, 'Beware lest anyone touch the young man Absalom (II Samuel 18:12)!'"

Notice how the young man stated that he would not accept silver for killing Absalom. This story is thematically connected to Ahithophel's death and Ahithophel, like Judas, betrayed his master. Judas betrayed Yeshua for silver! Once again, the connections between our two stories are dizzyingly accurate.

Lastly, I'd like to note an interesting thematic connection concerning II Samuel 17:23-25 and Acts 1:18-26. Let's look at these two passages more closely.

²³ Now when Ahithophel saw that his advice was not followed, he saddled a donkey, and arose and went home to his house, to his city. Then he put his household in order, and hanged himself, and died; and he was buried in his father's tomb. ²⁴ Then David went to Mahanaim. And Absalom crossed over the Jordan, he and all the men of Israel with him. ²⁵ *And Absalom made Amasa captain of the army instead of Joab* (II Samuel 17:23-25).

Now this man *purchased a field with the wages of iniquity*; and falling headlong, he burst open in the middle and all his entrails gushed out. [19] And it became known to all those dwelling in Jerusalem; so that field is called in their own language, *Akel Dama, that is, Field of Blood*. [20] "For it is written in the Book of Psalms: '*Let his dwelling place be desolate, And let no one live in it*'; and, '*Let another take his office.*' [21] "Therefore, of these men who have accompanied us all the time that the Lord Jesus went in and out among us, [22] beginning from the baptism of John to that day when He was taken up from us, *one of these must become a witness with us of His resurrection.*" [23] And they proposed two: Joseph called Barsabas, who was surnamed Justus, and Matthias. [24] And they prayed and said, "You, O Lord, who know the hearts of all, show which of these two You have chosen [25] to take part in this ministry and apostleship from which Judas by transgression fell, that he might go to his own place." [26] And they cast their lots, and the lot fell on Matthias. And he was numbered with the eleven apostles *(Acts 1:18-26).*

The author of II Samuel informs us that Absalom made Amasa captain of his army, *taking the place of Joab*. This occurs right after the story concerning Ahithophel's suicidal death and burial. I find it extremely interesting that right after Luke informs us of Judas' suicidal death and burial, he recorded how *someone was chosen to take his place*! Very interesting.

Where Are We?

We have just analyzed one of many small chiastic structures (II Samuel 17:14-23) nested within our master chiastic structure which forms the basis for this book. According to our master chiastic structure, we are at points G through J. In other words, our small chiastic structure (II Samuel 17:14-23) occurs at a point equivalent to points G through J in our master chiastic structure. At this point you should be wondering, "What about all of the other information within II Samuel 17:14-23 (excluding verses 14 and 23, which pertain to Ahithophel's suicide)? Does the information in II Samuel 17:15-22 have anything to do with the Messiah?" It most certainly does. However, please remember the introductory remarks to this chapter where I stated, "Although the story of David's flight from Absalom will continue in chronological order, soon we will discover that the second story, presenting us with a thematic presentation of the Gospel, will meander from its chronological course." The events recorded in II Samuel 17:14-23—excluding the information concerning Ahithophel's death—is the place where the thematic presentation of the Gospel meanders from chronological order. Therefore, I will deal with it later in this chapter.

David's Prophetic Picture

The next point in our chiastic structure is the central axis, point L (II Samuel 17:27-29).

F
G
H
I

J) II Samuel 17:23—*Ahithophel's suicide by hanging*

The Scroll of the Gospel of David

      K) II Samuel 17:24-25—Absalom appointed Amasa over his army in place of Joab; David's position in Mahanaim
       L) II Samuel 17:27-29—Three men brought David and his servants all sorts of provisions because they *were hungry, exhausted and thirsty in the desert*
      K`) II Samuel 18:1-5—David appointed officers and divided his camp into thirds; David's position near the city gate
     J`) II Samuel 18:9-15—*Absalom hanging* in the elm tree; David's servant refusing to accept bribery of silver; Absalom's death
    I'
   H'
  G'
 F'

  As you may remember, the central axis is the most important point of the chiastic structure, but for different reasons. The central axis often is the most important point because it functions as the turning point or point of contrast between the two halves of the chiastic structure. When the central axis functions as the turning point, you will usually see contrasts between elements in the two halves of the story. Or, the events that occur in the second half of the story reverse the direction of events that occurred in the first half of the story. This is exactly the situation in our master chiastic structure. In II Samuel 17:27-29, David's three friends bring food and provisions for him and his servants. Before the central axis, David was humiliated, defeated, weak, on the run, fleeing for his life and his enemies were planning how to kill him. Immediately after the central axis, David, seemingly strengthened and encouraged from the provisions of his three friends, began to formulate a battle plan. Furthermore, he engaged the enemy, was strengthened, victorious, loved and admired by all. Clearly, the central axis functions as the turning point in our story!

  II Samuel 17:27-29 should remind you of an earlier event in our story. This is not the first time someone has brought provisions for David. The provisions brought by David's three friends are thematically connected to II Samuel 16:1-4, which recounts how Ziba, Mephibosheth's servant, brought provisions for David and his servants. At that time, we determined that Ziba's gifts of food and wine were given *to provide David and his servants with the physical strength* they needed to overcome their plight. Furthermore, Ziba brought them donkeys. The donkeys were used as beasts of burden to carry loads and for people to ride as well. In other words, the donkeys were given to help David and his servants *preserve their physical strength*. I suggest the same is true here. II Samuel 17:29 astutely notes that David and his servants were "hungry and weary and thirsty in the wilderness." Therefore, we should conclude that the gifts were given to help give physical strength to David and his servants.

Yeshua's Prophetic Fulfillment

  We have already seen how our central axis is thematically connected to II Samuel 16:1-4 at the literal level. Therefore, I suggest we review the prophetic/thematic fulfillment of these verses as well. After all, if the literal interpretation of II Samuel 16:1-4 is so closely connected to the literal interpretation of II Samuel 17:27-29, shouldn't we expect that the thematic interpretation of II Samuel 16:1-4 might shed light on the thematic interpretation of II Samuel 17:27-29? Previously, we learned that the physical provisions supplied by Ziba for David (the Messianic figure) were prophetic pictures thematically connected to the spiritual strength Yeshua received from angels! We demonstrated this quite clearly. Therefore, I suggest that the presentation of gifts to David by his three friends is associated with an event where the Messiah was strengthened and received help from some outside source. We simply need to determine the next point in the Gospel where Yeshua received physical strength/help from someone else.

The answer is found in John 19:17 and Mark 15:21.

And He, bearing His cross, went out to a place called *the Place* of a Skull, which is called in Hebrew, Golgotha (John 19:17).

Then they compelled a certain man, Simon a Cyrenian, the father of Alexander and Rufus, as he was coming out of the country and passing by, to bear His cross (Mark 15:21).

These passages relate how Yeshua received help to carry the cross upon which He was to be nailed. He had been beaten and was extremely tired, thirsty and weary, even as II Samuel 17:29 relates how David and his servants were, "hungry and weary and thirsty in the wilderness." Not able to bear the load, Simon the Cyrenian was compelled to help Yeshua carry the cross; therefore, just as David received physical help and strength at a moment of weakness, so too, Yeshua received help to carry His burden.

We have now made it to the halfway point in the thematic presentation of the Gospel. Excluding a major portion of the small chiastic structure of II Samuel 17:14-23, we have seen how II Samuel 15:10-17:23 has been thematically related to the chronological presentation of the Gospel accounts of Yeshua's sufferings. Now, it's time to deal with the portion of II Samuel 17:14-23 which was skipped earlier.

The Problem With II Samuel 17:14-23

As stated earlier, II Samuel 15:10 – 20:2 is simply a chronological presentation of the events surrounding David's flight from Absalom (at the literal or pashat level of interpretation). However, through thematic analysis, we've found that there are actually two stories being told in this passage of scripture. II Samuel 15:10 – 20:2 is also presenting us with a thematic presentation of the Gospel in chronological order. Until II Samuel 17:14-23, the thematic presentation of the Gospel proceeded in chronological harmony with the four Gospel accounts. However, most of II Samuel 17:14-23[17] pertains to events in the Gospel that are not in correct chronological order![18] At this point, we need to make a small digression in our thematic study to accomplish the following tasks.

♦ Many significant events within the chiastic structure of II Samuel 17:14-23 require a solid understanding of Messianic prophecy and a firm grasp of the theology of thematic

connections. Therefore, we need to take the time to develop some concepts pertaining to Messianic prophecy and thematic analysis.
- ♦ We need to understand the thematic/Messianic significance of the events in II Samuel 17:14-23.
- ♦ We need to understand why Samuel's thematic presentation of the Gospel departs from chronological order.
- ♦ We need to present a justification for the departure from chronological order of the thematic presentation of the Gospel.

More Messianic Theology

A Review of the Sign of the Messiah, A Foundational Messianic Teaching

The first chapter presented the foundational teaching concerning Messianic prophecy. Here is a summary of that teaching, which I call the Sign of the Messiah. It is based on Matthew 12:38-40.

Then some of the scribes and Pharisees answered saying, "***What sign*** do You show to us, since You do these things?". . . But He answered and said to them, "***For as Jonah was three days and three nights in the belly of the great fish, so will the Son of Man be three days and three nights in the heart of the earth*** (Matthew 12:38-40)."

Note how Yeshua connected His death, burial and resurrection with the story of Jonah and the big fish! In other words, Yeshua stated that the story of Jonah was actually the story of His death, burial and resurrection. How so? Well, what should have happened to Jonah when he was swallowed by the big fish? Obviously, he should have died. But instead of dying, he came forth alive in three days. The significance? It's a picture of death, burial and resurrection. Please note the thematic connections between the events in Jonah's life and Messiah Yeshua's life found in the following table.

Events in Jonah's Life	Messianic Significance
Jonah was swallowed by a large fish	A picture of death
Jonah was in the fish's belly for three days and three nights	A picture of burial in the earth for three days and three nights
Jonah was spewed forth from the fish's belly	A picture of resurrection

Remember, Yeshua stated the story of Jonah was a sign. A sign is a marker telling you, "Here is what you're looking for." In other words, the story of Jonah and the big fish is a sign telling us, "Look in this story for a picture of the work of the Messiah." So what is the sign of Jonah? It's the sign of resurrection! *Now here's what's most exciting—this sign is not unique to Jonah! The sign of resurrection is found in the life of every Messianic figure in the Tanakh.* There are many people who were confronted with death, then their lives were spared and the number three is visible. This thematic formula (life, death and the number three) is a sign indicating when a passage has Messianic significance. The number three is important because it is the number of resurrection. This should not come as a great surprise to you. Most people know that Adonai teaches us things with numbers. For example, when someone hears the number seven they usually think of completion, Sabbath and/or creation. Well, three is the number that teaches resurrection!

As you read the Tanakh, anytime you see 1) pictures of *resurrection* or 2) pictures of renewed *life* as a result of deliverance from impending *death,* the Tanakh is about to present a teaching concerning the Messiah. I call these themes **The Resurrection and the Life,** and they are especially strengthened when coupled in some manner with the number *three* (3, 30, 300, 3000, etc.).

I went on to show you the sign of the Messiah in Joseph's and David's lives. In each instance, we saw the themes of death, life and the number three. However, the teaching on the Sign of the Messiah is only the foundation of Messianic theology. Let us once again look deeper into this study, using Jonah as our object lesson. The reason we want to look deeper into the Sign of the Messiah is because we will be able to apply the wisdom gained from this teaching to the story at hand.

The Significance of Pits and Assorted Holes in the Earth

At this point we need to take a close look at the story of Jonah, because it is a treasure chest of Messianic theology. We have already seen the sign of the Messiah in his life; therefore, we know his life teaches us about the Messiah. Let's take a look at those verses reminding us of Jonah's sojourn in the belly of a great fish.

> ¹ Then Jonah prayed to the LORD his God *from the fish's belly*. ² And he said: "I cried out to the LORD because of my affliction, and He answered me. "*Out of the belly of Sheol I cried*, and You heard my voice. ³ For You cast me *into the deep, into the heart of the seas*, and the *floods surrounded me*; All Your billows and Your waves passed over me. ⁴ Then I said, 'I have been cast out of Your sight; yet I will look again toward Your holy temple.' ⁵ The waters surrounded me, even to my soul; *the deep closed around me*; weeds were wrapped around my head. ⁶ I went down to the moorings of the mountains; *the earth with its bars closed behind me* forever; yet You have *brought up my life from the pit*, O LORD, my God. ⁷ "When my soul fainted within me, I remembered the LORD; and my prayer went up to You, Into Your holy temple. ⁸ "Those who regard worthless idols, forsake their own Mercy. ⁹ But I will sacrifice to You with the voice of thanksgiving; I will pay what I have vowed. Salvation is of the LORD."
>
> ¹⁰ So the LORD spoke to the fish, and it vomited Jonah onto dry land (Jonah 2:1-10, NKJV).

As is so often the case, these verses are part of a chiastic structure, which I have organized below:

The Chiastic Structure of Jonah 1:15 – 2:11[19]

A) Jonah 1:15—They lifted Jonah and *heaved him into the sea*
  B) Jonah 1:16—They feared Adonai; *sacrificed and made vows*
    C) Jonah 2:1—Jonah was in the fish for three days and three nights
      D) Jonah 2:2-3a—Jonah *prayed* from the fish's innards; "I called *in my distress*"
        E) Jonah 2:3b—I cried *out from the belly of the grave (literally Sheol)*
          F) Jonah 2:4a—You cast me *into the depth/heart of the seas*; the river *surrounds me*
            G) Jonah 2:4b—Your breakers and waves *passed over me*
              H) Jonah 2:5—*I was driven from before Your eyes but I will gaze at Your Holy Temple again*
            G') Jonah 2:6—Waters *encompassed me*; the *deep whirled around me*
          F') Jonah 2:7a—I descended to *the base of the mountain*; the *earth's bars were against me*
        E') Jonah 2:7b—You lifted my life *from the pit*
      D') Jonah 2:8—When *I was faint* I remembered Adonai; my *prayer* came to your temple
    C') Jonah 2:9—Those who give heed to lying vanities forsake their own mercy
  B') Jonah 2:10—With thanksgiving I will make *sacrifice to you and fulfill my vow*
A') Jonah 2:11—Adonai addressed the fish and it *spewed Jonah onto dry land*

Chiastic structures are analyzed by comparing and contrasting the points that are thematically related (compare A to A', B to B', etc.). With the exception of C and C' all of the elements in the first half are clearly thematically connected to those in the second half. For example, points B (sacrifice and vows), D (prayer) and G (trapped in water) are thematically equivalent to points B' (sacrifice and vows), D' (prayer) and G' (trapped in water) because they essentially present the same information with no major differences. I have bolded and italicized the important words in each point of the structure so that you can easily see the thematic connections.

On the other hand, some points, although thematically equivalent, offer interesting differences or slight modifications of the main theme. For example, although points A and A' are thematically connected through the chiastic structure, the phrase from element A), *heaved him into the sea,* and the phrase from element A'), *spewed Jonah onto dry land*, are not exactly the same. There is a slight modification because A) pertains to Jonah being *thrown into* something, whereas A') involves Jonah being forcefully *ejected from* something. Although slightly different, it is still easy to see why they are thematically equivalent because both of them share the common theme of Jonah being forcefully taken from one place to another! Chiastic elements that are either exactly thematically equivalent (such as B-B', D-D' and G-G') or thematically equivalent with a slight modification of the theme (such as A-A`) are not the most interesting elements of a chiastic structure because they do not present any new information. They are very important, though, for the following reason. The fact that their themes match so well is the greatest proof that the two passages under comparison are thematically equivalent and meant to be compared! Who can compare points A-A', B-B', D-D' and G-G' and not see that the Holy One inspired their thematic equivalence?

The most interesting elements of a chiastic structure are those that *do not seem to match thematically* (such as points C-C', E-E' and F-F'). Why? Let's review what we've learned so far. Within the context of the chiastic pattern, the fact that A-A', B-B', D-D' and G-G' match so perfectly should be proof enough for us to understand that points C-C', E-E' and F-F' are related somehow, *even though they may not appear to be so at first glance*. In other words, chiastic structures are one of the means the Holy One uses to demonstrate that points C-C', E-E' and F-F' *are thematically equivalent in some manner*. There are many doctrines and pieces of wisdom our Father wants to teach, and the main way He teaches is through chiastic structures, parallelisms and thematic connections. While it is easy to thematically connect themes that are similar, it would be very difficult to connect certain themes that are very dissimilar. Yet, many times this is exactly what we need to do. Chiastic structures and parallelisms are the main tools Adonai uses to help us see the connections between themes that are inherently dissimilar. Our job is to make the connections, understand the thematic equivalences and apply the understanding. For our purposes, we'll only consider points E and E'.

From our chiastic structure, we may surmise that the Holy One wants us to see a connection between the E) **belly of the grave** and E') **the pit**. He has done this by thematically connecting them to each other through the chiastic structure. Now, why are these two passages thematically connected? What does their connection teach?

Let's review some basic math so that we can understand *one* of the main reasons thematic connections exist. Math, you may ask? Well, as a teacher, I'm constantly searching for ways to bring understanding and simplicity to what I teach, which is not exactly elementary. There are some postulates of mathematics that will help you understand how thematic connections function. The first postulate is entitled, the Symmetric Property of Equality. It states the following:

$$\text{If } a = b, \text{ Then } b = a$$

Now that seems simple enough. It's basically stating that if $a = b$, then you can also state that $b = a$. Said in a slightly different manner, if we know that *a* is equivalent to *b*, then we can also state that b is equivalent to a. This is one of the major reasons thematic connections exist. **It's the Holy One's way of showing equivalence between people, things, actions, concepts, etc.** Now, let's apply this understanding. It's easy to see how elements B and B' fulfill the Symmetric Property of Equality because . . .

B) **sacrificed** and made **vows** = B') **sacrifice** to you and fulfill my **vow**

$$A \quad = \quad B$$

It is intuitive because these two statements are essentially the same, using the same words. However, it's not as easy to see the following:

E) **belly of the grave** = E') **the pit**.

$$A \quad = \quad B$$

Why? Because a grave is a grave and a pit is a pit. Furthermore, I can show you pits that aren't graves and I can show you graves that aren't pits. Yet they are thematically connected to enable us to see that in Adonai's eyes, they are the same. This is the Holy One's way of teaching us that the grave is equivalent to the pit and the pit is equivalent to the grave (if a=b then b=a). By thematically connecting them through the chiastic structure, the Holy One has taught us that when we see a passage mentioning a pit it could actually be talking about the grave! And this is the case at hand. Jonah is likening his stay in the belly of the grave to a stay in a pit!

Our math lesson doesn't stop here though. Thematic connections are closely related to another mathematical property, the Transitive Property of Equality.

$$\text{If } A = B \text{ and } B = C, \text{ then } A = C$$

I know this may seem trite or boring, but these two mathematical postulates are used hundreds (if not thousands) of times to thematically connect scriptures, especially Messianic prophecies. Let's see this property in action.

²Jonah prayed to HaShem, his God *from the fish's innards* (*belly*), ³and said, "I called in my distress, to HaShem and He answered me; **From the belly of the grave** I cried out—You heard my voice (Jonah 2:2-3)."

According to Jonah 2:2, from where did Jonah state he cried out? "From the fish's innards/belly," you would have to say. According to Jonah 2:3, from where did Jonah state he cried out? "From the belly of the grave," would be the correct answer. Literally, we know that Jonah was in the fish's innards/belly when he cried out. His statement that he cried out from the "belly of the grave" is a poetic/symbolic statement, not a literal one. Therefore, the scripture has just taught us that belly of the grave is equivalent to the fish's belly! This is an A = B statement.

$$\text{fish's innards/belly} = \text{belly of the grave}$$

$$A \quad = \quad B$$

However, elements E) and E') of our chiastic structure taught us that the belly of the grave is equivalent to the pit! This is a B = C statement.

$$\text{belly of the grave} = \text{the pit}$$

$$B \quad = \quad C$$

If A = B and B = C, then A = C. In other words, if the fish's innards/belly is equivalent to the belly of the grave (A = B) and the belly of the grave is equivalent to the pit (B = C), then the fish's innards/belly is equivalent to the pit (A = C).

If	the fish's innards/belly = the belly of the grave	
	A = B	

And	the belly of the grave = the pit,	
	B = C	
Then	the fish's innards/belly = the pit	
	A = C	

Let's take inventory. We've seen that the chiastic structure of Jonah 1:15 – 2:11 thematically connects the *belly of the grave* to the *pit*, thus, making them equivalent. But we've also seen, through thematic connections that the *grave*, *pit* and *innards/belly of the fish* are all equivalent! Adonai has done this so that we can see the pictures He's trying to paint for us through the stories of the scriptures. We have already seen how the story of David's flight from Absalom is actually two stories in one. At the literal level, it's simply the story of the flight of David from Absalom. However, it is also a thematic presentation of the Gospel! In other words, the Holy One is actually giving a thematic presentation of the Gospel ***through*** the literal story of David's flight from Absalom. In order for us to be able to see a thematic story behind a literal story, we need to be able to see allusions to the thematic story being painted by the literal story. In the case of Jonah, once we understand that the innards/belly of a fish is equivalent to the grave, the thematic story behind the literal story of Jonah being swallowed by a big fish becomes abundantly clear. As Yeshua confirmed, the story of Jonah's literal stay in the innards/belly of the big fish is actually a picture of the thematic presentation of Messiah's stay in the grave! This is clear because of the thematic connections equating the innards/belly of the fish to the grave.

The story of Jonah and the big fish is not the only place in scripture that equates a pit with Sheol (the grave). Look at the following verses. All of them reinforce what we've learned from Jonah.

- Psalm 88:4— I am counted with those who go down to the ***pit*** (by implication, the grave); I am like a man who has no strength.
- Proverbs 1:12—Let us swallow them alive like **Sheol** and whole, like those who go down to the ***pit***
- Isaiah 14:15—Yet you shall be brought down to **Sheol**, To the lowest depths of the ***pit***.
- Isaiah 38:18—For **Sheol** cannot thank You, **death** cannot praise You; Those who go down to the ***pit*** cannot hope for Your truth.

As you can see, these verses clearly make a thematic connection between the grave (Sheol) and a pit. Furthermore, Isaiah 38:18 shows that Sheol and the pit are equivalent to death! The Holy One is teaching us that a pit is equivalent to the grave/death (If A=B, Then B=A). Thus, when you see someone actually go into a pit, there's the possibility that it's really a thematic picture of their death. We've seen this lesson from the prophets and the writings (Jonah, Isaiah, Psalms and Proverbs); however, it's the Torah that gives us the foundational teaching of the equivalence of a pit and the grave/death. Let us review the story of Joseph's encounter with a pit.

I'm sure you remember the particulars concerning Joseph's brothers' plot to kill him. As Joseph approached his brothers, note what they said.

> [20] "Come therefore, *let us now **kill him*** and ***cast him into some pit***; and we shall say, 'Some wild beast has devoured him.' We shall see what will become of his dreams (Genesis 37:20)!"

Now, I could stop here because this one verse proves my point. The pit has once again been equated to a place of death, because a pit was to be the means of Joseph's death! And what was the final conclusion based upon the brothers' original plan to kill Joseph by throwing him into a pit?

> [33] And he recognized it and said, "It is my son's tunic. A wild beast has devoured him. Without doubt Joseph is torn to pieces." [34] Then Jacob tore his clothes, put sackcloth on his waist, and mourned for his son many days. [35] And all his sons and all his daughters arose to comfort him; but he refused to be comforted, and he said, "For I shall go down *into the grave to my son* in mourning." Thus his father wept for him (Genesis 37:33-35).

The final conclusion (in Jacob's eyes) was that his son had died and gone into the grave! But we know that Joseph was actually in a pit, not the grave. As you can see, the Torah has painted a picture of Joseph dying. It started with his brothers wanting to throw him into a pit (a picture of the grave/death) and it ended with his father pronouncing that Joseph was indeed dead and *in the grave*! In fact, from this point on, Joseph, for all intents and purposes is considered dead by his own family. Note, when Joseph's brothers appeared before Joseph, they considered him dead!

> [19] My lord asked his servants, saying, 'Have you a father or a brother?' [20] And we said to my lord, 'We have a father, an old man, and a child of his old age, who is young; *his brother is dead*, and he alone is left of his mother's children, and his father loves him (Genesis 44:19-20).'

Now, let's take a closer look at Genesis 37:24.

> [24] Then they took him and cast him into a pit. And *the pit was empty; there was no water in it*.

From a western point of view, the statement in Genesis 37:24 of there being no water in the pit should seem rather curious. So what? Why should a pit have water in it? The reason the scripture states that the pit had no water in it is because it was actually a cistern! Water was scarce in that area of the world and rain water was often collected and stored in cisterns, or holes dug out of the earth. Note, this is not the same as a well, which actually has a source of water in it! The Hebrew word used throughout the narrative of Genesis 37:22-30 is the word bōr בּוֹר (SEC H953), which can be translated as *pit, cistern, well, dungeon or prison*. Hebrew words are derived from a three-letter, consonantal, verbal/action root. The Hebrew word bōr (בּוֹר) is derived from the following three-letter consonantal root; בור (SEC H952), which means to bore. Note the following passages where the word בּוֹר is translated as cistern—Jeremiah 2:13 and Isaiah 36:16.

> " For My people have committed two evils: They have forsaken Me, the fountain of living waters, and hewn themselves *cisterns*—broken cisterns that can hold no water (Jeremiah 2:13).

> Do not listen to Hezekiah; for thus says the king of Assyria: 'Make peace with me by a present and come out to me; and every one of you eat from his own vine and every one from his own fig tree, and every one of you drink the waters of his own *cistern* . . . (Isaiah 36:16)

Closely connected to the word cistern/pit בּוֹר is the Hebrew word translated as *well, b'eir* בְּאֵר (SEC H875). A well, בְּאֵר, was a deep shaft bored below the surface of the earth until it connected to a source of water, such as the ones dug by Jacob in the book of Genesis. The Hebrew word *b'eir* (בְּאֵר) is derived from the following three-letter consonantal root; באר (SEC H874), which means to dig. A contrast of the words for cistern and well are found in Proverbs 5:15.

> Drink water from your own cistern (בּוֹר, a hole or pit to hold water), and *running water* from your own well (בְּאֵר, a shaft dug to a source of water).

As you can see, the words for cistern and well have similar verbal roots, which mean to bore or dig. This makes sense and it is easy to see why the words cistern/pit and well/pit have similar roots. They're both holes the ground! Finally, what is the significance of a pit with no water in it? We know that water is essential for life. Therefore, the fact that the cistern contained no water is another hint of death residing in the pit.

Earlier in this chapter, we learned that a pit is a picture of the grave. It is a place harboring death. We learned this from 1) the chiastic structure and thematic connections in the story of Jonah and 2) the thematic connections from the prophets and writings. Whether or not you know it, we have just stumbled onto another amazing thematic connection. We now have four concrete pieces of evidence *to thematically connect **pits to wells and cisterns***.

1. Textual Support—The story of Joseph's "death" teaches us that the pit was actually a cistern.
2. Linguistic Support—The Hebrew words for well/pit and cistern/pit originate from similar three-letter consonantal root words (one meaning to bore, the other, dig), thus confirming their close relationship.
3. Linguistic Support—The Hebrew words for cistern and well are often translated as pit.

4. Thematic Support—We know that a cistern was simply a hole in the earth just like a pit.

Earlier, we saw that the *grave, pit* and *innards/belly of the fish* are all equivalent! Now, we can add wells/cisterns to that group of thematically connected entities.

$$\text{pit} \equiv \text{grave} \equiv \text{belly of the fish} \equiv \text{cistern} \equiv \text{well}$$

Wow! The thematic connections keep piling up.

Two More Examples of the Pit as a Place of Death

The Story of Joseph

If you are still not convinced that Joseph's descent into the pit was a picture of his descent into the grave (and hence an allusion to his "death"), then please examine the significance of the verses *immediately* following that event where Joseph was thrown into the pit.

> [24] Then they took him and cast him into a pit. And the pit was empty; there was no water in it. [25] And they sat down to eat a meal. Then they lifted their eyes and looked, and there was a company of Ishmaelites, coming from Gilead with their camels, bearing spices, balm, and *myrrh*, on their way to carry them down to Egypt (Genesis 37:24-25).

Immediately after Joseph was thrown into a pit, we are confronted with the story of Ishmaelite traders who burst onto the scene carrying spices—balm and myrrh. Do you know the significance of myrrh? It is a burial spice! It was one of the spices used to anoint Yeshua's body.[20] Is it a coincidence that immediately after Joseph was thrown into a pit (a picture of death) Ishmaelite traders came bearing a burial spice? I think not. In fact, the reason why the scripture mentions them and their cargo immediately after Joseph's descent into the pit is to help complete the picture of Joseph's death. It's as if the Ishmaelites brought the burial spices for Joseph's funeral!

The Story of Daniel

As you begin to develop the habit of reading and thinking thematically you will not be able to keep up with the vast number of thematic connections waiting to be discovered in the Scriptures. For example, let's create a simple outline of the events surrounding Joseph's exaltation from prison.

- ◆ Pharaoh had a dream that deeply troubled him.
- ◆ None of his magicians could interpret the dream.
- ◆ A Hebrew lad was brought before him to interpret the dream.
- ◆ The Hebrew lad interpreted the dream properly.
- ◆ The Hebrew lad was exalted to the position of first-in-command under Pharaoh.

Now, can you think of another person whose life is almost a mirror image of the points above? I can. His name is Daniel! If you read Daniel 2:1-49 you will notice numerous thematic connections between Daniel's life and Joseph's! Note the following thematic connections. In both stories:

- Pagan kings had a prophetic dream concerning future events about the entire world.
- A Hebrew slave interpreted the dream and gave glory to Adonai for revealing the dream.
- A Hebrew slave received gifts after properly interpreting the dream.

The question should immediately arise—Why are these two stories related so closely? To answer that question we need to rely on our second mathematical postulate, the Transitive Property of Equality.

$$\text{If } A = B \text{ and } B = C, \text{ then } A = C$$

Anyone who has studied the scriptures (whether Jewish or non-Jewish) knows that Joseph is a major Messianic figure. We saw this in Chapter 1 where I showed you the Sign of the Messiah in his life. So let's use this information with our postulate. The examples above clearly connect Daniel to Joseph thematically.

$$\text{Daniel} = \text{Joseph}$$

$$A = B$$

However, we also know that Joseph is a picture of the Messiah. Or, stated another way, Joseph is thematically connected to the Messiah.

$$\text{Joseph} = \text{Messiah}$$

$$B = C$$

Therefore, Daniel is also a picture of the Messiah.

$$\text{Daniel} = \text{Messiah}$$

$$A = C$$

If this is true, we should be able to look to Daniel's life and discover Messianic significance even as we've done with Joseph, Moses and David. Let's give it a try. First, let's see if we can discover the Sign of the Messiah in Daniel's life. Daniel 6 is the story of Daniel in the lions' den. Let me ask you a question. What was supposed to happen to Daniel once he was thrown into the lions' den? Surely, he was supposed to die. But instead, he came forth alive! As for the number three, note how many times the number three occurs throughout Daniel 6:1-23.

- Daniel 6:2—Daniel was one of *three* governors who ruled over the 120 satraps of the kingdom.
- Daniel 6:7 and 12—No one was to pray to anyone other than King Darius for *thirty* days.
- Daniel 6:10—Daniel prayed *three* times a day as was his custom.
- Daniel 6:13—Daniel continued to pray *three* times a day despite the king's decree.

This is the Sign of the Messiah in Daniel's life. This is a second witness to the fact that events in Daniel's life have Messianic significance.

I'm going to dispense with the suspense and suggest to you that the story of Daniel's trip to the lions' den is actually a prophecy of the Messiah's suffering, death, burial and resurrection.[21] Daniel 6:1-4 informs us that Daniel was exalted above his comrades, the satraps (wise men) of Babylon. As a result, the Babylonian satraps were extremely jealous of him (Daniel 6:5-6) and took counsel to determine how they could defame his character. Let's take note of the following thematic connections between Daniel 6:5-6 and the Gospel account of Yeshua.

- The Babylonian satraps were contemporaries of Daniel.
  - We know the religious leaders were contemporaries of Yeshua.
- The Babylonian satraps were jealous of Daniel's wisdom and position.
  - The religious leaders were extremely jealous of Yeshua's successful ministry.
- The Babylonian satraps gathered together to take counsel on how to have Daniel killed.
  - The religious leaders took counsel to determine how to kill Messiah Yeshua.
- According to Daniel 6:5-6, the satraps could not find any fault in Daniel!
  - According to Matthew 26:59-61, the religious leaders could not find fault in Yeshua.

Are these thematic connections coincidental? Of course not! According to Daniel 6:11-12, the satraps found Daniel praying after the king made a decree prohibiting prayer to anyone but him. Isn't it amazing to note that when the religious leaders confronted Yeshua, He too was in prayer in the Garden of Gethsemane? Furthermore, please note the wording in Daniel 6:10 and Luke 22:39-41 concerning the habits of Daniel and Yeshua.

> [10] Now when Daniel knew that the writing was signed, *he went* home. And in his upper room, with his windows open toward Jerusalem, *he knelt down on his knees* three times that day, and *prayed* and gave thanks before his God, <u>*as was his custom*</u> since early days (Daniel 6:20).
>
> [39] Coming out, *He went* to the Mount of Olives, <u>*as He was accustomed*</u>, and His disciples also followed Him. [40] When He came to the place, He said to them, "Pray that you may not enter into temptation." [41] And He was withdrawn from them about a stone's throw, and *He knelt down* and *prayed.*

As you can see, Daniel's story is a perfect thematic picture of Yeshua's story. But wait, there's more!

Daniel 6:13-15 records the actions of the satraps as they brought charges against Daniel before King Darius. Please note King Darius' reaction. He didn't want to execute Daniel! In fact, the scripture states that King Darius tried until sundown to free Daniel. However, the satraps *zealously* pressed the king, reminding him that according to the law of the Medes and Persians, his prior decree could not be revoked. In an amazing parallel, the religious leaders *zealously* brought charges against Yeshua before Pontius Pilate and he didn't want to kill Yeshua! Please note the following dramatic thematic connections.

- Daniel, a Jewish man, was brought before a pagan king.
  - Yeshua, a Jewish man, was brought before a pagan ruler!
- Charges were brought against Daniel.
  - Charges were brought against Yeshua!
- The satraps diligently pressed King Darius to execute Daniel.
  - The religious leaders diligently pressed Pilate to execute Messiah Yeshua!
- According to Daniel 6:14, King Darius tried (until nightfall) to do his best to free Daniel because he knew Daniel was righteous.
  - According to John 19, Pilate tried to release Yeshua three times, not wanting to kill Him because he felt that Yeshua was innocent!
- According to Daniel 6:14-15, when the satraps saw that King Darius was trying to free Daniel, they appealed to the law of the Medes and Persians, of which they said, "__It is the law of the Medes and Persians__ that no decree or statute which the king establishes may be changed."
  - According to John 19:7, when the religious leaders saw that Pilate was trying to free Yeshua, they appealed to the Torah (law) of God, of which they said, "__We have a law, and by our law He ought to die__..."!
- According to Daniel 6:18-19, King Darius fasted and could not sleep during the night that Daniel spent in the lions' den.
  - According to Matthew 27:19, Pilate's wife suffered many things in a dream (while she slept) because of Yeshua!
- According to Daniel 6:17, King Darius sealed the stone over the lions' den with his signet ring.
  - According to Matthew 27:65-66, Pilate ordered that Yeshua's sepulcher be made secure by sealing the stone!

Hopefully, I have your attention. These thematic connections are absolutely amazing! They've been in the scriptures for centuries and yet most of us have been totally unaware of how intimately they're connected. Furthermore, we haven't understood the purpose of stories like Jonah and the big fish and Daniel in the lions' den. They were written to teach us about the ministry of the Messiah so that when He came we would be able to verify that He fulfilled the prophecies.

The last few details I'd like to bring to your attention concern Daniel's "execution." First, let's read these verses according to the New King James Version.

[16] So the king gave the command, and they brought Daniel and cast him into the ***den of lions***. But the king spoke, saying to Daniel, "Your God, whom you serve continually,

He will deliver you." ¹⁷ Then a stone was brought and laid on the mouth of *the den*, and the king sealed it with his own signet ring and with the signets of his lords, that the purpose concerning Daniel might not be changed (Daniel 6:16-17, NKJV).

In an unmistakable manner, Daniel was placed into the lions' den to provide us with a picture of Yeshua being placed into His sepulcher. Furthermore, a stone was rolled over the mouth of the den, a prophecy of the fact that a stone was rolled over Messiah Yeshua's grave! Could the picture be any clearer? Daniel's descent into the lions' den is a picture of the Messiah's death!

Actually, the picture can be clearer. According to the NKJV, Daniel was placed into a den of lions. Now, let's look at a Jewish translation.

Then the king commanded and they brought Daniel and threw him into the *lions' pit*. The king exclaimed to Daniel, "May your God, Whom you serve continually, save you!" A stone was brought and was placed over the opening of *the pit*, and the king sealed it with his signet ring and with the signet rings of his nobles, so that his will regarding Daniel could not be changed (Daniel 6:16-17).²²

The Artscroll Tanakh states that Daniel was thrown into a lions' *pit*! The word translated as *den* (NKJV) and *pit* (Artscroll Tanakh) is taken from the Hebrew word גֹּב (SEC# H1358), which means a *pit/den* (for wild animals). It is derived from a prime root corresponding to the Hebrew word goov גּוּב (SEC# H1358), which means to dig. As you can see, this Hebrew word has a three-letter verbal root whose meaning is similar to the three-letter verbal roots for the Hebrew words pit, cistern and well! And I'm sure you know where I'm going with this. Just as Joseph descended into and ascended from the pit (an empty cistern), so likewise, Daniel descended into and ascended from a pit (den for wild animals). Both of these men's lives are clear pictures of Messiah Yeshua's life. Their descent into pits was a picture of the Messiah's death because the Messiah was placed in a sepulcher, which, like a pit, is a <u>**hole in the earth**</u>.

As you can see, there is Messianic significance whenever a Messianic figure descends into and ascends from a pit. Clearly, a pit is the Tanakh's picture of the grave. The thematic connections found within the stories of Joseph and Daniel confirm this beyond a shadow of doubt!

Concerning our list of thematic connections, we can now add *animal dens* to our list of equivalent expressions representing the grave or death.

grave ≡ pit ≡ belly of the fish ≡ cistern ≡ well ≡ animal den

In summary, we have learned how the Tanakh teaches us about the death of the Messiah. When we see a Messianic figure go into a pit, belly of a fish, cistern, well or animal den, we know that this is simply a picture of the Messiah's death. By inference, we should understand another point. When Jonah descended into the belly of the fish, shouldn't he have died? When Joseph was thrown into the pit with no water, wasn't it for the purpose of killing him? When Daniel was thrown into the lions' pit, wasn't he supposed to die? But of course! Well, what is the significance of their emergence from those places of death? It is a picture of victory over death! And that's just a phrase for the word RESURRECTION! The Tanakh has taught us about the death, burial and resurrection of the Messiah by using the pictures of Messianic figures descending into and ascending from *pits and other assorted holes in the earth*. With this foundation, we are now ready to interpret another portion of II Samuel 17:14-23.

David's Prophetic Picture

We will now examine the events recorded in II Samuel 17:15-21, the story of how Hushai sent messengers to warn David of Absalom's plans. According to II Samuel 17:17, Hushai would send messages to David by first telling a female servant. She would then bring the message to Jonathan and Ahimaaz, the sons of Abiathar and Zadok, respectively. Finally, they would carry the news to David. This time however, one of Absalom's cronies saw Jonathan and Ahimaaz and the mission was jeopardized. This event is recorded as follows:

¹⁸ Nevertheless a lad saw them (Jonathan and Ahimaaz), and told Absalom. But both of them went away quickly and came to a man's house in Bahurim, who had a well in his court; and they went down into it. ¹⁹ Then the woman took and spread a covering over the well's mouth, and spread ground grain on it; and the thing was not known. ²⁰ And when Absalom's servants came to the woman at the house, they said, "Where *are* Ahimaaz and Jonathan?" So the woman said to them, "They have gone over the water brook." And when they had searched and could not find *them,* they returned to Jerusalem. ²¹ Now it came to pass, after they had departed, that they came up out of the well and went and told King David, and said to David, "Arise and cross over the water quickly. For thus has Ahithophel advised against you."

At this point, I'd like to ask you a question. What would have happened to Jonathan and Ahimaaz had Absalom's servants found them? Certainly, it would have meant death! This is very important to our interpretation of this story. Jonathan and Ahimaaz were faced with death. Had it not been for the presence of the well into which they descended, they surely would have been murdered by Absalom. How did they escape death? They escaped death by descending into a well, or *b'eir* בְּאֵר in Hebrew. Now, isn't that interesting? Let me tell this story in another fashion. Jonathan and Ahimaaz were about to face death as Absalom's servants ventured forth searching for them. It was under this specter of potential death that they descended into a well. After the woman sent Absalom's servants away, the threat of death was over. Having escaped death, Jonathan and Ahimaaz emerged from the well.

Lastly, note how the actions of Jonathan and Ahimaaz—their descent into and ascent from the well—are beautifully emphasized in the chiastic structure of II Samuel 17:14-23 (points E and E')!

E) II Samuel 17:18—A lad saw them and ***told Absalom***. But both of them went away quickly and came to a man's house in Bahurim, who ***had a well in his court, and they went down into it***
  F) II Samuel 17:20a—Absalom's servants asked, "***Where are Ahimaaz and Jonathan?***"
    G) II Samuel 17:20b—So the woman said to them, "They have gone over the water brook."
  F') II Samuel 17:20c— . . . and when ***they had searched and could not find them***

E') II Samuel 17:21a—Now it came to pass, after they had departed, *that they came up out of the well* and went and *told King David.*

Yeshua's Prophetic Fulfillment

I want to focus on the fact that Jonathan and Ahimaaz were able to elude detection by going down into a well. Now, on the surface, this may not seem significant. However, you must remember that the writer of II Samuel is recording information about the Messiah throughout this narrative. This is where the foundational teachings concerning the death, burial and resurrection of the Messiah will pay huge dividends. What is the significance of Messianic figures descending into and ascending from pits/wells/animal pits/bellies of fish? They are pictures of death, burial and resurrection. The thematic significance of the story of Jonathan's and Ahimaaz's trip into and out of the well is that *it is a prophetic act symbolizing the death, burial and resurrection of the Messiah.*

Jonathan and Ahimaaz descended into and ascended from a well just as Joseph descended into and ascended from a pit/cistern. Jonathan and Ahimaaz descended into and ascended from a well just as Daniel descended into and ascended from a pit. Finally, Jonathan and Ahimaaz descended into and ascended from a well just as Jonah went into and emerged from the belly/innards of a great fish, which, is likened to a pit and the grave. Individually, each of these stories echoes the truth of the death, burial and resurrection of the Messiah. Collectively, they strengthen each other and confirm that our interpretation is correct.

Some of you may be thinking, "How do we know that Jonathan and Ahimaaz are Messianic figures?" There are two reasons. The first reason I will present in this chapter. The second reason, which is thematically more exciting because it involves a wonderful play on thematic connections, I will save for the next chapter. We reviewed the sign of the Messiah earlier in this chapter. Remember? You could be in the middle of Messianic prophecy when you see someone who is supposed to die but somehow escapes impending death. This is exactly what happened to Jonathan and Ahimaaz! They escaped death by descending into a well (a picture of the grave/death). Then, they emerged alive as they ascended from the well. Oh my, what an awesome picture! And the number three? In the next chapter we'll see how cleverly the Holy One will bring the number three to bear on this story. We will also study the thematic significance of the remaining verses that lead up to the central axis (II Samuel 17:21-24). These also contain another veiled prophesy of the death, burial and resurrection of the Messiah.

Tying up Loose Ends

If it is true that Jonathan's and Ahimaaz's actions are prophetic pictures of the death, burial and resurrection of the Messiah, then we have a glitch in the chronological order of the thematic presentation of the Gospel. Refer to the Running Chart of Thematic Connections. The last event in the chart is none other than the central axis of our chiastic structure. We've already seen that the provisions given to David and his servants provide a prophetic/thematic basis for how Simon the Cyrenian provided help for Messiah Yeshua as He carried the crossbar. Obviously, Simon's actions occurred *before* the death, burial and resurrection of Messiah Yeshua. Therefore, II Samuel 17:15-24, which contains two separate prophesies of the death, burial and resurrection of the Messiah, is out of proper chronological order. The pictures of death, burial and resurrection should occur sometime after the prophetic picture of Simon helping the Messiah. Clearly, the chronological order of the thematic presentation of the Gospel has been "compromised." But, there is a reason for the departure.

Here is a preview of the next three chapters.

1. Chapter 5 will cover more Messianic and thematic theology. I will use that knowledge to prove even further that Jonathan and Ahimaaz are Messianic figures. I will also demonstrate the Messianic significance of II Samuel 17:21-24.
2. Chapter 6 will present an explanation of why Samuel's thematic presentation of the Gospel departed from chronological order in II Samuel 17:15-22 and a justification for the departure.
3. In the remaining chapters, we will continue our chronological journey of the second half of the chiastic structure of II Samuel 15:10 – 20:2, showing how the remaining events continue to show a chronological presentation of the Gospel.

Running Chart of the Thematic Connections Between II Samuel 15:10 – 20:2 and the Gospels

II Samuel		The Gospels
II Samuel 17:14 and 23—Ahithophel committed suicide by hanging himself; details concerning Ahithophel's burial;		**Matthew 27:3-10**—Judas hanged himself; details concerning Judas' burial place;
II Samuel 17:15-24—Jonathan and Ahimaaz eluded capture by descending into a well; David eluded capture by crossing the Jordan	*The thematic significance of these prophecies in II Samuel 17:15-24 (The death, burial and resurrection of the Messiah) are out of chronological order when compared to the Gospel accounts.*	*Prophetic pictures of the death, burial and resurrection of the Messiah*
II Samuel 17:27-29—Three men brought David and his servants all sorts of provisions because they were hungry, exhausted and thirsty in the desert, needing physical help		**Matthew 27:32 and Mark 15:21**—Simon the Cyrenian was compelled to help Yeshua carry the cross-bar, thus helping Him at a time He needed physical help

Thematic Moments

I think Adonai desperately desires for us to know and understand the truth about Yeshua the Messiah. There is no shortage of thematic evidence pointing to Him! If you have never been exposed to thematic study, I'm sure you have been pleasantly surprised at how much information Adonai has placed in the Scriptures concerning the truth of Yeshua's death, burial and resurrection. His death, burial and resurrection should be the most prophesied event in all of the Tanakh. After all, it is the truth that will determine every man's eternal destiny.

I would like to take a moment to re-visit the story of Jonah. Earlier we learned that his story (Jonah 1:15 – 2:11) was told chiastically. Furthermore, we have seen enough information to know that he is a Messianic figure. As a matter of fact, of all the Messianic figures, Yeshua chose Jonah as His main example for understanding Messianic prophecy.

> [38] Then some of the scribes and Pharisees answered, saying, "Teacher, we want to see a sign from You." [39] But He answered and said to them, "An evil and adulterous generation seeks after a sign, and no sign will be given to it except the sign of the prophet Jonah. [40] For as Jonah was three days and three nights in the belly of the great fish, so will the Son of Man be three days and three nights in the heart of the earth. [41] The men of Nineveh will rise up in the judgment with this generation and condemn it, because they repented at the preaching of Jonah; and indeed a greater than Jonah is here (Matthew 12:38-41).

We can learn even more about Yeshua if we simply continue to make the proper thematic connections. While meditating in II Samuel, I noticed that David and Jonah made very similar statements.

> Then I said, 'I have been cast out of Your sight; *yet I will look again toward Your holy temple* (Jonah 2:4).'

> Then the king said to Zadok, "Carry the ark of God back into the city. If I find favor in the eyes of the LORD, *He will bring me back and show me both it and His dwelling place* (II Samuel 15:25).

Clearly, the statement by Jonah and David are equivalent expressions. They both stated that Adonai would bring them back to His dwelling place/His holy temple. It was not a coincidence that two strong Messianic figures would say the same thing! When it comes to Messianic prophecy, Adonai leaves nothing to coincidence and every thematic connection is significant. After seeing these two equivalent expressions from these two Messianic figures, it dawned on me that perhaps I could find other Messianic passages by noting (in those passages) phrases and/or sentences used by Messianic figures elsewhere. For example, while in the belly of the great fish, Jonah exclaimed the following:

> But I will sacrifice to You with the voice of thanksgiving; *I will pay what I have vowed*. Salvation is of the LORD (Jonah 2:9)."

At first glance, this statement doesn't seem too important; however, note how this phrase is repeated in Psalm 22.

> ◆ My praise shall be of You in the great assembly; *I will pay My vows* before those who fear Him (Psalm 22:25).

This is just one clue that Psalm 22 may be Messianic. When you consider the Messianic content of Psalm 22, it's easy to see that finding the phrase "I will pay my vows," in Psalm 22 and connecting it to Jonah was a good lead to discovering that Psalm 22 was Messianic. Here is *a small sampling* of some of the Messianic content of Psalm 22.

- My God, My God, why have You forsaken Me?
- All those who see Me ridicule Me; they shoot out the lip, they shake the head, saying, "He trusted in the LORD, let Him rescue Him; let Him deliver Him, since He delights in Him!"
- I am poured out like water, and all My bones are out of joint; my heart is like wax; it has melted within Me. My strength is dried up like a potsherd, and My tongue clings to My jaws; You have brought Me to the dust of death.
- For dogs have surrounded Me; the congregation of the wicked has enclosed Me. They pierced My hands and My feet; I can count all My bones. They look and stare at Me. They divide My garments among them, and for My clothing they cast lots.

But this revelation doesn't stop here. The following Psalms all contain references to statements made by Jonah when he was in the belly of the great fish – Psalms 18, 20, 22, 31, 35, 42, 55, 56, 61, 69, 88, 107 and 116! Furthermore, they all contain Messianic themes. Another example is the statement by Jonah concerning lying vanities.

Those who regard *worthless idols* forsake their own Mercy (Jonah 2:8).

The phrase, lying vanities, is a translation of the Hebrew words, מְשַׁמְּרִים הַבְלֵי־שָׁוְא. This same Hebrew phrase is translated as useless idols in Psalm 31:6.

I have hated those who regard *useless idols*; but I trust in the LORD (Psalm 31:6).

And how can we confirm that Psalm 31 is Messianic? Yeshua's last words were taken from Psalm 31:5.

And when Jesus had cried out with a loud voice, He said, *"Father, into Your hands I commit My spirit."* Having said this, He breathed His last (Luke 23:46).

Into Your hand I commit my spirit; You have redeemed me, O LORD God of truth (Psalm 31:5).

The last example I'd like to share pertains to Psalm 69. Please note the following thematic connections that lead me to believe this psalm is Messianic.

- Psalm 69:1-2 states, "¹ Save me, O God! For *the waters have come up to my neck*. ² I sink in deep mire, where there is no standing; *I have come into deep waters*, where the *floods overflow me*." This passage is thematically connected to Jonah 2:3 and 5a which state, "³ For You *cast me into the deep*, into the heart of the seas, and *the floods surrounded me*; all *Your billows and Your waves passed over me* . . . ⁵ *The waters*

surrounded me, even to my soul; ***The deep closed around me.***" The thematic connections between these statements by Jonah (a Messianic figure) and the psalmist hint that Psalm 69 is Messianic.
- Psalm 69:14-15 states, "¹⁴ Deliver me out of the mire, and ***let me not sink***; Let me be delivered from those who hate me, and ***out of the deep waters***. ¹⁵ ***Let not the floodwater overflow me, nor let the deep swallow me up; and let not the pit shut its mouth on me***. These verses are thematically connected to Jonah 2:3 and 5 above as well as to Jonah's story in general. Jonah was swallowed by a great fish. Remember, Jonah likened the belly of the fish to a pit. The psalmist's allusion to Jonah's fish shutting his mouth on Jonah, locking him into the pit of his belly, is inescapable.

Having identified Psalm 69 as being Messianic by its numerous thematic connections to Jonah (one of our primary Messianic figures), we can note the following Messianic prophecies within it.

- Psalm 69:4 - ***Those who hate me without a cause*** are more than the hairs of my head; they are mighty who would destroy me, ***being my enemies wrongfully***; though I have stolen nothing, I still must restore it. Yeshua Himself quoted this Psalm in John 15:25!
  o John 15:25 - But this happened that the word might be fulfilled which is written in their law, '***They hated Me without a cause.***'
- Psalm 69:9 - ***Because zeal for Your house has eaten me up***, and the reproaches of those who reproach You have fallen on me. Yeshua's disciples remembered Psalm 69:9 as being Messianic.
  o ¹⁵ When He had made a whip of cords, He drove them all out of the temple, with the sheep and the oxen, and poured out the changers' money and overturned the tables. ¹⁶ And He said to those who sold doves, "Take these things away! Do not make My Father's house a house of merchandise!" ¹⁷ Then His disciples remembered that it was written, "***Zeal for Your house has eaten Me up*** (John 2:15-17)."
- Psalm 69:21 - They also gave me ***gall for my food, and for my thirst they gave me vinegar to drink***. Yeshua was given gall as He languished on the tree.
  o There they offered Jesus wine to drink, ***mixed with gall; but after tasting it, he refused to drink it*** (Matthew 27:34).
  o Immediately one of them ran and got a sponge. ***He filled it with wine vinegar, put it on a stick, and offered it to Jesus to drink*** (Matthew 27:48).
- Psalm 69:25 - ***Let their dwelling place be desolate; Let no one live in their tents***. This passage was mentioned by the apostles as referring to Judas.
  o Now this man purchased a field with the wages of iniquity; and falling headlong, he burst open in the middle and all his entrails gushed out. ¹⁹ And it became known to all those dwelling in Jerusalem; so that field is called in their own language, Akel Dama, that is, Field of Blood.²⁰ "For it is written in the Book of Psalms: '***Let his dwelling place be desolate, And let no one live in it***'; and, 'Let another take his office (Acts 1:18-20).'

As you can see, Adonai knows how to get our attention. The only question is, "Are we listening?"

Chapter 5

Death, Burial, Resurrection . . . and Salvation!

Introduction

In the last chapter, we continued our trek through the chiastic structure of II Samuel 15:10 – II Samuel 20:2. We were able to analyze this chiastic structure all the way until the central axis (II Samuel 17:27-29), noting the amazing parallels between David's flight from Absalom and Yeshua's suffering. At the pashat, or literal level of interpretation, this story pertains to the events that fulfill Nathan's prophecy that the sword would not depart from David's house. However, by studying the scriptures thematically, we have seen that another story is being told—the Gospel—the story of Messiah Yeshua's suffering, death, burial and resurrection. *Just as importantly, the thematic presentation of the Gospel told through David's flight from Absalom matches the chronological presentation of it in the four Gospel accounts!* However, as we discovered in the last chapter, the chronological presentation of the Gospel has developed a glitch. We observed that II Samuel 17:15-24 departed from chronological order! At that time, I stated that there were two thematic presentations of the death, burial and resurrection of the Messiah in II Samuel 17:15-24. We analyzed one of the stories—the actions of Jonathan and Ahimaaz—and stated that their descent into and ascent from the well was a picture of Yeshua's death, burial and resurrection. If it is true that their actions are prophetic pictures of the death, burial and resurrection of the Messiah, then the departure from chronological order becomes evident. Refer to the **Running Chart of Thematic Connections** to help you see this. As you can see, the last event in the chart is none other than the central axis of our chiastic structure. In chapter four, we saw that the provisions given to David and his servants provide a prophetic/thematic basis for how Simon the Cyrenian provided help for Messiah Yeshua as He carried the cross. Obviously, Simon's actions occurred *before* the death, burial and resurrection of Messiah Yeshua. Therefore, II Samuel 17:15-24, which contains two separate prophecies of the death, burial and resurrection of the Messiah, is out of proper chronological order. *The pictures of death, burial and resurrection should occur sometime after the prophetic picture of Simon helping the Messiah!* Clearly, the chronological order of the thematic presentation of the Gospel has been "compromised." The reason for the departure will be discovered in Chapter 6. For the remainder of this chapter, I want to 1) present another proof that Jonathan and Ahimaaz's actions were pictures of death and burial, 2) prove that Jonathan and Ahimaaz are actually Messianic figures and 3) demonstrate how II Samuel 17:21-24 is a thematic picture of salvation won by the Messiah as a result of His death, burial and resurrection.

Jonathan and Ahimaaz, Pictures of the Messiah

Jonathan's and Ahimaaz's "Death and Burial"

In chapter four, Jonathan and Ahimaaz gave us a picture of the Messiah's death, burial and resurrection through their descent into and ascent from a well. Now, let us return to the main chiastic structure for more evidence suggesting that Jonathan's and Ahimaaz's descent into the pit was a picture of death and burial. Please look at the portion of our main chiastic structure below, paying particular attention to elements I and I`.

I) II Samuel 17:18-19—Jonathan and Ahimaaz *descended into a well*; a woman *spread a curtain over the well*
  J) II Samuel 17:23—Ahithophel's suicide by hanging
    K) II Samuel 17:24-25—Absalom appointed Amasa over his army in place of Joab; David's position in Mahanaim
      L) II Samuel 17:27-29—Three men brought David and his servants all sorts of provisions because they were hungry, exhausted and thirsty in the desert
    K`) II Samuel 18:1-5—David appointed officers and divided his camp into thirds; David's position near the city gate
  J`) II Samuel 18:9-15—Absalom hanging in the elm tree; David's servant refusing to accept bribery of silver; Absalom's death;
I`) II Samuel 18:17—Joab's men throw *Absalom's body into a large pit* and erected a *mound of stones over him*

There are two specific themes connecting II Samuel 17:18-19 to II Samuel 18:17. Jonathan and Ahimaaz's *descent into the well* is clearly thematically connected to Absalom's dead body being *thrown into a large pit*. Furthermore, the *curtain being spread over the well* is thematically connected to the *mound of stones spread over Absalom*. In chapter four, I demonstrated that Jonathan and Ahimaaz's actions were a picture of death, burial and resurrection by appealing to the Torah's teaching concerning the equivalence of pits, cisterns, animal dens and wells as pictures of the grave. In this section, I have shown that Jonathan and Ahimaaz's actions were pictures of death and burial by appealing to our main chiastic structure where their descent into the well is thematically connected to Absalom's (**DEAD**) body being thrown into a large pit as a burial ground! The image is very clear. Jonathan and Ahimaaz's descent into the well has been thematically connected to an actual dead person's burial! Once again, Adonai has led us to the correct interpretation through connecting the themes. Baruch HaShem Adonai! This is why studying thematically is so important. As one develops the habit of allowing the Ruach to help make thematic connections, he will notice that Adonai will confirm a truth once, twice, thrice and sometimes four or more times in different ways. Yet each witness will confirm the same truth. It is like a theological quality assurance plan. Adonai is thoroughly committed to ensuring that we see His truths. That's why His themes are so important and useful.

The Scroll of the Gospel of David

Connecting Jonathan and Ahimaaz to the Messiah

We have seen that Jonathan and Ahimaaz have given us a picture of death, burial and resurrection, but we have not actually connected them to the Messiah. Let us now prove that Jonathan and Ahimaaz are Messianic figures. In order to see this truth, we need to make a thematic connection to another story that is almost a mirror image of II Samuel 17:15-24. Can you think of another story where a woman hid two people from their pursuers? The story I'm thinking of is found in Joshua 2:1-24. If you carefully read Joshua 2:1-24 and II Samuel 17:15-24, comparing and contrasting them, you will find the following amazing thematic connections:

II Samuel 17:15-24	*Joshua 2:1-24*
Jonathan and Ahimaaz are two spies for David	The two Israelites are spies for Joshua
Jonathan and Ahimaaz were given military intelligence and told to deliver the message to King David (a military leader)	The two spies were given military intelligence and told to deliver the message to Joshua (a military leader)
Jonathan and Ahimaaz came to a house in Bahurim	The two spies came to Rachav's house in Jericho
A girl gave Jonathan and Ahimaaz military intelligence	Rachav gave the two spies military intelligence
A young man saw Jonathan and Ahimaaz and told Absalom	It was told to the king of Jericho that the two spies had come in
A woman helped Jonathan and Ahimaaz hide in a well	Rachav helped the two spies hide on the roof
A woman covered the well Jonathan and Ahimaaz went into with groats	Rachav covered the two spies (on the roof) with stalks of flax
Absalom's servants inquired about Jonathan and Ahimaaz	The king of Jericho's servants inquired concerning the two spies
A woman told Absalom's servants that Jonathan and Ahimaaz had fled	Rachav told the king of Jericho's servants that the two spies had fled
Absalom's servants searched for Jonathan and Ahimaaz but couldn't find them	The king of Jericho's servants searched for the two spies but couldn't find them

Jonathan and Ahimaaz emerged from hiding after Absalom's servants left	The two spies emerged from hiding after the king of Jericho's servants left
The woman said that Jonathan and Ahimaaz had gone across a body of water (the Jordan)	The spies crossed over the Jordan
Jonathan and Ahimaaz delivered military intelligence to David	The two spies delivered military intelligence to Joshua

The large number of thematic connections assures us that these two stories are thematically connected. The beauty of our discovery is that Adonai inspired the writers of the books of Joshua and II Samuel to record the events as they did, enabling us to make the connections. More importantly, these two stories were real events that happened to real people. What an awesome testimony to the sovereignty of our Elohim! For it is He Who controls all events on earth so that they fulfill His will.

There is one more connection. According to II Samuel 15:35-37, Jonathan and Ahimaaz were the sons of Abiathar and Zadok, respectively. Thus, we may assume that they were *relatively young men*, being sons of the two priests. Furthermore, according to II Samuel 17:18, Jonathan and Ahimaaz descended into the well at a man's house in a place called Bachurim. It just so happens that Bachurim means *young men*! It is the plural of bachur (בחור) which means *young man*. With that in mind, note the description of the two spies recorded in Joshua 6:22-23.

Joshua said *to the two men who had spied out the land*, "Go into the prostitute's house and bring her out and all who belong to her, in accordance with your oath to her." [23] So ***the young men*** who had done the spying went in and brought out Rachav (Rahab), her father and mother and brothers and all who belonged to her. They brought out her entire family and put them in a place outside the camp of Israel.

As you can see, the two spies are referred to as *young men*. The Stone Edition of the Tanakh[23] translates Joshua 6:23a as:

So they entered—*the youthful ones, the spies*—and they brought out Rachav...

Thus, it seems that Jonathan and Ahimaaz are thematically connected to the two spies because both pairs were young men! We have clearly seen that Adonai wants us to connect Jonathan and Ahimaaz to the two young spies in the story of Rahav the harlot, but why?

In chapter four, we learned two important hermeneutic tools pertaining to WHY thematic connections are made. We were able to understand these hermeneutic tools by making use of two postulates of mathematics. The first postulate is entitled, the symmetric property of equality. It states the following:

If A = B, Then B = A

We learned that one of the reasons passages are thematically connected is to show equivalence between people, places, things, situations, events, etc. Therefore, applying that reasoning to II Samuel 17:15-24 and Joshua 2:1-24 we can easily state that Ahimaaz and Jonathan are equivalent (thematically connected) to the two young spies.

Jonathan and Ahimaaz = The two young spies

A = B

The other postulate is called the Transitive Property of Equality.

If A = B and B = C, then A = C

Sometimes, the Ruach does not make a *direct connection* between two people via the *if A = B, then B = A* principle. Sometimes, the connection between some people is *indirect*, via the *if A = B and B = C, then A = C* principle. We saw how this property is used to connect people to the Messiah *through someone else*! Remember, the primary purpose of the Tanakh is to teach us about the Messiah. It does this by providing images of the Messiah through the lives of people in the Tanakh. There are two primary ways in which it "informs" us that someone is a Messianic figure. The first is the Sign of the Messiah. The other way is through usage of the Transitive Property of Equality. In this method, person A is thematically connected to person B (A = B). Then person B is thematically connected to the Messiah[24] (B = C). This is done to connect person A to the Messiah (A = C) as follows:

If   Person A = Person B

A = B

And   Person B = Messiah Yeshua

B = C

Then   Person A = Messiah Yeshua

A = C

So, why does Adonai want us to equate Jonathan and Ahimaaz with the two spies? The reason why they are connected to them is most likely because the two young spies are somehow thematically connected to the Messiah, thus, making them Messianic figures. It just so happens that the story of the two young spies is thematically connected to another story! Can you think of another story where someone from the nation of Israel stayed in the house of a harlot in a heathen nation? Please read Judges 16:1-3 along with Joshua 2:1-24 noting how many similar themes appear. In fact, if you look very closely at these two passages, you'll notice that they are arranged in a chiastic structure!

A) Joshua 2:1-5 — A') Judges 16:1-3[25]

A Joshua 2:1—The spies went to *observe (see)* Jericho
  B Joshua 2:1—The spies *stayed at the house of an harlot*
    C Joshua 2:1—The spies *lodged* at Rachav's house
      D Joshua 2:2—The king of Jericho was *told that Israelites had come into Jericho*
        E Joshua 2:3—The *pursuers tried to capture* the two Israelite spies
          F Joshua 2:4—The *spies remained hidden* from their pursuers
            G Joshua 2:5—Rachav told the king that the spies *had left through the city gate* when it was *dark* and the city gate was about to close.
              H Later in Joshua, the Israelites *breached the wall* around Jericho when the entire wall fell down
              H' Judges 16:3—Samson *breached the wall* around Gaza by taking its city gate.
            G' Judges 16:3—Samson *left through the city gate* at *midnight*
          F' Judges 16:3—Although the Gazites laid in wait at the city gate, *Samson was hidden* from them for we read of no resistance from the Gazites at the city gate
        E' Judges 16:2—*Gazites lay in wait* for Samson to catch him
      D' Judges 16:2—The Gazites were *told that Samson had come into Gaza*
    C' Judges 16:3—Samson *slept* with the harlot (he arose from sleep at midnight)
  B' Judges 16:1—Samson *stayed with an harlot*
A' Judges 16:1—Samson went to Gaza and *saw* an harlot

Clearly, the two young spies have been thematically connected to Samson! Now, we must ask, "What's so special about Samson?" Well, as you might have guessed, Samson is a Messianic figure. In fact, he is one of the major Messianic figures of the Tanakh. Let us demonstrate this fact.

Samson's life is recorded for us in Judges 13 – 16. Judges 14:1-20 is the story of how Samson took a wife from among the Philistines. According to Judges 14:5-7, Samson was met by a roaring lion as he went to Timnah to fetch himself a bride. Samson killed the lion with his bare hands! Now, what, may I ask you, is supposed to happen to the average person (who isn't carrying a weapon) who is attacked by a roaring lion? Obviously, he/she should be killed! However, Samson escaped death. This is the Sign of the Messiah in his life. He was supposed to die; however, his life was spared. And where is the number three? The number three occurs in Judges 14:11 where we are informed that Samson was given **30** companions for his wedding. This completes the Sign of the Messiah in Samson's life—life, death and the number three.[26] Before going on with a discussion concerning the thematic connections pertaining to Jonathan, Ahimaaz, the two spies and Samson, let's see two more examples of how Samson's life is a picture of Messiah Yeshua's life.

Judges 13:2-7 describes the angelic prophecy of Samson's birth.[27] If you read this passage, it will seem as if you read certain facts twice. There are no idle repetitions in the Scriptures. This is a common Hebrew literary technique called a parallelism. A parallelism is very similar to a chiastic structure except that the themes of the first half of the story are repeated in the second half in the same order. Whenever you see a parallelism, you should thematically compare and contrast the two halves to uncover any veiled wisdom. I have divided the parallelism for you so that you can compare each repetition.

> A) Judges 13:2—The description of a barren woman
> B) Judges 13:3a—Appearance of an angel
>   C) Judges 13:3b—Promise of a son
>   D) Judges 13:4-5a—Stipulations of the Nazirite vow
>   E) Judges 13:5b—*He will save Israel*
> A1) Judges 13:6a—Description of a man and woman
> B1) Judges 13:6b—Appearance of an angel
>   C1) Judges 13:7a—Promise of a son
>   D1) Judges 13:7b—The Nazirite vow
>   E1) Judges 13:7c—*His death*

Although parallelisms may seem unimportant, they often pay huge dividends, as in this case. Have you noticed how each theme of this parallelism is essentially a mirror image of its counterpart...except in E)? In other words, the theme of A matches A1, B matches B1, C-C1, and D-D1 very easily. However, E doesn't seem to match E1! Since A1 - D1 are simply thematic restatements of A - D, the real wisdom will be found in comparing E - E1. And what is the message we are to glean by thematically connecting E to E1? How about this:

The promised son (whom we know to be Samson) will...

E) Save Israel through E1) His Death

As you can see, this is actually a prophecy of Samson's death which will occur later in Judges 16:23-31 where he killed more Philistines (thus saving Israel)[28] *through his death* than he did in his lifetime. But more importantly, do you realize the Messianic significance of this connection? Isn't this what Messiah Yeshua came to do? He saved Israel (and all who believe) *through His death*! Absolutely amazing! Yes, Samson's triumph over the 3000+ Philistines *through His death* was a prophetic picture of the work of Messiah Yeshua, who destroyed hasatan—the true roaring lion[29]—*through His death*. How so? Colossians 2:15 states the following:

And having spoiled principalities and powers, he made a show of them openly, *triumphing over them in it* [on the execution stake/cross] (Colossians 2:15).

This verse teaches us *that Yeshua won his greatest battle against His enemies (hasatan and his minions) through His death on the execution stake*! In fact, note how Judges 16:30b is emphatic that Samson killed more in his *death* than in his *life*!!! Beloved, this is a picture of how Yeshua's greatest victory occurred *through His death*! Although Samson had destroyed many of Am Yisrael's enemies during his lifetime, his greatest victory came as a result of his death. So likewise, although Yeshua destroyed many of the works of hasatan (sickness, etc.) during His life, it was through His **DEATH** that He won the greatest victory over hasatan and secured eternal **LIFE** for us!!! The story of Samson's final battle in Judges 16 is how the Holy One teaches us that Messiah Yeshua will obtain His greatest victory over the enemy of mankind through His death. Therefore, Samson's death in the temple of Dagon is a prophetic picture of the death of Messiah Yeshua on the execution stake. This thematic connection is also taught in the following verse.

> [14]Inasmuch then as the children have partaken of flesh and blood, He Himself likewise shared in the same, *that **through death*** He might ***destroy*** him who had the power of death, that is, ***the devil***, [15]and release those [us] who through fear of death were all their lifetime subject to bondage (Hebrews 2:14-15).

This verse clearly shows us two things. First, hasatan was defeated through Yeshua's death—just as Samson's greatest victory came through His death. Secondly, it teaches that we were freed from fear through Yeshua's death, just as Am Yisrael was freed from fear of the Philistines through the death of Samson! Lastly, note the following picture. When Samson pushed the two pillars, what motion did he make with his hands and what was the Messianic significance? He *stretched his hands out* just like Yeshua stretched out His hands to be nailed to the execution stake!

Now, we can piece together this great Messianic teaching.

- The two young spies are thematically connected to Samson (A = B)
- Sampson is thematically connected to (or a picture of) Yeshua the Messiah (B = C)
- Therefore, the two young spies are thematically connected to (or a picture of) Yeshua the Messiah (A = C)

But . . .

- Jonathan and Ahimaaz are thematically connected (equivalent) to the two young spies (A = B)
- The two young spies are thematically connected to (or a picture of) Yeshua the Messiah (B = C)
- Therefore, Jonathan and Ahimaaz are thematically connected to (or a picture of) Yeshua the Messiah (A = C)

If   the two young spies = Samson

$$A = B$$

And   Samson = Yeshua

$$B = C$$

Then   the two young spies = Messiah Yeshua

              A   =   C

But...

If   Jonathan and Ahimaaz = The Two Young Spies

              A   =   B

And   The Two Young Spies = Yeshua

              B   =   C

Then   Jonathan and Ahimaaz = Messiah Yeshua

              A   =   C

Beloved, this is how thematic connections work and how Adonai will teach you about the Messiah. This is not the only instance of this type of analysis of Scripture. There are many, many more examples in scripture where a person is thematically connected to the Messiah through others who are themselves Messianic figures. The thematic connections are Adonai's pointers, pointing you to the truth. Our job is to simply follow the connections.

We have only one more task to accomplish concerning these two Messianic figures. Where was the number three in their story? Many times the number three (**3**, **3**0, **3**00, **3**,000, etc.) will be found in the story of the Messianic figures' life. However, sometimes it will seem to be missing, as in our present instance, where there was no mention of the number three in II Samuel 17:15-21. When this is the case, you will usually find the number three in a story that is intimately thematically connected to the one lacking the number three. Remember, one of the reasons passages are thematically connected is because all the information you need to interpret it may not be located there. Sometimes, extra information needed to interpret one passage (like the number three in our instance) will be found in another passage thematically connected to it. We have already seen that the story of the two young spies (Joshua 2:1-24) is a virtual mirror image of the story of Jonathan and Ahimaaz. Therefore, since Jonathan and Ahimaaz are equivalent to the two young spies, it only stands to reason that we may find the number three in the story of the young spies who are equivalent to Jonathan and Ahimaaz. If you examine the chiastic structure of Joshua 2:16-22, you will find the number three in elements A and A'!

Joshua 2:16-22

A) Joshua 2:16—Rachav said "***Go to the mountains*** lest the pursuers see you"; "***Hide THREE days until the pursuers turn back***"
  B) Joshua 2:17-18a—Spies said, "You shall ***tie this cord of scarlet thread in the window***"; spies said "We are ***absolved of this oath*** unless…"

  C) Joshua 2:18b—Spies said, "Bring your father and his entire house, your mother and brothers *into the house*"

   D) Joshua 2:19a—The spies said, "Anyone who leaves the doors of your house for the outside, his blood will be on his own head and we'll be absolved"

  C') Joshua 2:19b—"Anyone who stays with you *in the house*"

 B') Joshua 2:20-2:21—The spies said, "If you relate this discussion we will be *absolved of our oath*"; Rachav *tied a scarlet cord in the window*

A') Joshua 2:22—After *arriving at the mountain*, the spies *hid THREE days until the pursuers turned back*; pursuers couldn't find them because they were hiding

The number three—necessary to complete the picture of Jonathan and Ahimaaz's death, burial and resurrection—is found in Joshua 2:1-24, which relates the story of the two young spies who are clearly thematically connected to Jonathan and Ahimaaz. Thus, in the last two chapters we have demonstrated that Jonathan and Ahimaaz are Messianic figures and their story in II Samuel 17:15-21 is a thematic portrait of the death, burial and resurrection of Messiah Yeshua.

This portion of our story is now complete. Now, let us lay the foundation for understanding the Messianic significance of II Samuel 17:21-24.

The Torah's Foundational Definition of Salvation

Why We Need to Understand the Torah's Foundational Definition of Salvation

At this time, I'd like to reveal the Messianic significance of II Samuel 17:21-24; however, I need to acquaint you with another foundational teaching concerning salvation through the Messiah. Anytime you want to understand a subject in the Bible you should immediately ask, "What does the Torah teach about this?" This is especially true concerning salvation. Unlike most believers who think that salvation is primarily taught in the New Testament, we should seek to understand salvation by first learning what the Torah teaches about it. Why is the subject of salvation so important? I will answer that question with another. Who is it that we expect to bring salvation? The Messiah is the One who will bring us salvation. This is so important because in chapter one, we saw that the Messiah is the primary subject of the Tanakh. The following verses support this assertion.

- John 5:46—For if you believed Moses, you would believe Me; for <u>**he wrote about Me**</u>.
- John 5:39—You search the Scriptures, for in them you think you have eternal life; <u>**and these are they which testify of Me**</u>.
- Psalm 40:6-8—Sacrifice and offering You did not desire; My ears You have opened. Burnt offering and sin offering You did not require. Then I said, "Behold, I come; <u>**In the scroll of the book it is written of me**</u>. I delight to do Your will, O my God, And Your law is within my heart."
- Luke 24:27, 44-48—And beginning at <u>**Moses and all the Prophets**</u>, He expounded to them in all the Scriptures **the things concerning Himself**…Then He said to them, "These are the words which I spoke to you while I was still with you, that <u>**all things**</u>

must be fulfilled which were written in the Law of Moses and the Prophets and the Psalms concerning Me." And He opened their understanding, that they might comprehend the Scriptures. Then He said to them, "Thus it is written, and thus it was necessary for the Messiah to suffer and to rise from the dead the third day, and that repentance and remission of sins should be preached in His name to all nations, beginning at Jerusalem. And you are witnesses of these things.

If the Messiah is the One who will bring salvation, it stands to reason that we can learn about Him when we study passages dealing with salvation! In other words, as we study the stories in the Tanakh that pertain to salvation we are actually studying about the work of the Messiah! With that thought, let's see what we can glean from the Tanakh about salvation, the work of the Messiah.

Let's begin by seeing if we can find a good definition of salvation in the Torah. To do this, we'll study the story of the Red Sea crossing found in Exodus 14:1-31. As you can see, this passage relates the account of the splitting of the Red Sea and the word *salvation* is mentioned in Exodus 14:13-14.

And Moses said to the people, "Do not be afraid. Stand still, and see the ***salvation*** of the LORD, which He will accomplish for you today. For the Egyptians whom you see today, you shall see again no more forever. The LORD will fight for you, and you shall hold your peace (Exodus 14:13-14).

This is a very important passage to understand in our quest for the Torah's foundational definition of salvation. Moses told Am Yisrael (the people of Israel) to "Stand still, and *see the salvation of the LORD*." In other words, the Holy One was about to give Am Yisrael a picture/definition of salvation and all they needed to do was stand back and *watch it unfold* before their eyes! How simple can the Holy One make it? So what happened? ***What did the people see that can be equated with salvation?*** Were their sins forgiven? Did they inherit eternal life? Were they healed? Did they receive their new, resurrected bodies and enter into the eternal state? Well, not exactly. So what happened that can be equated with salvation? In a nutshell, the people saw two things:

1. They were ***delivered*** from the hand of their enemy.
2. Their enemy was ***destroyed*** by the hand of the Almighty.

Based on Moses' statement, "Stand still, and see the salvation of the LORD," and the ensuing story, I suggest that ***the Torah's foundational definition of salvation*** can be summarized as follows:

- Your enemy is about to annihilate you.
- You are powerless to help or defend yourself.
- The Holy One delivers you from the hand of your enemy.
- The Holy One destroys your enemy.

That's it. Based on Exodus 14:13-14 and the ensuing story of the splitting of the Red Sea, you have just been taught the Torah's *foundational definition of salvation*.[30] Why is this important? Because, as I said earlier, it's the Messiah who will bring about the Holy One's great salvation. Therefore, if we want to understand how the Messiah will bring this about, we simply need to study those stories that define it. And it just so happens that the splitting of the Red Sea is the foundational passage defining salvation.

By now, some of you may be saying, "What does the story of the splitting of the Red Sea have to do with the salvation Yeshua brought through His death on the tree?" To see the true significance of the splitting of the Red Sea, remember that *the Torah is a shadow* of good things to come. Most of the Torah's pictures of the Messiah are black and white snapshots of His redemptive work. Through thematic analysis, we will soon see a wealth of information concerning the Messiah and gain a tremendous understanding of His mission. This understanding will help us see the Messianic significance of II Samuel 17:21-24.

Salvation Through Yeshua

The story of the splitting of the Red Sea occurs in Exodus 14. As you have already seen, Moses stated that Am Yisrael were about to see the salvation of **Yahweh**. This section of Scripture contains some jewels that you will never see unless you understand Hebrew.

Moses said to the people, "Do not fear! Stand fast and *see the salvation* of YHVH (Exodus 14:13)."

The Hebrew word used for *salvation* is yeshuat, יְשׁוּעַת. Does the word yeshuat sound familiar? You bet it does. It is the word from which we derive the Savior's Name, Yeshua, יֵשׁוּעַ! Let's take another look at this verse substituting the Savior's name in it.

Moses said to the people, "Do not fear! Stand fast and *see the Yeshua* of YHVH (Exodus 14:13)."

It's not many times that the Torah outright tells you that *you are about to see Yeshua*, so this must be important. This is a remez (hint) level teaching that salvation will come through Yeshua! Now isn't that amazing! By knowing the Torah's definition of salvation, and mining it for its wisdom, we are able to see a remez level teaching on the Messiah's Name!

Salvation Through the Name Yahweh

Speaking of names, it just so happens that the Holy One's name, YHVH (יהוה), actually gives a word-picture of how salvation will come. All the Hebrew letters were given their form from the shapes of objects found in nature.

- The letter yod י comes from the picture of a hand.
- The letter hey ה comes from the picture of a window, meaning revelation, or that which comes forth.
- The letter vav ו comes from the picture of a nail or hook.

Knowing that salvation will come through the name YHVH (יהוה), can we glean any understanding concerning salvation (yeshuat) through Yeshua? I think so. In hindsight, we know that our redemption and salvation was paid for by Yeshua because of His being hung on a tree. We can immediately see a thematic connection between the letters of the Name YHVH (יהוה) and the work of Messiah Yeshua. Just as the letters yod (י) and vav (ו) come from the picture of a *hand* and *nail*, respectively, so likewise, we understand that Yeshua's pierced *hands* were *nailed* to the tree to bring us salvation! This is the second major revelation (ה) we've received simply by studying the splitting of the Red Sea, the Holy One's foundational picture of salvation. But wait, there's more!

The Outstretched Hand

In Exodus 14:16, 21 and 26-27 we learn that salvation would occur through Moses' outstretched hand. The Holy One commanded Moses to stretch forth his hand over the Red Sea in Exodus 14:16 and 26. The first time he did this, the Holy One delivered Am Yisrael by splitting the Red Sea so they could escape from their enemy (Exodus 14:21). The second time he stretched forth his hand, the Egyptian army was destroyed (Exodus 14:27-28). Thus, we see that two events occurred as a result of the stretching forth of Moses' hands. Am Yisrael was ***delivered*** from the hand of their enemy and the Egyptian army was ***destroyed***. Since we have already learned that—according to Torah—salvation occurs when you are delivered from your enemy while they are destroyed, we can easily state that *salvation occurred as a result of Moses stretching forth his arm/hand*!

Now let's ask another pertinent question. What was in Moses' hand when he stretched it forth to bring salvation? A staff! More precisely, a wooden staff. Knowing that Messiah is the chosen One to bring forth salvation, the last two revelations teach us that salvation will occur through the outstretched hand of Messiah. Furthermore, should we not expect Messiah's outstretched hand to be associated with wood in some manner? Yes, indeed we should. In fact, in hindsight we know this to be the case, because *Messiah Yeshua's outstretched hand was nailed to the tree*! Once again we see that the story of the Red Sea crossing contains a wealth of foundational information pertaining to salvation through the Messiah. These are the Torah's shadows of the redemption to come. They were hidden within the narrative of the Torah. Although they were hidden, Adonai revealed their true significance (salvation through the Messiah) at the appropriate time and in the appropriate manner. Moses is acting as a picture of the Messiah stretching forth His hand to bring salvation. Yeshua is His name.

Did you notice how much work Am Yisrael had to do in order to help the process of salvation along?

> ***Do not be afraid. Stand still***, and *see* the salvation of the LORD, which He will accomplish for you today. For the Egyptians whom you see today, you shall see again no more forever. ¹⁴***The LORD will fight for you***, and you shall ***hold your peace*** [be silent] (Exodus 14:13-14)."

As you can see, they weren't required to do much. In fact, they did nothing. This teaches us that the Messiah will perform the great work of salvation all by Himself—not by works of righteousness which we have done (Titus 3:5).

Now, let us take inventory of what we have learned thus far through the story of the splitting of the Red Sea concerning our salvation.

- Salvation will occur through one named salvation.
- Salvation will occur through the Name YHVH (יהוה). This salvation will be revealed (ה) through a nail- (ו) pierced hand (י).
- Salvation will occur through an outstretched hand.
- Salvation will occur through an outstretched hand associated with wood in some manner.
- Salvation will not depend on the works of any man.

Now we can see the big picture. The Red Sea crossing is simply a thematic picture of salvation through the sacrificial death of Messiah Yeshua. Moses' staff-laden, outstretched hand is simply a prophetic/Messianic picture of the outstretched hand of Messiah Yeshua that was nailed to the tree (a piece of wood). With this as a foundation, pay attention to any reference to the outstretched hand. We should now know that it is a clear reference to salvation secured by the Messiah! And now, for the rest of the story…

Chiastic Revelations

The Torah has many thematic lessons to teach. It does this by hiding its wisdom within certain literary schemes/paradigms. We have already seen that one of the most fascinating literary techniques of the Torah involves the usage of chiastic structures and parallelisms. These two techniques are the Holy One's way of demonstrating which Scriptures have thematic relevance to each other. Let's see how these literary devices can be used as extraordinary hermeneutic tools.

Most of you are familiar with the story of how Am Yisrael crossed the Jordan River in route to the Promised Land. As you remember, the Holy One stopped the flow of the Jordan River so they could pass through on their way to destroy Jericho and obtain their inheritance. There is an obvious thematic parallel between the splitting of the Red Sea and the splitting of the Jordan, right? However, there is much more to these two stories than you may think. Please read the account of the crossing of the Jordan River (Joshua 3-5). Now compare it to Exodus 14-16. Do you see any parallels? In case you didn't see it, please note the following parallelism thematically linking the crossing of the Red Sea to the stopping of the Jordan River.

The Parallelism of Joshua 3:9-5:12 and Exodus 14:13-16:4

A) Exodus 14:13-14—Moses said, "Don't fear…stand still *and see the salvation of YHVH*… He will *destroy the Egyptians*; He will fight for you"
  B) Exodus 14:15-20—Adonai told Moshe ahead of time what would happen; *the angel of God and pillar of cloud that went before them* went behind them
    C) Exodus 14:21-22—Moses stretched out his *hand over the sea*; Adonai turned the sea into dry land; the waters were *divided*; Am Yisrael went into the *midst of the Red Sea on dry ground*; the water was a heap on the left and right

  D) Exodus 14:26—Adonai commanded Moses what to do so that the water would return
   E) Exodus 14:27-28—Moses stretched his *hand over the sea* and the water returned
    F) Exodus 15:8 and 19—The waters heaped up; *the deep congealed*; Am Yisrael *walked on dry ground*
     G) Exodus 15:14-15—The people *heard and feared*; may they fear the greatness of Your mighty arm
      H) Exodus 16:4—The manna began coming down

A`) Joshua 3:9-10—Joshua said, "He shall *destroy the inhabitants*; you shall *know the living God is among you*"
 B`) Joshua 3:11-14—Joshua told the people ahead of time what would happen; the *ark of the covenant went before the people*
  C`) Joshua 3:15-17—The priests *feet dipped into the edge of the Jordan*; the *water split*; the people crossed *on dry ground*; the priests stood on dry ground in the *midst of the Jordan*
   D`) Joshua 4:15—Adonai commanded Joshua what to do so that the water would return
    E`) Joshua 4:16-18—As the priests *feet touched the dry ground* the water returned
     F`) Joshua 4:19-24—Tell your children Israel *crossed on dry ground*; Adonai *dried up the water* of the Jordan
      G`) Joshua 5:1—The Amorite and Canaanite kings *heard* how Adonai dried up the Jordan's waters *and feared*
       H`) Joshua 5:12—The manna ceased

  Is this not amazing? Parallelisms are <u>*extremely*</u> valuable because they teach numerous thematic lessons that are not readily apparent at the pashat (literal) level. Parallelisms are analyzed by comparing and contrasting the points that are thematically related (compare A to A`, B to B`, etc.). Usually, most of the points in a parallelism are thematically equivalent. For example, points D, F and G are thematically equivalent to points D`, F` and G` because they essentially present the same information with no major differences. I have bolded and italicized the important words in each point of the structure so that you can easily see the thematic connections. On the other hand, some points, although thematically equivalent, offer interesting differences or slight modifications of the main theme. For example, although points A and A` are clearly thematically related through the phrases *destroy the Egyptians* and *destroy the inhabitants, respectively,* the other two points of thematic equivalency are not as straightforward— *and see the salvation of YHVH* versus *know the living God is among you*. Although different, it is easy to see that they are thematically equivalent because Am Yisrael will understand that *the living God is among* them when they *see* and experience *His great salvation*. Points H and H` also fit this second category of chiastic elements where they are thematically equivalent with a slight modification of the main theme. They are both thematically equivalent because each pertains to the feeding of Am Yisrael with manna. However, the slight modification is that point H pertains to the initiation of the supply of manna, whereas, point H` pertains to the cessation of the supply of manna. Elements that are either exactly thematically equivalent (such as D-D`, F-F` and G-G`) or thematically equivalent with a slight modification of the theme (such as A-A` and H-H`) are not the most interesting elements of a chiastic structure because they do not present any new information. They are very important, though, for the following reason. The fact that their themes match so well is the greatest proof that the two passages under comparison are thematically equivalent and part of a Divine literary scheme! Who can compare points A- A`, D-D`, F-F` G-G` and H-H` and not see that the Holy One 1) inspired their thematic equivalence and 2) intended for us to take note of them?

The most interesting elements of a parallelism are those that *do not seem to match thematically*! Why? Let's review what we've learned so far. The fact that A- A`, D-D`, F-F` G-G` and H-H` match so perfectly should be proof enough for us to understand that points B-B`, C-C` and E-E` are related in some manner even though they may not appear to be so at first glance. In other words, the parallelism is the Holy One's way of showing us that points B-B`, C-C` and E-E` *are thematically equivalent in some manner*. Our job is to make the connection, understand the thematic equivalence and apply the understanding. Let's start with points B-B`. In point B, the Torah emphasizes how the angel of God and the pillar of cloud were originally in front of Am Yisrael. Then, when it was time to confront the Egyptians, the angel of God and the pillar of cloud went behind Am Yisrael to confront them. This paints the picture of the function of the angel of God and the pillar of cloud as follows: 1) they go before Am Yisrael, leading the way [Divine guidance] and 2) they fight Am Yisrael's enemies [Divine protection]. Note how these two specific functions of the Angel are mentioned later in the book of Exodus.

- Exodus 23:20—"Behold, I send an Angel before you to keep you in the way and to bring you [Divine guidance] into the place which I have prepared."
- Exodus 23:23—"For My Angel will go before you and bring you in to the Amorites and the Hittites and the Perizzites and the Canaanites and the Hivites and the Jebusites; and I will cut them off."
- Exodus 33:2—"And I will send My Angel before you, and I will drive out [Divine protection] the Canaanite and the Amorite and the Hittite and the Perizzite and the Hivite and the Jebusite."

Since the *angel of God and the pillar of cloud* are thematically related to *the ark of the covenant* through the parallelism, the Torah is trying to teach us that *the angel of God and pillar of cloud* are thematically equivalent to *ark of the covenant*, which represents the presence of the Holy One. Remember, He dwelled between the cherubim (angels) on the top of the mercy seat.

We can also connect them thematically in other ways. The Ark of the Covenant had two cherubim (*angels*) upon its cover and on Yom Kippur, the High Priest could enter the Holy of Holies only after he had made a *cloud* in front of the Ark with the incense. As you can see, the last sentence clearly connects the cloud of incense (within the veil on Yom Kippur) and the cherubim (covering the mercy seat) of the Ark with the angel of God and the pillar of cloud that led Am Yisrael. Thus, we see that the angel of God and the pillar of cloud together function as a "primitive" Ark or its prototype, representing the presence of Adonai over the mercy seat.

We know the Ark of the Covenant *went before Am Yisrael* from the book of Numbers.

So they *set* out from the mountain of the LORD and traveled for three days. The **ark** of the covenant of the LORD went before them during those three days to find them a place to rest (Numbers 10:33).

Whenever the *ark set* out, Moses said, "Rise up, O LORD ! May your enemies be scattered; may your foes flee before you (Numbers 10:35)."

Furthermore, the Ark was crucial in ensuring that Am Yisrael would defeat their enemies just as the angel of God and the pillar of cloud 1) safely led Am Yisrael [by going before them] and 2) destroyed Egypt at the Red Sea. Numbers 10:35 beautifully captures both themes of Divine guidance and Divine protection in one verse.

Now let us turn to points C-C` and E-E`. The main idea of point C is that the Holy One split the Red Sea as a result of Moses stretching forth his hand over it. The main idea of point E is that Moses caused the waters of the Red Sea to return by stretching forth his hand over it. Now note the beautiful thematic parallel found in points C` and E`. In those points, the Jordan River was stopped when the *feet* of the priests went into it, whereas, the waters of the Jordan were allowed to flow again as a result of the priest's *feet* leaving the water. The connection could not be any clearer. Moses' *outstretched hand over the sea* is thematically connected to the priest's *feet dipping into the edge of the Jordan*. Just as it was Moses' *outstretched hand* that opened the Red Sea for Am Yisrael (delivering/saving them) and brought the waters of the Red Sea down on Am Yisrael's enemies (destroying them), it was the *feet of the priests* which stopped the flow of the Jordan so Am Yisrael could cross it, and it was the *feet of the priests* that caused the Jordan to flow again.

So what are we to make of this connection? Clearly, the Holy One wants us to view Moses' hand as thematically equivalent to the priest's feet! But why? May I suggest that we can find the answer when we apply the Messianic significance of Moses' outstretched hand to the feet of the priests? Earlier, we saw quite clearly that the splitting of the Red Sea teaches the following: Moses' staff-laden outstretched hand, bringing salvation through the Name of YHVH, is a prophetic picture of the salvation secured for us by Messiah Yeshua's outstretched hand that was pierced to the tree. That is the Messianic significance of Moses' outstretched hand. Now that the Torah has clearly thematically connected Moses' outstretched hand to the priest's feet, we can apply the same Messianic understanding to the priest's feet, namely, that the Messiah's feet will also play some role in securing salvation! Wow! What a revelation! We've already seen that Messiah's pierced outstretched hands will bring about salvation. Could it be that points C-C` and E-E` of the parallelism relating the Red Sea crossing to the Jordan crossing have taught us that the Messiah's feet will also be outstretched and pierced? Yes, this is exactly the case. Through the story of the Red Sea crossing and its thematic connection to the Jordan crossing, the Torah has accurately shown us that salvation will occur through the outstretched, pierced <u>***hands and feet***</u> of the Messiah! This is how these connections work to reveal that which is not obvious.

The parallelism relating the Red Sea crossing to the Jordan crossing has truly been a treasure chest. Apart from the clear thematic relationship between these two events, we wouldn't have known that the priest's feet served the same purpose as Moses' outstretched hand. Maybe this is why Joshua 4:21-24 states that these two events were to be remembered ***together***.

²¹Then he spoke to the children of Israel, saying: "When your children ask their fathers in time to come, saying, 'What are these stones?' ²²then you shall let your children know, saying, 'Israel crossed over this Jordan on dry land'; ²³for ***the LORD your God dried up the waters of the Jordan before you until you had crossed over, as the LORD your God did to the Red Sea,*** which He dried up before us until we had crossed over, ²⁴that all the peoples of the earth may know the hand of the LORD, that it is mighty, that you may fear the LORD your God forever."

The Ubiquitous Nature of the Red Sea Crossing

The Red Sea crossing is actually a *blueprint for salvation* that weaves its path throughout the Scriptures all the way into the Brit Chadasha (New Testament Scriptures). The Jordan crossing is only the beginning point of the Tanakh's thematic parallels to the Red Sea crossing! *Many of the stories of the Tanakh make clear thematic connections to the Red Sea crossing.* Why? Because the splitting of the Red Sea is a picture of salvation through Messiah Yeshua. Therefore, other stories in the Tanakh will make clear allusions (thematic connections) to the splitting of the Red Sea because Adonai wants us to know that those stories also pertain to the salvation won for us by Messiah Yeshua! Remember the Transitive Property of Equality from chapter four?

$$\text{If } A = B \text{ and } B = C, \text{ then } A = C$$

It applies here also.

Salvation through the Messiah = The story of the splitting of the Red Sea

$$A \quad = \quad B$$

However, another story somewhere else will be thematically connected to the splitting of the Red Sea.

The story of the splitting of the Red Sea = Some other story in the Tanakh

$$B \quad = \quad C$$

If $A = B$ and $B = C$, then $A = C$. In other words, if salvation through the Messiah is taught by the story of the splitting of the Red Sea ($A = B$) and the story of the splitting of the Red Sea is thematically connected to another story in the Tanakh ($B = C$), then salvation through the Messiah is taught by the other story in the Tanakh ($A = C$).

Salvation through the Messiah = Another story in the Tanakh

$$A \quad = \quad C$$

Let's see how other stories in the Tanakh thematically point us to the splitting of the Red Sea. Some of Joshua's battles contain images of the events that transpired at the crossing of the Red Sea. For example, Joshua 8 records Am Yisrael's victory over the city of Ai. In this battle, the Scripture records that Joshua *descended into a valley* (Joshua 8:13) the *night before* his battle with Ai. This is reminiscent of Am Yisrael's *descent* into the Red Sea the night *before Egypt* was annihilated. Joshua 8:15-16 records that Am Yisrael *fled toward the wilderness* to lure the men of Ai into attacking them. This also occurred at the splitting of the Red Sea when Pharaoh was lured to attack (Exodus 14:1-8) by Am Yisrael's planned "meandering" as they left Egypt. In Joshua 8:18, the Holy One commanded Joshua to *stretch forth the spear in his hand* just as He had commanded Moses *to stretch out his hand and staff* to initiate the Red Sea crossing. During the battle, the men of Ai were trapped in a valley. They were *in the midst* of the army of Am Yisrael who were attacking them from both sides, just as Egypt's army was slaughtered *in the midst* of the "valley" of the Red Sea. Am Yisrael's army attacking them in a valley from both sides is thematically equivalent to the waters of the divided Red Sea crashing in upon the Egyptian army! And why does the battle for Ai contain so many allusions to the splitting of the Red Sea? Because, like the splitting of the Red Sea, it contains information to help us understand the salvation brought about by Messiah Yeshua.

Joshua's defeat of the five Amorite kings (Joshua 10) is also connected to the Red Sea crossing. The Scripture states that Joshua and his men had *marched all night* from Gilgal to engage the Amorite kings. This is thematically connected to the fact that Am Yisrael *"marched" all night* through the Red Sea (Exodus 14:19-22). Just as the Holy One *overthrew the Egyptians in the morning* after Am Yisrael had "marched" all night long, so likewise, He *overthrew the Amorite kings in the morning* after Am Yisrael had marched all night. The Scripture states that the Holy One rained large hailstones (solidified water!) upon the attacking armies. This is thematically connected to the waters of the Red Sea crashing down upon the Egyptians. Finally, in an inescapable allusion to the Red Sea crossing, the *sun and moon stood still so that Joshua could defeat his enemy*. This is thematically equivalent to the fact that the *pillar of fire provided light to Am Yisrael during the night* enabling them to have enough time to cross the Red Sea! In both instances, light was provided during a time period that normally would have been dark. Why does Joshua's defeat of the five Amorite kings contain so many allusions to the splitting of the Red Sea? Because, like the splitting of the Red Sea, it contains information to help us understand salvation brought about by Messiah Yeshua.

The same lesson is taught elsewhere by one of David's mighty men named Elazar. He fought valiantly against the Philistines after the Israelites had run off. The Scripture states "he arose and attacked the Philistines until *his hand was weary, and his hand stuck to the sword. The LORD brought about a great salvation that day* (II Samuel 23:10)." Note how his victory occurred because his hand was *stretched forth* against his enemies. As you can see, Elazar's *sword-laden outstretched hand* is reminiscent of Moses' *staff-laden outstretched hand*. Why does Elazar's victory contain this allusion to the splitting of the Red Sea? Because, like the splitting of the Red Sea, it contains information to help us understand the salvation brought about by Messiah Yeshua.

This lesson on salvation is also taught by Samson. One of his great victories occurred when he killed 1,000 men with the jawbone of an ass.

He found a fresh jawbone of a donkey, ***stretched out his hand*** and took it, and killed a thousand men with it...And so it was, when he had finished speaking, that *he threw the jawbone from his* ***hand***, and called that place Ramath Lehi (Judges 15:15-17).

Note how the Scripture describes his actions. Observe how carefully his victory was accomplished by *stretching forth his hand* to grA *an unusual instrument* with which to wage battle, the jawbone of an ass! Did not Moses win his battle at the Red Sea Crossing by *stretching forth his hand* which contained *an unusual object* of warfare, a staff?

Finally, when the Holy One delivered Jehoshaphat from Ammon, Moab and Mount Seir, note the clear thematic connection to the Red Sea Crossing (Exodus 14:13) in the Holy One's exhortation to king Jehoshaphat.

> You will not need to fight in this battle. Position yourselves, ***stand still and see the salvation of the LORD***, who is with you, O Judah and Jerusalem!' Do not fear or be dismayed; tomorrow go out against them, for the LORD is with you (II Chronicles 20:17)."

Moses said to the people, "Do not fear! ***Stand fast and see the salvation*** of YHVH (Exodus 14:13)."

With so many clear thematic connections (and these examples are just the tip of the iceberg) to the original act of salvation canvassing the Scriptures, we must ask why the Holy One is so diligent in prodding us to see them. The reason the Scriptures make so many thematic allusions to the Red Sea Crossing is because the Holy One is aggressively teaching us about our salvation through the Messiah! In order to do this, He wants to focus our attention on the foundational passage that teaches salvation through the Messiah. When Moses recorded the Red Sea Crossing, he prophetically recorded the picture of our salvation through the Messiah. With that as a foundation, let us return to the story of David's flight from Absalom and discover another picture of our great salvation through Messiah Yeshua.

Allusions to the Splitting of the Red Sea

David's Prophetic Picture

At this point, I'd like to analyze II Samuel 17:22-26 with the goal of showing how often this story makes allusions (thematic connections) to the splitting of the Red Sea (Exodus 14)!

- Hushai, David's trusted friend who was an undercover agent, sent a message to David *warning him to cross the Jordan River* to escape from Absalom. In Exodus 14:15-16, Adonai *commanded Moses to cross the Red Sea.*
- After Jonathan and Ahimaaz delivered their message from Hushai, David made his escape. This is recorded for us in II Samuel 17:22.

"So David and all the people with him set out and crossed the Jordan. By daybreak, no one was left who had not crossed the Jordan."

The connection is very simple. *David and his followers were fleeing for their lives from Absalom just as Moses and Am Yisrael fled for their lives from Pharaoh!* Although David had a large number of people with him,[31] Absalom probably had more. At this time, the nation was divided into two groups, the children of Judah (some of whom followed David) and the children of Israel (most of whom followed Absalom). You must also remember, according to II Samuel 15:1-6, Absalom stole the hearts of the men of Israel through deceit. Thus, *David and his followers, outnumbered, on the run and lacking adequate provisions, fled for their lives* by crossing the Jordan River. In Exodus 14, Moses and *the nation of Israel found themselves at a military disadvantage and on the run, fleeing from Pharaoh.* Furthermore, the Egyptians were trained warriors and seasoned in battle, whereas Am Yisrael was simply a nation of ex-slaves who had no military skills.

- II Samuel 17:22b states, "By daybreak, no one was left who had not crossed the Jordan." Therefore we know for sure that *David and his servants crossed the Jordan during the night*. Amazingly, *Moses and Am Yisrael also crossed the Red Sea at nighttime*, for we read in Exodus 14:19-22 that Adonai split the Red Sea and gave Am Yisrael light during the night to aid their escape.
- After David and his servants crossed the Jordan River, they went on to Mahanaim. According to II Samuel 17:24, Absalom pursued David by crossing the Jordan River!

Then David went to Mahanaim. And **Absalom crossed over the Jordan**, he and all the men of Israel with him (II Samuel 17:24).

At this point, you probably already know the next connection. Yes, Absalom's hot pursuit of David—by *crossing the Jordan River after him*—is thematically connected to Pharaoh's hot pursuit of Moses and Am Yisrael when the Egyptian army attempted to *cross the Red Sea*!

- This next connection requires that we fast forward to the battle between David and Absalom's armies in II Samuel 18:1-8. II Samuel 18:8 is a very peculiar verse.

For the battle there was *scattered over the face of the whole countryside*, and the *woods devoured more people* that day than the sword devoured (II Samuel 18:8)

What does the scripture mean that "the woods devoured more people that day than the sword?" My Stone Edition of the Tanakh has tried to clear the confusion concerning this verse by offering the following note pertaining to II Samuel 18:8."

The soldiers constantly became entangled in the thick branches of the trees (Radak), or they were attacked by the wild animals of the forest (Targum).[32]

By stating that the woods devoured more than the sword, the Scripture seems to indicate that more people died as a result of events associated with the woods than from fighting! In other words, the suggestions from the sage Radak and the Targum is probably right on the mark. For example, we know that Absalom's death was indirectly caused by the woods when his hair got caught in the thick branches of a tree. After his mule walked from under him, he was left suspended in the air (easy prey for Joab and his men). I believe we should take this Scripture quite literally—the woods devoured more than the sword. Through numerous circumstances, the forces of nature in the woods of Ephraim actually killed more soldiers than were killed by the sword. Since David's men defeated Absalom's we can probably be sure that most of Absalom's soldiers were actually killed by mishaps in the woods of Ephraim. This is thematically connected to the fact that Pharaoh's army was defeated not by Am Yisrael's sword, but by nature itself—the Red Sea! What a connection! In both stories, it was the forces of nature that destroyed the enemy. Now you know the real significance of the strange statement that the woods devoured more than the sword. It is one of many thematic connections intended to help you see the connection between David's flight from Absalom and Am Yisrael's flight from Pharaoh. Furthermore, note that it was the *woods* that devoured more than the sword. At the splitting of the Red Sea, didn't Moses lift a *wooden* staff that caused the destruction of Am Yisrael's enemies? Yes, it was. The connection is clear. In both stories, *wood* caused the overthrow of the enemy!

Our last connection is icing on the cake. Hopefully, you remember the Torah's foundational definition of salvation which was developed earlier in this chapter. Remember the anatomy of salvation?

- Your enemy is about to annihilate you.
- You are powerless to help or defend yourself.
- The Holy One delivers you from the hand of your enemy.
- The Holy One destroys your enemy.

Wasn't that the scenario in Exodus 14? Yes, it was. Remember, when Moses told Am Yisrael that they were about to see Adonai's salvation?

And Moses said to the people, "Do not be afraid. Stand still, and see the ***salvation*** of the LORD, which He will accomplish for you today. For the Egyptians whom you see today, you shall see again no more forever. The LORD will fight for you, and you shall hold your peace (Exodus 14:13).

It's pretty easy to see examples of salvation when the Scriptures clearly state that a particular story is an example of such. Well, let's see how the writer of II Samuel characterized the events pertaining to David's victory over Absalom.

The ***salvation*** of that day was transformed to mourning for all the people ... (II Samuel 19:3)[33]

The writer of II Samuel referred to David's victory as a salvation! Now, you know why he would call such an event salvation. You see, beloved, when your enemy comes to annihilate you, when you are outnumbered and at a disadvantage, and when Adonai delivers you and destroys your enemy, you have experienced salvation![34] Beyond a shadow of doubt, David experienced salvation, not just victory or deliverance!

Yeshua's Prophetic Fulfillment

We know that salvation will come through the Messiah; therefore, whenever we see pictures of salvation, we know we are getting a lesson concerning Him. Therefore, I suggest to you that II Samuel 17:22-24 is actually a thematic presentation of the truth of salvation through Messiah Yeshua! According to Matthew 1:21, from what will the Messiah save us?

And she will bring forth a Son, and you shall call His name Yeshua (יֵשׁוּעַ), for He will **save** His people from their sins (Matthew 1:21)."

He will save us from our sins. We have already learned that Yeshua's name means *salvation* in Hebrew. According to Matthew 1:21, this is why Joseph was told to name Him Yeshua. The following verses also associate Yeshua with our great salvation.

- And has raised up a horn of *salvation* for us in the house of His servant David (Luke 1:69).
- To give knowledge of *salvation* to His people by the remission of their sins (Luke 1:77).
- For my eyes have seen Your *salvation* (Luke 2:30).
- And all flesh shall see the *salvation* of God (Luke 3:6).

How was Yeshua able to bring us salvation by delivering us from our sins? Through His death, burial and resurrection! Salvation was obtained through the death, burial and resurrection of Messiah Yeshua when He defeated hasatan in an unusual manner. He stretched forth His hands and died. Thematically, II Samuel 17:15-21 presents us with a picture of the *death, burial and resurrection* of the Messiah through the lives of Jonathan and Ahimaaz, while II Samuel 17:22-24 presents us with a picture of *salvation* through the Messiah. Thus our picture is complete and we have successfully interpreted the thematic significance of the first half of our master chiastic structure, noting how it matches the chronological order of the Gospels![35]

Our Next Task

As stated before, II Samuel 17:15-24 represents a glitch in the thematic presentation of the Gospel, because the pictures of Messiah Yeshua's death, burial, resurrection and the picture of salvation should occur sometime after the central axis, which is thematically equivalent to when Simon the Cyrene helped Yeshua carry the crossbar. Therefore, in chapter six we will 1) continue our thematic presentation of the Gospel through the story of David's flight from Absalom, 2) present an explanation of why the thematic presentation of the Gospel departed from chronological order in II Samuel 17:15-22 and 3) propose a justification for the departure.

So far, analysis during the first five chapters has clearly shown that the writer of II Samuel is presenting us with a chronological, thematic picture of Messiah Yeshua's death, burial and resurrection. Therefore, as we begin to thematically analyze the second half of our chiastic structure, *we should surely expect to see a definite thematic presentation of the death, burial and resurrection of the Messiah in its proper chronological place*!

Thematic Moment

Earlier in this chapter, I made some very important thematic connections to the two young spies that Joshua sent to spy out Jericho. I have studied quite a bit of the book of Joshua thematically and would like to share with you some more information that will enhance what we've learned in this chapter. First of all, I'd like to share a beautiful chiastic structure/parallelism that I found at the beginning of the book of Joshua. Please note how Joshua 1:1 – 1:5 forms a parallelism with Joshua 1:10 – 1:18. Sandwiched between the parallelism is a beautiful chiastic structure from Joshua 1:5b – 1:9c.

Joshua 1:1-18

A) Joshua 1:1-2—Adonai commanded the people to prepare to take the land
  B) Joshua 1:3—Am Yisrael will receive the land spoken of by Moses
    C) Joshua 1:4—Adonai gave the boundaries of the land with respect to water barriers (the Mediterranean and Euphrates rivers); "towards the setting of the sun"
      D) Joshua 1:5—Adonai promised to be faithful to Joshua; Adonai will be with Joshua as He was with Moses; no man will be able to stand up to him

E) Joshua 1:5b—As I was with Moses, I'll be with you
  F) Joshua 1:5c—I will not forsake you
    G) Joshua 1:6a—Be strong and courageous
      H) Joshua 1:6b—I will cause the people to inherit the land
        I) Joshua 1:7a—Observe the Torah
          J) Joshua 1:7b—You shall not deviate from it (a negative commandment)
            K) *Joshua 1:7c—You will succeed wherever you go*
          J') Joshua 1:8a—The Torah shall not depart from your mouth (a negative commandment)
        I') Joshua 1:8b—Observe the Torah
      H') Joshua 1:8c—You will make your way successful and act wisely
    G') Joshua 1:9:a—Behold, I have commanded you 'be strong and courageous'
  F') Joshua 1:9b—Do not fear or lose resolve
E') Joshua 1:9c—I am with you wherever you go

A') Joshua 1:10-12—Joshua gave the command (mitzvah) to prepare to possess the land
  B') Joshua 1:13—Remember what Moses told you: Adonai will give you the land
    C') Joshua 1:14—Joshua gave the boundaries of the inheritances of Gad, Reuben and the ½ tribe of Manasseh with respect to the Jordan river two times; "toward the rising of the sun"

D') Joshua 1:16-18—Am Yisrael promised to be faithful to Joshua; they will heed Joshua as long as Adonai is with him as He was with Moses; They will even kill anyone who rebels

Please notice the beautiful teaching contained in the parallelism. The main theme of elements A-D refers to Adonai's support for Joshua, whereas, the main theme of elements A`-D` refer to Am Yisrael's support for Joshua. Notice how most of the elements of the chiastic structure are related very easily except for element H/H'. A comparison of H/H' helps us understand Adonai's definition of success for Joshua. Success = Taking possession of the land! Notice how the central axis refers to the establishment of Joshua's leadership. It's a promise that he will be successful. Overall, this portion of Scripture pertains to the establishment of Joshua's leadership by Adonai for the people of Israel. Another significant chiastic structure is found in Joshua 2:3-7.

Joshua 2:3-7

A) Joshua 2:3—The king sent people to Rachav *looking for the spies*
  B) Joshua 2:4a—Rachav *hid the spies*
    C) Joshua 2:4b—Rachav stated "*I don't know where they are from*"
      D) Joshua 2:5a—The spies left Jericho through the city gate when it was about to close at dark
    C') Joshua 2:5b—Rachav stated "*I don't know where they went*"
  B') Joshua 2:6—Rachav *hid the spies* on her roof in stalks of flax
A') Joshua 2:7—Men of Jericho *pursued the spies*

If you compare elements A-C to A`-C` you will notice that the themes are pretty much equivalent. Therefore, we should expect for our central axis to function not as the turning point, but as the most important part of our chiastic structure. This means that Adonai wants us to know that Joshua 2:5a – Rachav's statement that the spies left through the city gate when it was dark – is very, very important because the two spies are thematically connected to Samson who actually left through the city gate (of Gaza) at midnight (when it was dark). Is that not beautiful? Apart from thematically connecting the two spies to Samson it is rather mysterious that Adonai would make Joshua 2:5a the central axis of a chiastic structure. In other words, analyzed in a vacuum, the statement found in Joshua 2:5a seems rather uninteresting and one would be tempted to wonder why Adonai would make it a central axis. However, by thematically connecting the two spies to Samson, the importance of Joshua 2:5a becomes apparent. It serves as yet another confirmation that Samson and the two spies have been connected thematically by the hand of the Ruach HaKodesh. Another chiastic structure can be found in Joshua 2:6-16.

Joshua 2:6-16

A) Joshua 2:6-7—Rachav *hid* the spies on the *roof* in stalks of *flax*; the pursuers chased them towards the Jordan crossing; the pursuers went in the wrong direction

B) Joshua 2:8-12a—Rachav said, "I know Adonai has **given you the land**"; "**Swear** to me by Adonai"

   C) *Joshua 2:12b-13—Give me a sign that you will keep alive my father, mother, brothers, sisters and all that's theirs by saving our souls from death*

B') Joshua 2:14—Spies said, "When **Adonai gives us the land**"; **our souls will die in place of yours**

A') Joshua 2:15-16—Rachav lowered the spies by a **rope**; she lived **high on the city wall**; she told spies to **hide** for **three days** until the pursuers turn back, then continue; pursuers went in wrong direction

Note how point A/A' thematically connects the rope to the flax. Remember, there's a connection between the rope and the flax!

Earlier in this chapter, I connected the two spies to Samson. I also stated that oftentimes Adonai will teach you a truth more than once to make sure you get it. Please note the following parallelism connecting Samson to the two spies!

The Parallelism of Joshua 2:10-15 and Judges 15:13b-20

A Joshua 2:10—Rachav stated "We've heard how Adonai **dried up the waters** of the Red Sea." Sihon and Og, Am Yisrael's **enemies were utterly destroyed**

 B Joshua 2:10—This was done by **splitting the Red Sea**.

  C Joshua 2:11—Rachav stated "**No spirit remained in any man** because of you."

   D Joshua 2:12-14—Rachav requested that the spies **take an oath** to spare her life

    E Joshua 2:15—Rachav lowered the spies by a **rope** and told them to go to a mountain to hide. *Note: Joshua 2:6-16 is chiastically related. The **flax** of Joshua 2:6 is thematically related to the **rope** of Joshua 2:15!*

A' Judges 15:15-18—Samson **killed 1,000 Philistines** with the jawbone of an ass. Samson became very **thirsty** and stated, "You have granted this great salvation through the hand of your servant, and now, **shall I die of thirst**…"

 B' Judges 15:19a— This was done by **splitting the hollow in the jawbone**[36]

  C' Judges 15:19b—**His spirit returned to him** and he was revived

   D' Judges 15:12b-13a—Samson had the tribe of Judah **swear** they wouldn't kill him

    E' Judges 15:13b-14—They bound Samson with ropes and brought him up from a **rock**. The **ropes** on Samson's hands became like **flax**!

Although this parallelism isn't as neat and orderly as most are, I believe you can still see the connections. Do you think perhaps Adonai wants us to connect the two spies and Samson? He most certainly does, and He's doing quite a bit to get us to see it! Now you can see the significance of the rope and the flax in the story of the two spies. It shows up again in the story of Samson where it states that *the **ropes** became like **flax** singed in the fire*! Oh, the riches of the wisdom of our great God!!! He has truly set a bountiful meal before us!

At this point, I'd like to consider Rachav's story. The most interesting verses appear in Joshua 2:17-21. Do you see any thematic connection between this portion of Scripture and a great event that occurred in the lives of Am Yisrael? Pay particular attention to the scarlet cord in window. Got it yet? Pay attention to the necessity of staying *in the house*. Let me summarize events in Joshua 2:17-21:

- Rachav lowered the spies through a window. Thematically, the window has become a place of *entrance/exit.*
- A red/scarlet/crimson cord was placed *in* the window.
- Rachav and her family had to *stay in the house* during the siege against Jericho.
- During the siege there was death in every household in Jericho except for Rachav's.
- The *scarlet cord was a sign* to Am Yisrael not to kill those in that house.

Do you see the thematic lesson being taught in this passage? All these points are thematically connected to the Passover of the book of Exodus by the following connections:

- The window through which Rachav lowered the two spies is thematically connected to the doors of the houses of Am Yisrael in Egypt.
- The scarlet cord in the window is thematically connected to the blood on the doorposts and lintels.
- Rachav and her family must stay inside just as the Israelites had to stay inside when Adonai destroyed the firstborn of Egypt.
- There was death in every house of Jericho except Rachav's because she had the sign in her window.
- The scarlet cord is thematically connected to the blood of the lambs.

These connections teach us that Rachav had her own Passover experience! She was born again as it states in the book of James—*Likewise, was not Rachav the harlot also justified by works when she received the messengers and sent them out another way* (James 2:25)? As you can see, many times Adonai is trying to teach us deeper truths that we can only see if we exercise the practice of studying thematically.

Lastly, I'd like to share with you a little more of the beauty of Samson's story. It just so happens that his story is told in a chiastic structure. Please, enjoy.

The Chiastic Structure of Judges 13:25 – 16:31

A) Judges 13:25—Activity of the Ruach began in Samson between **Zorah and Eshtaol**
  B) Judges 14:1-8—Emphasis on and repetition of the words relating to Samson's **eyes, saw,** etc.
    C) Judges 14:5-6—<u>Samson conquered the roaring lion</u>
      D) Judges 14:10—Samson had a **feast**
        E) Judges 14:10-18—Samson **made sport of** the Philistines, who won in the end
          F) Judges 14:19-20—**Took** what didn't belong to him **and returned to Israel (Hebron)**
            G) Judges 15:1—Samson **desired to go into** his wife
              H) Judges 15:2-3—Samson's **unfulfilled desire**
                I) Judges 15:4-5—Usage of **animals** (foxes), fire **burning vegetation**

    J) Judges 15:6-7—Philistines **investigated cause of problem** and confronted cause
     K) Judges 15:8a—Samson **attacked**
      L) Judges 15:8b—Samson dwelt in rock of Etam
     K') Judges 15:9—Philistines **attacked**
    J') Judges 15:10-13—Judah **investigated cause of problem** and confronted cause
   I') Judges 15:14-16—Usage of **animal** (jawbone), image of **fire burning vegetation (flax)**
  H') Judges 15:18-20—Samson's **fulfilled desire** (thirst), water, well, wives?
  G') Judges 16:1—Samson **desired to go into** harlot
 F') Judges 16:2-3—Samson **took** what doesn't belong to him **and returned to Israel**
 E') Judges 16:4-20—Philistines **made sport of** Samson, who won in the end
 D') Judges 16:23—Philistines gathered for a sacrifice (feast) to their god
C') Judges 16:29-30—<u>Samson conquered 3000 Philistines</u>
B') Judges 16:28—Samson sought vengeance for his eyes
A') Judges 16:31—Samson is buried between **Zorah and Eshtaol**

Chapter 6

The Resurrection in Its Proper Chronological Position

Introduction

In the last chapter, we saw more evidence that Jonathan and Ahimaaz's actions were pictures of death, burial and resurrection. In fact, we were able to clearly demonstrate that they are Messianic figures through their connection to the two spies that visited Rahab the harlot. Lastly, we saw how II Samuel 17:21-24 is a thematic picture of salvation won by the Messiah as a result of His death, burial and resurrection. Thus, we were able to analyze the chiastic structure of II Samuel 15:10 – 20:2 up to its central axis (II Samuel 17:27-29) noting the amazing parallels between David's flight from Absalom and Yeshua's suffering. We also noted that the chronological presentation of the Gospel developed a glitch because II Samuel 17:15-24, which presents a picture of the Messiah's death, burial and resurrection, should occur after the central axis—which is a thematic presentation of the help Yeshua received as He carried the crossbar. Look towards the end of this chapter at the ***Running Chart of Thematic Connections*** to help you visualize this. ***The pictures of death, burial and resurrection should occur sometime after the prophetic picture of Simon helping the Messiah!*** I intend to show why this departure exists and to provide a thoroughly satisfactory explanation for it. First let's continue with our trek through David's flight from Absalom. Once we determine the Messianic significance of the next few events we will be in a better position to explain why the thematic presentation of the Gospel "meandered" from chronological order.

A Few Hints to Whet Your Appetite?

The next portion of Scripture to examine is II Samuel 18:1-18. As we venture past the central axis of our main chiastic structure (II Samuel 17:27-29), we should have a heightened expectation of seeing a picture of the death, burial and resurrection of the Messiah in its proper chronological sequence. Nonetheless, before we begin our study of II Samuel 18:1-18 in earnest, let's take a sneak peak at some selected passages occurring *after* this passage, looking for hints that the Messiah's great salvation may have occurred in these verses.

One of the Tanakh's most subtle ways of teaching its messages is to hint at them. There is a word that characterizes this technique—remez—a Hebrew word meaning *hint*. Using the technique of remez, the Scriptures may "hint" at a deeper meaning without stating so explicitly. For example, let's examine the following passage.

> I Kings 1:38-42 — So Zadok the priest, Nathan the prophet, Benaiah the son of Jehoiada, the Cherethites, and the Pelethites went down and had Solomon ride on King David's mule, and took him to Gihon (bursting forth). Then Zadok the priest took a horn of oil from the tabernacle and anointed Solomon. And they blew the horn, and all the people said, "Long live King Solomon!" And all the people went up after him; and the people played the flutes and rejoiced with great joy, *so that the earth seemed to split with their sound*. Now Adonijah and all the guests who were with him heard it as they finished eating. And when Joab heard the sound of the horn, he said, "Why is the city in such a noisy uproar?" While he was still speaking, there came Jonathan, the son of Abiathar the priest. And Adonijah said to him, *"Come in, for you are a prominent man, and bring good news."*

Let me draw your attention to the phrase, "Come in, for you are a prominent man, and bring good news." The words *good news* are translated from the Hebrew words וְטוֹב תְּבַשֵּׂר, v'tov t'baser. The word תְּבַשֵּׂר derives from the Hebrew primitive root בשר, basar, which means to bear news, bear tidings, publish, preach, and show forth. We've seen this Hebrew word before in Chapter 1 when we discussed the sign of the Messiah in David's life. This account is found in I Samuel 30:1-31, the story of how David and his men rescued their families and possessions from the Amalekites who had stolen them while David and his men were away with the Philistines. As they pursued the Amalekites, they came upon the Besor Brook as recorded in I Samuel 30:9-13:

> So David went, he and the six hundred men who were with him, and came to the **Brook Besor**, where those stayed who were left behind. But David pursued, he and four hundred men; for two hundred stayed behind, who were so weary that they could not cross the **Brook Besor**. And they found an Egyptian in the field, and brought him to David, and gave him bread, and he did eat; and they made him drink water; And they gave him a piece of a cake of figs, and two clusters of raisins: and when he had eaten, *his spirit came again to him: for he had eaten no bread, nor drunk any water, three days and three nights*. And David said unto him, "To whom belongest thou? and whence art thou?" And he said, "I am a young man of Egypt, servant to an Amalekite; and my master left me, because three days ago I fell sick."

Earlier, we saw that the events in I Samuel 30:11-13 are a shadowy picture of the death, burial and resurrection of the Messiah. These three verses contain the Sign of the Messiah! Notice the phrase *three days and three nights*. Does it sound familiar? It should. The Messiah was dead for three days and three nights in the grave before His resurrection. This picture is painted by the story of the Egyptian youth who had neither bread nor water for three days and three nights. Anyone can live on bread and water. The Tanakh is hinting at death by stating that the Egyptian hadn't eaten bread nor drank water for *three days and three nights*. It's painting a picture of the death of the Egyptian youth. Also, note the wording of verse twelve where it states, "His spirit came again to him." Now I know the Egyptian youth didn't actually die; however, the passage is written in such a manner as to hint at his "death." Therefore, let's follow through on the picture of death painted by the wording. In order for his *spirit to come to him again*, it had to have left him. What has happened if your spirit has left you? You died! Note what event occurred when the breath/spirit of God entered the two witnesses of the book of Revelation:

> ¹¹Now after the three-and-a-half days the **breath (spirit) of life from God entered them**, and they stood on their feet, and great fear fell on those who saw them (Revelation 11:11).

When the breath/spirit entered them, they rose from the dead! This is the picture being painted of the Egyptian youth when it states that his spirit came to him again. It's painting a picture of resurrection. Lastly, note that the Egyptian youth's master left him after he fell ill. Now why would someone leave their slave after he fell ill? The logical conclusion is that the Egyptian youth's sickness was nearly fatal. His master probably thought he was going to die and decided to leave him rather than bring him along. So, every way we analyze this story we see hints that the Egyptian youth was brought to death's door.

What you may not have noticed is that I Samuel 30:9 contains the word besor. Besor actually derives from the same Hebrew primitive root בשר (basar) as the word *news* in I Kings 1:42! What's interesting about I Samuel 30:9-13 is that the story teaching us about the death, burial and resurrection of the Messiah (I Samuel 30:11-13) follows I Samuel 30:9 which has a word in it meaning good news! *In other words, I'm suggesting to you that when the Scripture mentions the brook Besor in I Samuel 30:9, it is actually hinting to us that we are about to read something pertaining to **the gospel** (good news)!* Do you see the Tanakh's subtlety? To the unsuspecting reader, David is crossing the Besor Brook is just another fact added to the narrative. However, to those aware of the nuances and subtleties of the Hebrew text and its literary schemes, the word Besor, which means good news, is actually a neon light alerting us to the fact that something relating to the good news—the gospel of the death, burial and resurrection of the Messiah—is about to follow. And truly we aren't disappointed, because after the usage of the word Besor in I Samuel 30:9, we are treated to the sign of the Messiah, a veiled reference to the death, burial and resurrection of the Messiah! Baruch HaShem Adonai!

This was a great example of the usage of remez to hint at something deeper. In fact, this is exactly what's happening in I Kings 1:42! This is a story about how David hurriedly appointed Solomon as king in order to preempt a coup by his son Adonijah. Let's look at I Kings 1:38-42 more closely, noting its flow.³⁷

- ♦ Solomon was placed upon a mule
- ♦ He was anointed
- ♦ The people rejoiced before him at his coronation
- ♦ Adonijah inquired concerning the ruckus
- ♦ A statement concerning the good news

We have already seen – in the case of David (I Samuel 30:9-13) – how the mere mention of the words *good news* may be a hint at some type of deeper Messianic understanding. I'm also suggesting that the same phenomenon is occurring in I Kings 1:38-42. The Scripture is hinting at a great teaching concerning the Messiah. Do you know what it is? In order to see this teaching we need to take note of one more significant fact concerning Solomon's coronation. According to I Kings 1:40, the people made so much noise rejoicing before Solomon that "The earth seemed to split with their sound." Now that's an interesting phrase. What does it mean? It seems that the rejoicing of the people almost caused an earthquake! In order to see the Messianic significance of this passage we simply need to make an astute thematic connection to an event that occurred in one of the gospels. Do you know which gospel passage is thematically connected to I Kings 1:38-42? Here's one more clue. Another phrase describing an earthquake is *splitting of rocks*! Hopefully, you have been able to connect this passage with Yeshua's triumphal entry into Jerusalem. Please note the following thematic connections between I Kings 1:38-42 and Luke 19:28-40/Matthew 21:1-17.

- In both stories certain people want to crown a son of David as King of Israel
- Solomon and Yeshua both road into town on a donkey
- Zadok the priest, Nathan the prophet, Benaiah the son of Jehoiada, the Cherethites, and the Pelethites and all the people said, "Long live King Solomon!" Yeshua's disciples shouted, "Blessed is the King who comes in the name of the LORD! Peace in heaven and glory in the highest!"
- Adonijah and all his guests—enemies of Solomon—heard the tumult concerning Solomon's coronation and did not like it. The Pharisee's heard the tumult of Yeshua's disciples concerning their desire to see Him coronated and did not like it.
- The tumult concerning Solomon's coronation caused some to question the reason for it. The tumult concerning Yeshua's entry into Jerusalem caused some to question the reason for it.
- During Solomon's coronation, it states that the ground seemed to split with their sound.[38] The passage in Luke states that, "The stones would immediately cry out."

This passage in I Kings is actually a Messianic prophecy! In this instance, David is a shadowy picture of the Father in heaven and *Solomon is a picture of Yeshua*, His Son. The passages from Matthew and Luke above recount Yeshua's triumphal entry into Jerusalem.

In like manner, II Samuel 18:27 also mentions the phrase *good news*! II Samuel 18:19-28 is a story about how two runners came to bring King David news concerning the outcome of the war against Absalom. Could this verse also be a veiled reference to the actual gospel (good news) of the death, burial and resurrection of the Messiah, just as we saw in I Samuel 30:9-12? I'm suggesting that it is. Furthermore, something happened between our central axis, II Samuel 17:27-29 and II Samuel 18:27 that is thematically equivalent to the death, burial and resurrection of the Messiah. This is hint number one.

Another hint occurs in II Samuel 19:2 where the Scripture states the following:

So the **victory** that day was turned into mourning for all the people. For the people heard it said that day, "The king is grieved for his son."

Look at the word victory. So what does this verse have to do with the death, burial and resurrection of the Messiah? Well, the verse quoted above is from the New King James Version. The Artscroll Tanakh has the verse translated as such:

The *salvation* of that day was transformed to mourning for all the people, for the people heard it said on that day, "The king is saddened over his son" (II Samuel 19:3).

As you can see, the word translated victory in the New King James Version was translated salvation in the Stone edition of the Tanakh![39] The Hebrew word being translated as victory and salvation is תְּשׁוּעָה (te shuw`ah), which is usually translated as deliverance, help, victory, salvation and safety. Please note the definition of te shuw`ah given by the Crosswalk[40] Hebrew lexicon:

- salvation, deliverance
  - deliverance (usually by God through human agency)
  - salvation (spiritual in sense)

Notice how it states that the word can be translated as deliverance (usually by God through human agency). However, salvation is the meaning "in a spiritual sense." From the context, it's plain to see that David was delivered through human agency and maybe this is the reason why most popular English versions translate te shuw`ah as victory/deliverance. However, we know that the foundational definition of salvation is found in the story of the splitting of the Red Sea! There was nothing "spiritual" there. Therefore, I'm suggesting that the translators of the Tanakh did a better job of translating because they understood that David had experienced the Torah's foundational definition of salvation—deliverance from your enemies when the odds are against you!

The fact that II Samuel 19:2 states, "The salvation of that day was transformed to mourning," is proof that salvation occurred in the preceding story. In other words, something happened after our central axis (II Samuel 17:27-29) but before II Samuel 19:2 that can be considered salvation. If this is true, then we know that the act of salvation has something to do with the death, burial and resurrection of the Messiah. This is our second hint that we have come to a point in the story of David's flight from Absalom where we should see a very clear picture of the salvation secured for us through the death, burial and resurrection of Yeshua. Now, let us do away with any further suspense and see the salvation of YHVH!

A Picture of the Death, Burial and Resurrection of the Messiah

David's Prophetic Picture

Notice how often the number three is sprinkled throughout II Samuel 18:1-18. II Samuel 18:1-3 is a record of how David prepared his men for battle with the people of Israel. Notice how the number three is mentioned three times in II Samuel 18:2:

- Then David sent out *one third* of the people under the hand of Joab, *one third* under the hand of Abishai the son of Zeruiah, Joab's brother, and *one third* under the hand of Ittai the Gittite. And the king said to the people, "I also will surely go out with you myself."

Notice that Joab took three spears and thrust them through Absalom's heart (II Samuel 18:14). Finally, the word tree is mentioned three times (II Samuel 18:9, 10 and 14)! Concerning II Samuel 18:6-8, I explained its significance in Chapter 5. I stated that it was a clear thematic connection to the splitting of the Red Sea, the Torah's foundational definition of salvation!

- ♦ For the battle there was *scattered over the face of the whole countryside*, and the *woods devoured more people* that day than the sword devoured (II Samuel 18:8).

The phrase, "The woods devoured more people that day than the sword" meant that more people died as a result of nature itself (mishaps due to the thick forest) than from fighting! This is thematically connected to the fact that Pharaoh's army was defeated not by Am Yisrael's sword, but by nature itself—the Red Sea! In both stories, it was the forces of nature that destroyed the enemy. This connection is just one of many intended to help you see the parallels between David's flight from Absalom and Am Yisrael's flight from Pharaoh. In other words, this is a passage concerning SALVATION!

Although I could not detect a chiastic structure/parallelism in II Samuel 18:1-18, I did see some thematic connections between the first and second half of the passage.

- ♦ The phrase, "But you are worth *ten* thousand of us now," in II Samuel 18:3, is thematically connected to the phrase, "Would have given you *ten* shekels of silver and a belt," in II Samuel 18:11.
- ♦ II Samuel 18:5, *Now the king had commanded Joab, Abishai, and Ittai, saying, "Deal gently for my sake with the young man Absalom." And all the people heard when the king gave all the captains orders concerning Absalom,* is thematically connected to II Samuel 18:12b, *For in our hearing the king commanded you and Abishai and Ittai, saying, 'Beware lest anyone touch the young man Absalom.*
- ♦ The number three is mentioned in II Samuel 18:2 (one third) and 14 (Joab took three spears).
- ♦ Lastly, there is an obscure connection between David and Absalom. II Samuel 18:2b-5 is a discussion between David and his servants concerning their battle strategy. David wanted to go into battle with his servants; however, they did not want him to do this because they knew Absalom and his men would only care about pursuing David.
  o But the people answered, "You shall not go out! For if we flee away, they will not care about us; nor if half of us die, will they care about us. But you are worth ten thousand of us now. For you are now more help to us in the city (II Samuel 18:3)."

What is the connection? Amazingly, this conversation concerning the hypothetical case of David's capture is mirrored in Absalom's capture and demise. Notice that once Joab found out about Absalom's predicament he quit pursuing the people of Israel so he could kill Absalom. Furthermore, just as David's servants said that Israel wouldn't care about David's army if they could capture him, so likewise, Joab, after killing Absalom, commanded his troops to cease chasing after Israel.

So Joab blew the trumpet, and the people returned from pursuing Israel. For Joab held back the people (II Samuel 18:16).

Notice the peculiar phrase which describes Absalom's fate.

... so he was left hanging between heaven and earth (II Samuel 18:9b)

One has to wonder why the prophet described Absalom's position in this peculiar manner. What is the significance of Absalom hanging between the heaven and the earth?

Yeshua's Prophetic Fulfillment

Throughout our discussions concerning Messianic prophecy we have seen numerous times that the mere mention of the number three usually hints that Messianic prophecy is in the making. As noted previously, II Samuel 18:1-18 mentions the number three many times. This is a hint that this passage has Messianic significance.

In Chapter 5, we gained an understanding of the Torah's foundational definition of salvation. We learned that the Messiah is the One who will bring salvation; therefore, anytime we read a passage that has clear allusions to the splitting of the Red Sea (the foundational definition of salvation) we know we are into Messianic prophecy. This is the case at hand, where in the previous section we saw how the battle between the armies of David and Absalom were clearly thematically connected to the splitting of the Red Sea.

So where is the picture of the death, burial and resurrection we're looking for? II Samuel 18:1-18 says very little about David (our Messianic figure) after verse five. The remainder of the passage describes Absalom's capture and death. Remember one of our first lessons concerning Messianic prophecy. Sometimes, Messianic prophecy (actions and events associated with the Messiah) will be pictured in the life of someone associated with the Messianic figure. In Chapter 1, we saw Messianic prophecy in the lives of three individuals: Moses, Joseph and David. The sign of the Messiah (i.e., the sign of resurrection) was found <u>in</u> Moses' life. However, for Joseph and David, the sign of the Messiah and shadows of Messianic prophecy were found *in the lives of people associated with them*. In the story of Joseph, Messianic shadows were seen in the lives of the baker and cupbearer. In David's story, they were found in the life of the Egyptian youth. This is the nature of Messianic prophecy. The fact that pictures of the work of the Messiah are found in the lives of people associated with the Messianic figure represents a unique change in what we'd expect.[41] For example, Joseph and David are Messianic figures, but the Sign of the Messiah and significant Messianic prophecy were found in the lives of the baker, cupbearer and the Egyptian youth. The Holy One simply uses the lives of others to teach us about the work of the Messiah; however, when He does this, it is usually in connection with a true Messianic figure.

Whenever this occurs, there are usually some thematic connections between the Messianic figure and the one associated with him who actually demonstrates the sign of the Messiah and/or Messianic prophecy. Always remember that the primary reason the Scriptures makes thematic connections between people is to show equivalence (A = B)! In the case of Joseph, the text thematically connects him to the baker and the cupbearer in ways you may not have considered. Note how the lives of the cupbearer and baker (Genesis 40:1-23) are thematically connected to Joseph's.

- The cupbearer and baker both had a master whose name was Pharaoh. Joseph had a master whose name was Potiphar.
- Genesis 40:1—The cupbearer and baker transgressed against Pharaoh, whereas Joseph "transgressed" against Potiphar.
- Genesis 40:2—Pharaoh was enraged at the cupbearer and baker, whereas Potiphar's anger flared against Joseph (Genesis 39:19).
- Genesis 40:3—The cupbearer and baker were thrown into prison and so was Joseph.
- Genesis 40:5—The cupbearer and baker had dreams. Joseph also had dreams!
- Genesis 40:21—The cupbearer was restored to his position, whereas Joseph was exalted from his position.

All of these connections are intended for us to see that the cupbearer and baker are equivalent to Joseph.

Cupbearer and Baker = Joseph

This is why the sign of the Messiah in their lives is actually the sign of the Messiah in the life of Joseph! The same is true of David and the Egyptian youth.

- According to I Samuel 30:9-15, the exhausted Egyptian youth was found in a field. We know he was exhausted because he was sick and hadn't eaten bread nor drunk water for three days and nights. According to II Samuel 17:27-29, David was exhausted when fleeing from Absalom.
- According to I Samuel 30:11, David and his men gave the Egyptian youth bread (a product from grain), water, a cake of pressed figs and two raisin clusters. In II Samuel 17:27-29, three men brought David barley and wheat (grains which could be used to make bread), beans, lentils and many other items of food.

Once again, we can see clear thematic connections between David and the Egyptian youth. Thus, the sign of the Messiah in the life of the Egyptian youth is actually the sign of the Messiah in David's life, because, according to the thematic connections we've made…

The Egyptian Youth = David

Whenever the sign of the Messiah and/or pictures of the work of the Messiah are in the life of someone associated with the Messianic figure, you will see connections between them making them equivalent so that the sign of the Messiah and Messianic prophecy will apply to the actual Messianic figure. Adonai uses multiple people to teach us about the death, burial and resurrection of the Messiah. *He is very interested in us seeing the whole picture.* This is also the case with Isaac and Ishmael! We already know Isaac is a Messianic figure; however, the sign of the Messiah exists in Ishmael's life also! Please compare Genesis 21:9-20 (the story of the banishment of Ishmael) with Genesis 22:1-18 (the Akeida or binding of Isaac). Do you see any thematic connections between these two stories? Have you noticed that in both stories Adonai asked Abraham to part with a son whom he loved? Did you notice that both sons almost died and then were saved from death (the sign of the Messiah/resurrection)! In fact, these stories are so closely related that they form the parallelism shown below.

The Parallelism of Genesis 21:11- 20 and Genesis 22:1-24

A) Genesis 21:11-13—Abram's *strong affections for his son Ishmael* ("The matter was very displeasing in Abraham's sight because of his son*"); Adonai commanded Abraham to drive Ishmael away* ("Whatever Sarah has said to you, listen to her voice")

  B) Genesis 21:14—*Abraham awoke early in the morning*; *Abraham made preparations for a journey* (secured bread and water); a *parent leaves on a journey to an unknown place* with his/her child (Hagar and Ishmael head towards the desert)

    C) Genesis 21:15-16—*Separation* (Hagar separates herself from Ishmael); Scripture notes *lack of water (necessary for life)*, which is *a portent of Ishmael's impending death*; *association of Ishmael with wood* (he is placed under a tree/shrub); a *distance is given between her and the child* (she went and sat down across from *him* at a distance of about a bowshot); she waited for the child to die

      D) Genesis 21:17-18—The *angel of God called to Hagar from heaven*; Adonai *noticed the youth's state* (he was crying); *lift up the youth, grasp your hand upon him*

        E) Genesis 21:19—God *opened her eyes* and *she perceived a well*; saved the child's life by *providing water*

          F) Genesis 21:20-21—*Ishmael's life and the lineage of his wife*

A') Genesis 22:1-2—Abraham's *strong affections for his son Isaac* ("Take now your son, your only *son* Isaac, whom you love"); *Adonai commanded Abraham to sacrifice his son as an olah* (whole burnt offering)

  B') Genesis 22:3-4— *Abraham awoke early in the morning*; *Abraham made preparations for a journey* (split wood, saddled donkey and secured two servants); a *parent leaves on a journey to an unknown place* with his/her child (Abraham and Isaac head towards Mount Moriah)

    C') Genesis 22:5-10—*Separation* (Abraham and Isaac separated from the two youth; Scripture notes the *lack of a lamb (necessary for a sacrifice)*, which *is a portent of Isaac's impending death*; *the association of Isaac with wood* (Isaac carried the wood); *a distance is given between Abraham and Isaac and the two youth* (I and the lad will go yonder); Abraham lifted his hand ready to kill Isaac

      D') Genesis 22:11-12—The *angel of YHVH called to Abraham from heaven*; Adonai *noticed Abraham's faith*; "Do not *stretch out your hand against the lad*

        E') Genesis 22:13—Abraham *raised his eyes and saw a ram*; saved the child's life by *offering a ram in his place*

          F') Genesis 22:15-24—*A prophecy of Isaac's future, Isaac's descendants* and the *lineage of his wife*

The Scroll of the Gospel of David

The reason why the sign of the Messiah occurs in Ishmael's life is because there's information in the story of his life that is Messianic in significance and needs to be applied to the true Messianic figure, Isaac. By so clearly thematically connecting Isaac and Ishmael (A = B) we can more easily make the connections and apply the information gained from Ishmael's life to Isaac's.

These examples were cited to support my assertion that we actually need to look to Absalom to see the picture of the death, burial and resurrection of the Messiah, not David! Earlier, I showed you how David and Absalom were thematically connected when everything David's servants said about him and his army actually occurred to Absalom and his army! Ahithophel's plan was that Absalom's army would ignore David's army after killing him; however, in actuality, David's army ignored Absalom's army after killing him! Knowing that Absalom has been thematically connected to David, let's determine if there is a picture of death, burial and resurrection in his life.[42]

We know that Joab thrust three (hint) spears into Absalom's heart (II Samuel 18:14-16). But, did you notice something strange about what happened as a result of such punishment? Absalom didn't die! Can you believe that? Think about it folks. ***How many people do you think would survive three spears through the heart!?*** In fact, ten of Joab's armor bearers had to beat him to death because the three spears through the heart weren't enough to kill him! In other words, at that moment he exemplified a degree of power over death! It was not a full-fledged resurrection as we've seen in the past; however, the hint of power over death is surely there. Surely, we can see the connection to Messiah Yeshua who truly demonstrated victory over death. Also, please note that Messiah Yeshua was also pierced (with a sword) as He hung from the tree (John 19:34)![43]

After killing Absalom, we read that Joab's men took Absalom's body, threw it into a pit and covered it with stones. Surely this is a prophetic picture of Yeshua's body that was cast into the tomb and the stone that was rolled over the mouth of the grave. Interestingly enough, after we are informed of Absalom's death and burial, the Scripture goes on to relate how Absalom had built a monument to himself.

> Now Absalom in his lifetime had taken and set up a pillar for himself, which is in the King's Valley. For he said, "*I have no son to keep my name in remembrance.*" He called the pillar after his own name. And to this day it is called Absalom's Monument (II Samuel 18:18).

Let me ask you a question. Why did Absalom build a monument to himself? Because he didn't have a son to carry on his name. In other words, without a son (or the monument), he would cease to exist. How interesting. People build monuments to *immortalize* themselves. They want people to remember them even though they've died. Do you see a hint of resurrection in this action by Absalom? I do. The monument is his way of conquering death. It's his plan for *living on* in the minds of men even *after* his physical *death*. The picture's of Yeshua's death, as seen through the life of Absalom are shadowy indeed; however, I've saved the best and most convincing pictures for last.

The text we need to examine is found in II Samuel 18:9-10:

Then Absalom met the servants of David. Absalom rode on a mule. The mule went under the thick boughs of a great terebinth tree, ***and his head caught in the terebinth; so he was left <u>hanging between heaven and earth</u>***. And the mule which was under him went on. ¹⁰ Now a certain man saw it and told Joab, and said, "***I just saw Absalom <u>hanging in a</u> terebinth <u>tree</u>!***"

Earlier, I mentioned the peculiarity of the statement that Absalom was hanging "between heaven and earth." I believe this strange prepositional phrase was added to draw attention to what was happening to Absalom. Notice he was <u>hanging from a</u> terebinth <u>tree</u>. And what is a tree made of? Wood! Yes, this is it! This is the clearest prophetic picture of the death of the Messiah throughout II Samuel 1-18. Absalom hanging from the tree was a prophetic picture of Messiah Yeshua who was hung from a tree[44]—hanging between heaven and earth! Oh my, isn't Adonai awesome! What a picture. Could the prophecy be any clearer? The Messiah was executed by being hung from a tree (Matthew 27:35, 40; Mark 15:25, 30 and 32; Luke 24:20; and John 19:17, 23)! Once again, just like the cupbearer, the baker, the Egyptian youth, the two young spies, Ishmael, Ahimaaz and Jonathan and many others, pictures of the Messiah's death are seen in the lives of others we would not normally recognize or expect to be a Messianic figure.

There is another beautiful picture in these verses. Notice that Absalom's hair was entangled in the tree. The tree is part of vegetation on the earth. Quite literally, Absalom's head was encircled by vegetation. Did not Messiah Yeshua have vegetation wrapped around His head as did Absalom (Matthew 27:29, Mark 15:17 and John 19:2,5)? Yes, He did; it's called a crown of thorns. The Scripture states that Absalom's head was caught in the thick boughs of a tree and Yeshua had a crown of thorns placed on His head as He hung from a tree. This prophetic picture of Yeshua's crown of thorns is found in other places as well. Knowing that 1) Absalom's death is actually a prophecy of the death of Messiah Yeshua and 2) his hair caught in the elm tree is a picture of Yeshua's crown of thorns, you should be able to make another thematic connection to Absalom's "crown of thorns."

There is another instance of a picture of the Messiah's death which clearly presents a shadowy image of the Messiah's crown of thorns. Remember Isaac's probing question to Abraham at the Akeida (binding of Isaac)? *Look, the fire and the wood, but where is the lamb for a burnt offering* (Genesis 22:7b)? Abraham answered by stating that Adonai would provide the lamb Himself. And what happened? Genesis 22:13-14 states that Abraham saw "***. . . a ram caught in a thicket by its horns!***" We know for sure that the ram was a picture of Adonai's sacrifice – the Messiah – because the ram was an innocent substitute for Isaac, just as Yeshua is our innocent substitute! Just as the ram, with its horns caught in the thicket, is a picture of Yeshua, so likewise, Absalom's death pictures Yeshua's death. In both stories, we clearly see a shadow of the crown of thorns borne by Yeshua.

Remember Jonah's death? During his stay in the belly of the fish, which we know was actually a picture/shadow of Yeshua's burial in the grave, he prayed to Adonai. Note what he said in Jonah 2:5.

The waters surrounded me, even to my soul. The deep closed around me. ***Weeds were wrapped around my head*** (Jonah 2:5).

Beloved, there it is for the third time! The weeds that were wrapped around Jonah's head during the time of his stay in the belly of the fish were a perfect shadow of Yeshua's crown of thorns. We mustn't forget the picture of the baker's death in Genesis 40. Genesis 40:16b states that the baker informed Joseph that three white baskets were on his head. You should recall that it was the baker who presented us with a clear picture of the death of the Messiah because he was executed by being hung on a tree! Once again, a person showing us the death of the Messiah has vegetation on his head, thus providing us with our fourth prophetic picture of the fact that Yeshua would have a crown of thorns.[45]

It turns out that there is even more evidence supporting the fact that Absalom is giving us a picture of the Messiah's death. Can you make a thematic connection to another passage closely related to this story? I'll give you a hint—the book of Joshua. The incident is found in Joshua 10, the story of the defeat of the five Amorite kings. Please note the following thematic connections linking Joshua 10 to II Samuel 18:1-18.

- In both passages, a leader of Israel was attacked by someone else. In the story of II Samuel 15:10-20:2, David was attacked by Absalom. In the story of Joshua 10, Joshua was attacked by five Amorite kings led by ***Adoni-zedek, king of Jerusalem.***
- The passage in Joshua 10 is thematically connected to the splitting of the Red Sea as is the passage in II Samuel 18. We saw this in Chapter Five. Both passages are foundational pictures of salvation.
- In Chapter Five, I noted how in both passages Adonai overthrew His enemies using the forces of nature.
  - Joshua 10:11a—And it happened, as they fled before Israel and were on the descent of Beth Horon, that ***the LORD cast down large hailstones***[46] ***from heaven on them*** as far as Azekah, and they died.
  - II Samuel 18:8— For the battle there was scattered over the face of the whole countryside, ***and the woods devoured more people that day than the sword devoured.***
- Both passages use a common phrase!
  - Joshua 10:11b—. . . ***There were <u>more who died from the hailstones than the children of Israel killed with the sword</u>.***
  - II Samuel 18:8b—. . . ***and <u>the woods devoured more people</u>*** *that day <u>than the sword devoured</u>.*

Why does Joshua's defeat of the five Amorite kings and David's defeat of Absalom contain so many allusions to the splitting of the Red Sea? Because, like the splitting of the Red Sea, it contains information to help us understand the salvation brought about by Messiah Yeshua! As you can see, these passages are clearly thematically connected. Once again, however, I've saved the greatest connections for last!

- In both passages, the enemy was hung on a tree!
- In both passages, the enemy's body was thrown into some type of grave (a pit for Absalom and a cave for Adoni-zedek and his cohorts)!

♦ In both passages a mound of stones was used to cover the opening to the grave site!

The connections between these two passages are mind boggling! In case you doubted that Absalom's body hanging from the tree was a prophetic picture of the Messiah's death, hopefully, these last connections have helped you understand. This is another example of a thematic connection of the type similar to the Transitive Property of Equality (if A = B and B = C then A = C). We know that Absalom's death is a picture of the death of the Messiah who was hung on a tree; therefore . . .

Prophecy of Messiah's death = Pictured by Absalom's death

A   =   B

However, Absalom's death is thematically connected to the death of Adoni-zedek! This is a B = C statement.

Absalom's death = Adoni-zedek's death

B   =   C

If A = B and B = C, then A = C. In other words, if Messiah's death is equivalent to Absalom's death (A = B) and Absalom's death is equivalent to Adoni-zedek's death (B = C), then Messiah's death is equivalent to Adoni-zedek's death (A = C).

Prophecy of Messiah's death = Picture of Adoni-zedek's death

A   =   C

We know Adoni-zedek's death is actually a picture of Messiah Yeshua's death because of what the Gospels record for us. They both died by being hung on a tree. They were both thrown into a cave/tomb. Stone was placed over the mouth of their graves. You see beloved, Adoni-zedek's death is actually a veiled prophecy of the death of the Messiah! I know this may sound strange to you—the fact that Adonai would use the lives of sinners and heathen to give us a picture of the Messiah's death, burial and resurrection. However, let's consider this possibility in more detail.

Within this story about the capture of Adoni-zedek, there are many fascinating facts that hint at deeper truths. Therefore, I'd like to ask you some probing questions. Do you know what the name Adoni-zedek (אדני־צדק) means? It means *my lord is righteousness*! It is a contraction of two Hebrew words, אדני (adoni) meaning *my lord* and צדק (tsedeq) meaning *righteousness*. Now, have you ever wondered why a heathen king would be named ***my lord is righteousness***? Of all the names he could have been named, why a name meaning ***my lord is righteousness***? And why would the heathen king whose name means ***my lord is righteousness*** just so happen to be the ***king of Jerusalem*** of all places? I think you know why. It's prophetic! It is a prophetic picture of a future time when the true King of Jerusalem (Yeshua the Messiah) who can truly be called my Lord is Righteousness will, like Adoni-zedek, be hung on a tree, and buried in a cave/tomb with a large stone placed over its entrance.

Any way you look at it Adonai is trying (almost desperately) to show us pictures of the death, burial and resurrection of the Messiah—the most prophesied event in the Tanakh! He is using Messianic figures and people thematically connected to Messianic figures to teach us one important truth—the Messiah will need to 1) die by being hung on a tree, 2) be buried in a tomb and 3) rise again on the third day. Does the story of Adoni-zedek give us a picture of resurrection? It sure does. According to Joshua 10:15-19, the five kings were found hiding in a cave at Makkedah. Joshua commanded that 1) a large stone be rolled over the mouth of the cave and 2) the cave be made secure by the posting of guards at its entrance until they could return and deal with them.

One of the earliest references to a cave is found in Genesis 23:9. It was the cave of Machpelah that Abraham bought as a *burial place* for Sarah. This verse *thematically links a cave with a place of death*! Now we can see the picture of resurrection being painted for us in Joshua 10.

- Adoni-zedek, the king of Jerusalem, whose name means my lord is righteousness, was placed in a cave – a picture/place of death.
- A stone was placed over the mouth of the cave containing the body of the king of Jerusalem, whose name means my lord is righteousness.
- Guards were placed to secure the cave so that the king of Jerusalem whose name means my lord is righteousness could not escape.
- At a later time, the stone was removed and the king of Jerusalem named my lord is righteousness emerged alive from a place of death. Get the picture! Could it be any clearer?

I believe you can see my point. This is all a prophetic picture of the death, burial and resurrection of the Messiah, the true king of Jerusalem and the Lord our righteousness (Matthew 27:59-61, Mark 15:46 and Luke 23:53).

- Yeshua, the Lord of Righteousness, was placed in a cave/tomb.
- A large stone was rolled over the mouth of the tomb.
- Guards were posted to ensure that the true King of Jerusalem's body would not be taken out of the cave (Matthew 27:62-66).
- After three days, the stone was removed and the true King of Jerusalem, the Lord of Righteousness, emerged alive from a place of death (Matthew 28:1-8, Mark 16:1-8, Luke 24:1-7 and John 20:1-2).

At this time I'd like to show one final proof that the story found in II Samuel 18:1-18 is a story of death, burial and resurrection and it's based on our master chiastic structure. I will reproduce a small portion of the chiastic structure so that you can see the connection.

> I) II Samuel 17:18-19—Jonathan and Ahimaaz *descend into a well*; a woman *spread a curtain over the well*
> J) II Samuel 17:23—*Ahithophel's suicide by hanging*

> K) II Samuel 17:24-25—Absalom *appointed Amasa* over his army in place of Joab; ***David's position in Mahanaim***
>> L) *II Samuel 17:27-29—Three men brought David and his servants all sorts of provisions because they were hungry, exhausted and thirsty in the desert*
> K`) II Samuel 18:1-5—David *appointed officers* and divided his camp into thirds; ***David's position near the city gate***
> J`) II Samuel 18:9-15—Absalom *hanging in the elm tree*; David's servant refusing to accept bribery of silver; ***Absalom's death***
> I`) II Samuel 18:17—Joab's men throw ***Absalom's body into a large pit*** and erected a ***mound of stones over him***

Notice how the events of II Samuel 18:1-17 (elements I' – K') are thematically connected to the events in II Samuel 17:18-25 (elements I – K). Let's analyze each element individually.

- Elements I/I'—Notice how the act of throwing Absalom's body into a pit is thematically connected to the descent of Ahimaaz and Jonathan into the well. Once again, it is easy to see how this thematic connection teaches us that Jonathan and Ahimaaz are equivalent to Absalom (A = B)! We have already seen (Chapter Five) that Jonathan and Ahimaaz are Messianic figures and that their descent into the well was a picture of the death of the Messiah. Therefore, since Jonathan and Ahimaaz are thematically connected to Absalom, the action of throwing Absalom's body into a pit is also a picture of the death of the Messiah. This is exactly the point we've seen in numerous ways already.
- Elements J/J'—Here we see that Ahithophel and Absalom are thematically connected because they were both hanged. Does this mean that Ahithophel's death was a picture of the death of the Messiah? In this case, I would say no because we've already seen a clear connection between Ahithophel's suicide and Judas' suicide. Therefore, the hanging of Ahithophel is not a picture of the Messiah's death. It is simply another thematic connection to establish the chiastic structure.
- Elements K/K'—These do not bear on our current topic.

Understanding Why II Samuel 17:15-24 Was Out of Thematic Order

At this point, let us tidy up some unfinished business. In earlier chapters, we noted that the author of II Samuel was simply presenting a chronological presentation of David's flight from Absalom. This occurs in II Samuel 15:10 – 20:2. However, early on, we noted the amazing parallels between David's flight from Absalom and Yeshua's suffering. At the Pashat, or literal level of interpretation, this story pertains to the events that occurred as a fulfillment of Nathan's prophecy that the sword would not depart from David's house. However, by studying the Scriptures thematically, we have seen that another story is being told—the Gospel, the story of Messiah Yeshua's suffering, death, burial and resurrection. *Just as importantly, the thematic presentation of the Gospel told through David's flight from Absalom matches its chronological presentation in the four Gospel accounts!* Earlier, we discovered that the chronological presentation of the Gospel developed a glitch. We observed that II Samuel 17:15-24 departed from chronological order! I stated that there were two thematic presentations of the death, burial and resurrection of the Messiah in this passage. We analyzed one of the stories—the actions of Jonathan and Ahimaaz—and stated that their descent into and ascent from the well was a picture of Yeshua's death, burial and resurrection. If it is true that Jonathan's and Ahimaaz's actions were prophetic pictures of the death, burial and resurrection of the Messiah, then the departure from chronological order becomes evident. Look towards the end of this chapter at the ***Running Chart of Thematic Connections*** to help you see this. In chapter four, we saw that the provisions given to David and his servants provide a prophetic/thematic basis for how Simon the Cyrenian provided help for Messiah Yeshua as He carried the cross. Obviously, Simon's actions occurred *before* the death, burial and resurrection of Messiah Yeshua. Therefore, II Samuel 17:15-24, which contains two separate prophecies of the death, burial and resurrection of the Messiah, is out of proper chronological order. ***The pictures of death, burial and resurrection should occur sometime after the prophetic picture of Simon helping the Messiah!*** Clearly, the chronological order of the thematic presentation of the Gospel has been "compromised." The question we need to answer is this. Knowing that a thematic presentation of the death, burial and resurrection of the Messiah is being told through the story of David's flight from Absalom, why does a picture of the Messiah's death, burial and resurrection (II Samuel 17:15-24) occur "out of place," i.e., out of chronological order?

The answer has to do with the literary schemes of the Scripture. When we[47] write stories, we simply start at point A and go to point B in chronological order. But that's not how the prophets wrote their prophecies. Remember, the entire story of David's flight from Absalom was written as a chiastic structure! Therefore, all the themes of the first half MUST match the themes of the second half in reverse order. Look at the small portion of the chiastic structure above as you read through the following discussion.

Please note that the passage causing us chronological "trouble" in the thematic presentation of the death, burial and resurrection of the Messiah, II Samuel 17:15-24, is represented in our chiastic structure as point I. Although the chiastic structure only references II Samuel 17:18-19, most of the events pertaining to Jonathan and Ahimaaz's descent into and ascent from the well actually occur in II Samuel 17:15-22. The reason why a thematic picture of the death, burial and resurrection occurs here is because the prophet is writing the story thematically within the context of a chiastic structure, and a picture of this is needed at this point to thematically counterbalance the death, burial and resurrection of the Messiah that occurs in correct chronological order in points I' – J'! In other words, since I' – J' pertain to the death, burial and resurrection of the Messiah, then points I – J should too since the story is being told chiastically.

At this point, having seen the death, burial and resurrection of the Messiah, the remainder of the events in David's flight from Absalom should reflect events that happened after Yeshua's resurrection. This is exactly the case and in the next chapter we will discover events which occurred after Yeshua's resurrection that are prophetically pictured in II Samuel 18:19 – 20:2.

Running Chart of the Thematic Connections Between II Samuel 15:10 – 20:2 and the Gospels

II Samuel	The Gospels
II Samuel 18:9—Absalom was caught by his hair in an elm tree	Matthew 27:29, Mark 15:17 and John 19:2,5—Yeshua had a crown of thorns upon his head
II Samuel 18:9—Absalom was hanging from a tree between heaven and earth	Matthew 27:35, 40; Mark 15:25, 30 and 32; Luke 24:20; and John 19:17, 23—Yeshua was executed by being hung from a tree
II Samuel 18:14-18—Absalom was pierced with three spears through the heart; Absalom was killed, buried in a pit and stones were placed over the mouth of the pit	John 19:34; Matthew 27:59-66, 28:1-8; Mark 15:46, 16:1-8; Luke 23:53, 24:1-7; and John 20:1-2—Yeshua was pierced with a sword; Yeshua was killed, buried in a sepulcher and a large stone was placed over the mouth of the sepulcher

Thematic Moments

At this point, I'd like to demonstrate that Psalm 110 is Messianic. We've made extensive use of the story of how David rescued his family from the hand of the Amalekites. We know that David is a Messianic figure and that there is Messianic prophecy within I Samuel 30 (remember the Sign of the Messiah in I Samuel 30:9-13). Therefore any passage thematically connected to I Samuel 30:9-13 will probably be Messianic also. Please note the following thematic connections between I Samuel 30:1-31 and Genesis 14:1-20.

- Genesis 14:1-2 – At this time, Amraphel king of Shinar, Arioch king of Ellasar, Kedorlaomer king of Elam and Tidal king of Goiim *went to war against* Bera king of Sodom, Birsha king of Gomorrah, Shinab king of Admah, Shemeber king of Zeboiim, and the king of Bela (that is, Zoar).
  - I Samuel 30:1 – David and his men reached Ziklag on the third day. *Now the Amalekites had raided the Negev and Ziklag.* They had attacked Ziklag and burned it.
- Genesis 14:12 – *They also carried off Abram's nephew Lot and his possessions*, since he was living in Sodom.
  - I Samuel 30:2 – *. . . and had taken captive the women and all who were in it, both young and old.* They killed none of them, but carried them off as they went on their way.

- Genesis 14:14 – When Abram heard that his relative had been taken captive, *he called out the 318 trained men born in his household and went in pursuit* as far as Dan.
    - I Samuel 30:9-10 – . . . David and the six hundred men with him came to the **<u>Besor</u>** Ravine, where some stayed behind, for two hundred men were too exhausted to cross the ravine. *But David and four hundred men continued the pursuit.*
- Genesis 14:13 – *One who had escaped came and reported this to Abram the Hebrew.*
    - I Samuel 30:11-16 – . . . *They found an Egyptian in a field and brought him to David.* They gave him water to drink and food to eat—part of a cake of pressed figs and two cakes of raisins. He ate and was revived, for he had not eaten any food or drunk any water for three days and three nights . . . *"Can you lead me down to this raiding party? . . . I will take you down to them."*
- Genesis 14:16 – He recovered all the goods and brought back his relative Lot and his possessions, together with the women and the other people.
    - I Samuel 30:18-19 – . . . David recovered everything the Amalekites had taken, including his two wives. Nothing was missing: young or old, boy or girl, plunder or anything else they had taken. David brought everything back.
- Genesis 14:21-24 – The king of Sodom said to Abram, "Give me the people and keep the goods for yourself." But Abram said to the king of Sodom, "I have raised my hand to the LORD, God Most High, Creator of heaven and earth, and have taken an oath that I will accept nothing belonging to you, not even a thread or the thong of a sandal, so that you will never be able to say, 'I made Abram rich.' I will accept nothing but what my men have eaten and the share that belongs to the men who went with me—to Aner, Eshcol and Mamre. Let them have their share."
    - I Samuel 30:20-25 – He took all the flocks and herds, and his men drove them ahead of the other livestock, saying, "This is David's plunder." . . . But all the evil men and troublemakers among David's followers said, "Because they did not go out with us, we will not share with them the plunder we recovered. However, each man may take his wife and children and go. . . The share of the man who stayed with the supplies is to be the same as that of him who went down to the battle. All will share alike." David made this a statute and ordinance for Israel from that day to this.

It's easy to see that these two stories are similar by Divine design. Notice that Genesis 14:18-20 contains the passage about a mysterious person known as Melchizedek, king of Salem.

Then Melchizedek king of Salem brought out bread and wine. He was priest of God Most High, and he blessed Abram, saying, "Blessed be Abram by God Most High, Creator of heaven and earth. And blessed be God Most High, who delivered your enemies into your hand." Then Abram gave him a tenth of everything (Genesis 14:18-20).

So let's take inventory. We know that I Samuel 30:1-31 contains Messianic prophecy. Now we've seen that Genesis 14:1-20 is intimately thematically connected to I Samuel 30:1-31. Therefore, Genesis 14:1-20 must be Messianic in nature also. But the connections don't stop there. It just so happens that the name Melchizedek is mentioned in only one other place in the Tanakh – Psalm 110:4!

> The LORD has sworn and will not relent, "You are a priest forever according to the order of Melchizedek (Psalm 110:4)."

Beyond a shadow of doubt, Melchizedek, mentioned in Psalm 110, is thematically connected to the Melchizedek of Genesis 14. Thus, Psalm 110 is clearly Messianic in nature![48] Let's look at one more Messianic aspect of I Samuel 30:1-31, noting what happened in I Samuel 30:26-31!

> [26] Now when David came to Ziklag, he sent some of the spoil to the elders of Judah, to his friends, saying, "Here is a present for you from the spoil of the enemies of the LORD"— [27] to those who were in Bethel, those who were in Ramoth of the South, those who were in Jattir, [28] those who were in Aroer, those who were in Siphmoth, those who were in Eshtemoa, [29] those who were in Rachal, those who were in the cities of the Jerahmeelites, those who were in the cities of the Kenites, [30] those who were in Hormah, those who were in Chorashan, those who were in Athach, [31] those who were in Hebron, and to all the places where David himself and his men were accustomed to rove.

It seems that David has decided to share the spoils of victory with his brothers. This passage should remind you of another Messianic prophecy contained in the book of Psalms. If nothing comes to mind, think of I Samuel 30:1-31 in this manner. David's family was taken captive were they not? Therefore, when David rescued them, could we not say he took "captivity captive"? Does that sound familiar?

> You have ascended on high, You have led captivity captive; You have received gifts among men . . . (Psalm 68:18a)

Clearly, David's actions are a prophetic/thematic fulfillment of Psalm 68:18 as he took captivity captive and gave gifts to his men. This verse is given Messianic significance by the Apostle Paul and quoted by him in Ephesians 4:7-10.

> [7] But to each one of us grace was given according to the measure of Christ's gift. [8] Therefore He says: "When He ascended on high, He led captivity captive, and gave gifts to men." [9] (Now this, "He ascended"—what does it mean but that He also first descended into the lower parts of the earth? [10] He who descended is also the One who ascended far above all the heavens, that He might fill all things.)

Thus, it seems that Psalm 68 is Messianic also!

Chapter 7

What Is the Good News?

Introduction

In the last chapter, more undeniable *thematic* evidence of the death, burial and resurrection of Messiah Yeshua was presented. This chapter will provide even more evidence that the events of II Samuel 18:1-18 concern the Gospel – the story of the death, burial and resurrection of Messiah Yeshua. We will be able to make numerous thematic connections to other pertinent passages found throughout the Tanakh to bolster the already heavy accumulation of thematic evidence pointing to Yeshua's sufferings. However, the next two chapters will not only show us pictures of actions associated with Yeshua's sufferings, they will help us understand the heart of the Holy One—why He was pleased to bruise His only begotten Son.

What Is the Gospel (Good News)?

At this point, I'd like to ask you a question. What is the good news/gospel?[49] Some may think the answer is easy; however, it's not as easy as you may think. If you have been birthed into the Kingdom of God through the preaching of the gospel found in the New Testament, you will probably state, "The good news pertains to the facts concerning the death, burial and resurrection of the Messiah." However, if you were brought up in traditional Judaism, you would probably give a totally different answer! Why does this dichotomy exist? If you are Jewish and have only read what the Tanakh has to say about the good news, you will probably think it has something to do with the overthrow of Israel's enemies and the establishment of Adonai's kingdom. If you are like the average New Testament believer who primarily studies only the New Testament, you will think that it is essentially the death, burial and resurrection of the Messiah. Now, let me ask another question. If it's true that the New Testament writings primarily describe the fulfillment of prophecies in the Tanakh, then why would the definition of the good news be different for a Jewish person who studies the Tanakh and a good Bible-studying New Testament believer? Shouldn't they both arrive at the same conclusion? Why wouldn't the Jewish believer understand that the good news pertains to the death, burial and resurrection of the Messiah and why doesn't the New Testament believer understand that it concerns the overthrow of Israel's enemies and the establishment of the Kingdom of God? To answer these questions, let's take a look at what the Tanakh states concerning the good news and compare it to what the New Testament has to say about it.

I performed a search for the words 1) good news, 2) good tidings, 3) glad tidings and 4) Besor[50] in the New King James Bible (NKJB). There were seventeen separate occurrences of these words. The context of many of them clearly demonstrate how we should view the good news. I have divided the occurrences of these words into four categories. Category I includes those references that clearly give a definition or feeling for the concept of the good news. Category II includes those references that, although not very clear, can be thematically connected with the ideas demonstrated in Category I. Thus, although these verses do not clearly define the good news, they are thematically connected to those verses that do. Category III pertains to those verses that do not clearly teach us a definition of the good news. Finally, category IV lists those verses that, as we have discovered through thematic analysis, are actually veiled prophesies of events pertaining to the Messiah. Let's look at the four categories and see what we can glean.

Category I—A Clear Definition of the Good News

- Isaiah 52:7-10—⁷How pleasant are the footsteps of the herald upon the mountains announcing peace, *heralding **good tidings (good news)**, announcing salvation, saying unto Zion, 'Your God has reigned!'* ⁸The voice of your lookouts, they raise their voice, they sing glad song in unison; *with their own eyes they will see that HASHEM returns to Zion.* ⁹Burst out, sing glad song in unison, O ruins of Jerusalem, for HASHEM will have comforted His people; *He will have redeemed Jerusalem.* ¹⁰*HASHEM has bared His holy arm before the eyes of all the nations; all ends of the earth will see the salvation of our God!*

- Isaiah 40:9-11—⁹O Zion, *you who bring **good tidings**,* get up into the high mountain; O Jerusalem, *you who bring **good tidings**,* lift up your voice with strength, lift it up, be not afraid; *say to the cities of Judah, "Behold your God!"* ¹⁰Behold, *the Lord GOD shall come with a strong hand, and His arm shall rule for Him; behold, His reward is with Him, and His work before Him.* ¹¹*He will feed His flock like a shepherd; He will gather the lambs with His arm, and carry them in His bosom, and gently lead* those who are with young.

- Isaiah 61:1-7—¹"The Spirit of the Lord GOD is upon Me, because *the LORD has anointed Me to preach **good tidings** to the poor*; He has sent Me to *heal the brokenhearted*, to *proclaim liberty to the captives*, and the *opening of the prison to those who are bound*; ²To *proclaim the acceptable year of the LORD, and the day of vengeance of our God; to comfort all who mourn,* ³To *console those who mourn in Zion, to give them beauty for ashes, the oil of joy for mourning, the garment of praise for the spirit of heaviness; that they may be called trees of righteousness, the planting of the LORD, that He may be glorified."* ⁴And *they shall rebuild the old ruins, they shall raise up the former desolations, and they shall repair the ruined cities, the desolations of many generations.* ⁵*Strangers shall stand and feed your flocks, and the sons of the foreigner shall be your plowmen and your vinedressers.* ⁶But *you shall be named the priests of the LORD, they shall call you the servants of our God. You shall eat the riches of the Gentiles,* and in their glory you shall boast. ⁷Instead of your shame *you shall have* *double honor*, and instead of confusion *they shall rejoice in their portion.* Therefore in their land they shall possess double; *everlasting joy shall be theirs.*

- Nahum 1:15—¹⁵Behold, *on the mountains the feet of him who brings good tidings, Who proclaims peace!* O Judah, keep your appointed feasts, perform your vows. For *the wicked one shall no more pass through you; he is utterly cut off.*

Category II—Passages Clearly Thematically Connected to Passages Speaking of the Good News[51]

- I Chronicles 16:23—Sing to the LORD, all the earth; proclaim the ***good news*** of His salvation from day to day.
- Psalm 96:2—Sing to the LORD, bless His name; proclaim the ***good news*** of His salvation from day to day.

Category III—Those Passages That Don't Clearly Define the Good News Nor Connect to a Passage That Clearly Defines It

- 2 Kings 7:9—Then they said to one another, "We are not doing right. This day is a day of ***good news***, and we remain silent. If we wait until morning light, some punishment will come upon us. Now therefore, come, let us go and tell the king's household."[52]
- Psalm 40:9—I have proclaimed the ***good news*** of righteousness in the great assembly; indeed, I do not restrain my lips, O LORD, You Yourself know.
- Proverbs 25:25—As cold water to a weary soul, so is ***good news*** from a far country.

Category IV—Veiled Prophesies of the Work of the Messiah

- I Samuel 30:9-10—⁹So David went, he and the six hundred men who were with him, and came to the ***Brook Besor***, where those stayed who were left behind. ¹⁰But David pursued, he and four hundred men; for two hundred stayed behind, who were so weary that they could not cross the ***Brook Besor***.
- II Samuel 18:25-28 & 31—²⁵Then the watchman cried out and told the king. And the king said, "If he is alone, there is news in his mouth." And he came rapidly and drew near. ²⁶Then the watchman saw another man running, and the watchman called to the gatekeeper and said, "There is another man, running alone!" And the king said, "He also brings news." ²⁷So the watchman said, "I think the running of the first is like the running of Ahimaaz the son of Zadok." And the king said, "He is a good man, and comes with ***good news***." ²⁸ So Ahimaaz called out and said to the king, "All is well (peace)!" Then he bowed down with his face to the earth before the king, and said, "Blessed *be* the LORD your God, who has delivered up the men who raised their hand against my lord the king!" . . . ³¹Just then the Cushite came, and the Cushite said, "There is ***good news***, my lord the king! For the LORD has avenged you this day of all those who rose against you."
- I Kings 1:42—While he was still speaking, there came Jonathan, the son of Abiathar the priest. And Adonijah said to him, "Come in, for you are a prominent man, and bring ***good news***."

Looking at Categories I and II, one can easily see why a Jewish believer would think the good news pertained to the overthrow of Israel's enemies and the establishment of the Kingdom of God. In a nutshell, these verses describe the Messianic era! Note how prominently the following themes occur in the passages listed in Categories I and II:

- ◆ Salvation—Remember, in Chapter Five, we uncovered the Torah's foundational definition of salvation. We discovered that the Torah's definition of salvation meant deliverance from one's enemies against overwhelming odds. This is exactly what's pictured in these prophetic passages which clearly connect the concept of salvation to the good news.
- ◆ Peace—Notice how often peace is mentioned in these passages describing the good news. A Jewish person expects Adonai to usher in universal peace when the Messiah comes. This is part of the good news.
- ◆ Your God Reigns—Notice how often these prophesies of the good news mention the fact that Adonai will reign! The good news is that Adonai will return to Zion/Jerusalem to rule and reign over the earth with Israel as the head of the nations.
- ◆ Seeing Eyes—This event, Adonai's return to Jerusalem to establish His Kingship over Israel, will not go unnoticed. Every eye shall see when Adonai returns to redeem His people. It will be as spectacular as the splitting of the Red Sea.
- ◆ A Strong Arm—This speaks of the mighty deliverance Adonai has in plan for His people when He returns. The prophetic picture we should look to is the splitting of the Red Sea. This is the good news, my friend.
- ◆ Comfort For Zion—When the Messiah returns, He will comfort Zion.
- ◆ The Return of the Exiles—Adonai will gather the lost tribes of Israel from all lands and bring them back to Eretz Yisrael (the land of Israel). This is prophesied in Deuteronomy 30:4! This is one of the greatest events that will occur before Adonai sets up His eternal kingdom and it is a task that only the Messiah can fulfill.
- ◆ Wholeness For Israel—The good news is that there will be comfort, shalom (peace), joy, righteousness, liberty, abundance, joy and profound blessing for Zion when Adonai returns to Zion.
- ◆ The Day of Vengeance—The good news also includes the fact that Adonai will come to judge the enemies of Israel as well as those in Israel who haven't remained faithful to the covenant.

As you can plainly see, *the passages in Categories I and II clearly define the good news.* It is easy to understand why a Jewish person would think the good news refers to a time of 1) salvation, 2) peace, 3) the rule and reign of Adonai, 4) a time of profound blessing and comfort of Israel, 5) the return of the exiles and 6) the day of vengeance for all of Adonai's enemies. These are the obvious themes linked to the proclamation of the good news.

Have you noticed anything strange about what we've learned about the good news from passages in the Tanakh that clearly define it? Do you see anything about the death, burial and resurrection of the Messiah or anything about a suffering servant? No, you don't. Neither Isaiah 52:7-10, Isaiah 40:9-11, Isaiah 61:1-7 nor Nahum 1:15 give any explicit information about the death, burial and resurrection of the Messiah. This being the case, I would like to pose two more questions we need to answer.

1) Why do New Testament believers say the good news pertains to the death, burial and resurrection of the Messiah when the major prophesies of the Tanakh—which mention the concept of the good news—don't even hint at such a concept?
2) Since the New Testament speaks so much about the good news being the death, burial and resurrection of the Messiah, is it presenting a different message than the Tanakh?

Let's look at just two examples of how the New Testament defines the good news. During the Jerusalem council of Acts 15, Peter stood up and related how Adonai had chosen him to bear the gospel (good news) to the Gentiles.

And when there had been much dispute, Peter rose up and said to them: "Men and brethren, you know that a good while ago God chose among us, that by my mouth the Gentiles should hear *the word of the gospel* and believe (Acts 15:7).

This occurred in Acts chapter 10. Therefore, let's examine Peter's speech to the Gentiles in Acts 10 so that we can gain an understanding of which facts he considered to be the good news.

Then Peter opened his mouth and said: "In truth I perceive that God shows no partiality. But in every nation whoever fears Him and works righteousness is accepted by Him. *The word which God sent to the children of Israel*, preaching peace through Jesus Christ—He is Lord of all—*that word you know, which was proclaimed throughout all Judea*, and began from Galilee after the baptism which John preached: how God anointed Jesus of Nazareth with the Holy Spirit and with power, who went about doing good and healing all who were oppressed by the devil, for God was with Him. *And we are witnesses of all things which He did both in the land of the Jews and in Jerusalem, whom they killed by hanging on a tree. Him God raised up on the third day, and showed Him openly, not to all the people, but to witnesses chosen before by God, even to us who ate and drank with Him after He arose from the dead. And He commanded us to preach to the people,* and to testify that it is He who was ordained by God to be Judge of the living and the dead. To Him all the prophets witness that, through His name, whoever believes in Him will receive remission of sins (Acts 10:34-43)."

As you can see, the gospel/good news that Peter speaks of in Acts 15:7 is the truth of Messiah Yeshua's death, burial and resurrection! Paul also defines the gospel for us in I Corinthians 15:1-4.

Moreover, brethren, *I declare to you the gospel* which I preached to you, which also you received and in which you stand, by which also you are saved, if you hold fast that word which I preached to you—unless you believed in vain. For I delivered to you first of all that which I also received: *that Christ died for our sins according to the Scriptures, and that He was buried, and that He rose again the third day according to the Scriptures* (I Corinthians 15:1-4).

Thus, Peter and Paul both understood the gospel/good news to be the death, burial, and resurrection of the Messiah. But where did such a concept come from? It wasn't stated as such in the major prophesies of the Tanakh describing the good news. At this time, let's clear up this apparent contradiction and answer the two questions concerning why the New Testament writers seemed to have defined the good news in a manner inconsistent with Isaiah 52:7-10, Isaiah 40:9-11, Isaiah 61:1-7 and Nahum 1:15.

We must remember that the full extent of the good news was a mystery! That's right. Adonai only revealed certain aspects of the good news during the time period of the Tanakh. Categories I and II give this information. However, during the time period of the Tanakh, He did not want His people to fully understand the aspect of the good news that dealt with the death, burial and resurrection of the Messiah! It was a mystery and He did not want it to be fully revealed until the proper time. This was done so that He could ensure its fulfillment in His time.

> For this reason I, Paul, the prisoner of Christ Jesus for you Gentiles— ²if indeed you have heard of the dispensation of the grace of God which was given to me for you, ³how that by revelation He made known to me the mystery (as I have briefly written already, ⁴by which, when you read, you may understand my knowledge in *the mystery of Christ)*, *⁵which in other ages was not made known to the sons of men, as it has now been revealed by the Spirit to His holy apostles and prophets*: ⁶that the Gentiles should be fellow heirs, of the same body, and partakers of His promise in Christ through the gospel, ⁷of which I became a minister according to the gift of the grace of God given to me by the effective working of His power (Ephesians 3:1-7).

And how can we prove that the Tanakh does define the death, burial and resurrection of the Messiah as the good news? It's easy. Let's look at Category IV, the last set of Scriptures using the phrase, *good news*. I have written about each one of these passages in this book. Let's review what we learned about each passage remembering that in Chapter Six, I discussed the phenomenon of the scripture interpretation technique called remez. Remez means hint. In this technique, the Scriptures may "hint" at a deeper meaning without stating so explicitly. This was exactly the case in I Kings 1:38-42. On the surface, this passage detailed how King David hurriedly arranged for Solomon's coronation to preclude a coup attempt by his renegade son Adonijah. However, through thematic analysis, we saw that this story was actually a shadowy prophetic picture of Yeshua's triumphal entry into Jerusalem when the people wanted to coronate Him as the King!

- ♦ I Samuel 30:9-10—⁹So David went, he and the six hundred men who were with him, and came to the **Brook Besor**, where those stayed who were left behind. ¹⁰But David pursued, he and four hundred men; for two hundred stayed behind, who were so weary that they could not cross the **Brook Besor**.
- ♦ You may recall that I Samuel 30:1-31 is an account of how David and his men rescued their families and possessions from the Amalekites who had taken them while David and his men were away with the Philistines. In Chapter 1, we learned that this passage contained the Sign of the Messiah. It is a sign Adonai has given to teach us when we have come across Messianic prophecy. We saw that I Samuel 30:1-31 was a Messianic

prophecy of the death, burial and resurrection of the Messiah. Furthermore, we noted that the word Besor means good news, and it is used in a passage that presents a shadowy image of the Messiah's death, burial and resurrection.

- II Samuel 18:25-28 & 31—²⁵Then the watchman cried out and told the king. And the king said, "If he is alone, there is news in his mouth." And he came rapidly and drew near.

  ²⁶Then the watchman saw another man running, and the watchman called to the gatekeeper and said, "There is another man, running alone!" And the king said, "He also brings news." ²⁷So the watchman said, "I think the running of the first is like the running of Ahimaaz the son of Zadok." And the king said, "He is a good man, and *comes with good news*." - ³¹Just then the Cushite came, and the Cushite said, "There is *good news*, my lord the king! For the LORD has avenged you this day of all those who rose against you."

- Also, in Chapter Six, we saw how Absalom's death was actually a prophetic picture of the death of Yeshua Messiah. Furthermore, we were able to clearly thematically connect Absalom's picture of the Messiah's death to the good news delivered by the Cushite to David!

- I Kings 1:42—While he was still speaking, there came Jonathan, the son of Abiathar the priest. And Adonijah said to him, "Come in, for you are a prominent man, and bring *good news*."

Please note the following thematic connections between I Kings 1:38-40 and Luke 19:28-40/Matthew 21:1-17.

- In both stories, certain people want to crown a son of David as King of Israel
- Solomon and Yeshua both road into town on a donkey
- Zadok the priest, Nathan the prophet, Benaiah the son of Jehoiada, the Cherethites, and the Pelethites and all the people said, "Long live King Solomon!". Yeshua's disciples shouted, "Blessed is the King who comes in the name of the LORD! Peace in heaven and glory in the highest!"
- Adonijah and all his guests—enemies of Solomon—heard the tumult concerning Solomon's coronation and did not like it. The Pharisees heard the tumult of Yeshua's disciples concerning their desire to see Him coronated and did not like it.
- The tumult concerning Solomon's coronation caused some to question the reason for the tumult. The tumult concerning Yeshua's entry into Jerusalem caused some to question the reason for the tumult.
- During Solomon's coronation, it states that the ground seemed to split with their sound. The passage in Luke states, "the stones would immediately cry out."

As you can see, this passage in I Kings is actually a Messianic prophecy! In this instance, David is a shadowy picture of the Father in heaven and *Solomon is a picture of Yeshua*, His Son. Furthermore, I Kings 1:42 mentions the phrase good news.

Thus, we have two clear examples showing that the phrase *good news* was mentioned during a prophetic picture of the Messiah's death, burial and resurrection (I Samuel 30:1-31 and II Samuel 18:25-28 and 31), and one example of the phrase *good news* that was actually a veiled prophecy of an event that would occur later in the life of the Messiah (I Kings 1:38-42). All three examples make use of the remez technique, hinting at a deeper meaning than a surface reading of the text would reveal.

What's most important though is that we have discovered the answers to the two questions posed earlier.

1) First, we have discovered why the New Testament writers could say that the good news pertained to the death, burial and resurrection of the Messiah even though the major prophesies that define it most explicitly (Isaiah 52:7-10, Isaiah 40:9-11, Isaiah 61:1-7 and Nahum 1:15) don't actually mention anything about it. The reason why they have the authority to do so is because there are other prophecies that clearly link the good news to the death, burial and resurrection of the Messiah (I Kings 1:38-42 and II Samuel 18:25-28 & 31), albeit through the technique of remez. The good news in I Kings 1:38-42 and II Samuel 18:25-28 and 31 is actually the good news about the death, burial and resurrection of the Messiah, but the message is cloaked/hidden within the narrative of the characters. Thematic analysis brings these facts to light.
2) Secondly, we have discovered that the New Testament is not redefining the definition of the good news presented by the Tanakh. In actuality, it is unveiling one of the hidden aspects of the good news that was spoken of in the Tanakh, albeit in veiled terms.

We have now seen that the Tanakh actually presents two prophetic understandings of the good news. One aspect, which was veiled, spoke of the death, burial and resurrection of the Messiah. The other aspect, which was not veiled, spoke of the good news as a time of 1) salvation, 2) peace, 3) the rule and reign of Adonai, 4) a time of profound blessing and comfort for Israel, 5) the return of the exiles and 6) the day of vengeance against Adonai's enemies. How are we to understand these two streams of teachings concerning the good news? The veiled prophecies concerning the good news which teach of the death, burial and resurrection of the Messiah were fulfilled at His first advent. The clear prophecies concerning the good news which teach about 1) salvation, 2) peace, 3) the rule and reign of Adonai, 4) a time of profound blessing and comfort of Israel, 5) the return of the exiles and 6) the day of vengeance against Adonai's enemies will be fulfilled at His second advent.[53] To complete the picture, let us now examine how the New Testament also mentions the other aspect of the good news pertaining to Adonai's rule and reign.

Although the apostles seem to emphasize the death, burial and resurrection of the Messiah as if it was the only aspect of the gospel, as we have seen, the gospel is larger in scope. The Tanakh teaches this and so does the New Testament. We know that Yeshua taught the gospel, didn't He? The gospel writers often stated that Yeshua went about preaching the gospel. A brief perusal of the gospel accounts reveals many statements such as the following:

Then Jesus went about all the cities and villages, teaching in their synagogues, preaching the ***gospel of the kingdom***, and healing every sickness and every disease among the people (Matthew 9:35).

Now after John was put in prison, Jesus came to Galilee, preaching the ***gospel of the kingdom of God*** (Mark 1:14).

Although these verses mention the gospel, did you notice the slight nuance concerning the words describing it? It's called the *gospel of the* **kingdom**. Let me ask you a question. When Yeshua taught the gospel, did He go around preaching publicly that the gospel was His death, burial and resurrection? No, He did not. He taught that the Kingdom of God was at hand. In fact, His teachings were very much aligned with the gospel passages we examined from Category I. For example, note the message He preached in His home town as recorded in Luke 4:16-22.

> [16]So He came to Nazareth, where He had been brought up. And as His custom was, He went into the synagogue on the Sabbath day, and stood up to read. [17]And He was handed the book of the prophet Isaiah. And when He had opened the book, He found the place where it was written: [18]***"The Spirit of the LORD is upon Me, because He has anointed Me to preach the gospel to the poor; He has sent Me to heal the brokenhearted, to proclaim liberty to the captives and recovery of sight to the blind, to set at liberty those who are oppressed;* [19]*To proclaim the acceptable year of the LORD."*** [20]Then He closed the book, and gave it back to the attendant and sat down. And the eyes of all who were in the synagogue were fixed on Him. [21]And He began to say to them, ***"Today this Scripture is fulfilled in your hearing."*** [22]So all bore witness to Him, and marveled at the gracious words which proceeded out of His mouth. And they said, "Is this not Joseph's son?"

It has been stated that the prophecies of Category I are to be fulfilled at Yeshua's Second Advent. However, notice how Yeshua read a portion from Isaiah 61:1-7[54] and stated that it was fulfilled in their hearing! Does this mean that our analysis is flawed? No. Although the Category I passages will find their ultimate fulfillment at Yeshua's second coming, they actually began—in a spiritual sense—at His first advent. In other words, Yeshua actually ushered in the Kingdom of God at His first advent; however, He did not usher in its fullness, which must await His second coming. He has brought the power, healing and deliverance of the future Kingdom into the present age even though He hasn't actually begun to reign physically on the earth. When Yeshua came the first time, His mission was to usher the Kingdom of God within the hearts and minds of mankind and destroy His enemy (hasatan) through His death, burial and resurrection.

> Now when He was asked by the Pharisees when the kingdom of God would come, He answered them and said, "The kingdom of God does not come with observation; nor will they say, 'See here!' or 'See there!' *For indeed, the kingdom of God is within you* (Luke 17:20-21)."

Inasmuch then as the children have partaken of flesh and blood, He Himself likewise shared in the same, ***that through death He might destroy him who had the power of death, that is, the devil***, and release those who through fear of death were all their lifetime subject to bondage (Hebrews 2:14-15).

...having wiped out the handwriting of requirements that was against us, which was contrary to us. And He has taken it out of the way, having nailed it to the cross. Having *disarmed principalities and powers, He made a public spectacle of them, triumphing over them in it* (Colossians 2:14-15).

When He returns from heaven the second time, He will come to usher in the *fullness* of the Kingdom—the rule and reign of God on earth. He will judge the nations and establish the millennial kingdom, thus fulfilling the Category I passages to their fullest extent. With this understanding, let us continue our trek through David's flight from Absalom.

Bearing the Good News

David's Prophetic Picture

Let us begin by examining II Samuel 18:19-32. This passage details how news of the outcome of the war was delivered to David. The peculiar aspect of this story is that although Joab planned on sending a Cushite to herald the news, Ahimaaz, the son of Zadok, wanted to do it. The story unfolds as Ahimaaz begs for permission to do this task. The first interesting point I'd like to make concerns the usage of the word *news/tidings*. This word occurs in II Samuel 18:19, 20, 26 and 31. In each occurrence, the word *news/tidings* is a translation of the Hebrew verbal root בשר (basar), which means to bear news, bear tidings, publish, preach, and show forth. II Samuel 18:26 and 31 specifically states that the news was good news. At this point, please notice the location of the words new/tidings. It seems that the word is mentioned twice in the first half of our passage and twice in the second half. Also, notice that II Samuel 18:19 mentions "how the LORD has *avenged him of his enemies*," whereas II Samuel 18:32b states, "May *the enemies of my lord the king…be like that young man!*" These two verses are the first and last verses of this passage we're investigating. These are subtle clues that we may have happened upon another small chiastic structure within our main chiastic structure! The chiastic structure is below.

A) II Samuel 18:19b—"Let me run now and take the news to the king, how *the LORD has avenged him of his enemies*."
  B) II Samuel 18:20b-21—"But today you shall take no *news, because the king's son is dead*." Then Joab said to the Cushite, "*Go*, tell the king what you have seen." So *the Cushite bowed himself to Joab and ran*.
    C) II Samuel 18:22b-23—"Why will you run, my son, *since you have no news ready*?"; So *he said to him, "Run."*
      D) II Samuel 18:25—Then *the watchman cried out* and *told the king*. And the king said, "If he is alone, *there is news in his mouth*."
        E) II Samuel 18:26b—And *the king said*, "He also *brings good news*."
          F) II Samuel 18:27a—So the watchman said, "I think the running of the first is like the running of Ahimaaz the son of Zadok."
        E) II Samuel 18:27b—And *the king said*, "He is a good man, and *comes with good news*."
      D) II Samuel 18:28—So *Ahimaaz called out* and said *to the king*, "All is well!"
    C') II Samuel 18:29b-30—"…I saw a great tumult, but *I did not know what it was about*."; And *the king said*, "Turn aside and *stand here*."

B') II Samuel 18:31—Just then *the Cushite came*, and the Cushite said, "There is *good news*...the LORD *has avenged you this day of all those who rose against you.*"

A') II Samuel 18:32b—"*May the enemies of my lord the king*, and all who rise against you to do harm, *be like that young man!*"

Once again, we have been treated to another beautiful chiastic structure! They literally fill every page of the Scriptures. While analyzing the chiastic structure we see that each element in the two halves of the story is thematically connected to its partner by sharing similar words and/or themes. Let's begin a closer analysis of the chiastic structure by comparing elements B and B'. Note how element B states that the king's son Absalom is dead. This passage is thematically connected to B', where it states that Absalom has been killed (There is good news...the LORD has avenged you this day of all those who rose against you)! In other words, elements B and B' teach us that *Absalom's death is actually the good news*!

Most of the other thematic connections are pretty straightforward. Our central axis pertains to Ahimaaz's stride. We know that the central axis is usually the most important element or the reversal point of the structure. In this instance, the central axis is not functioning as the turning point of the story; therefore, we should assume that it is an important point in the story. But why? Why would Ahimaaz's stride be significant to this story? I believe it is the central axis because Adonai is trying to get us to thematically connect this story to a great prophecy concerning the Messiah.

Another reading of II Samuel 18:28a makes a tremendous thematic connection. According to the Artscroll Tanakh,[55] Ahimaaz called out the word *peace* to King David.

So Ahimaaz called out and said to the king, "Peace!"

The word *peace* is what triggered the connection. Can you think of how this story concerning the bearing of good news is thematically connected to a great prophecy of scripture? If not, here's a hint—remember Ahimaaz's stride. This passage (II Samuel 18:19-32) is thematically connected to the great prophecy of Isaiah 52:7-10 (NKJV)!

How beautiful upon the mountains are *the feet of him who brings good news*, who *proclaims peace, who brings glad tidings* of good things, *who proclaims salvation*, who says to Zion, "Your God reigns!" *Your watchmen shall lift up their voices*, with their voices they shall sing together; for they shall see eye to eye when the LORD brings back Zion. Break forth into joy, sing together, you waste places of Jerusalem! For the LORD has comforted His people, He has redeemed Jerusalem. *The LORD has made bare His holy arm* in the eyes of all the nations; and all the ends of *the earth shall see the salvation of our God.*

This is such a fascinating thematic connection. In many ways, II Samuel 18:19-32 is a fulfillment of Isaiah 52:7-10! Let's see how many ways these two passages are thematically connected. Here is the Artscroll Tanakh translation of these passages.

[19]Ahimaaz son of Zadok said, "I shall run and tell the king the news—that HASHEM has granted him justice from his enemies!" [20]But Joab told him, "You should not be the

bearer of news today. You can bring news another day; but do not bring news today, for the king's son is dead." [21]Joab then said to the Cushite, "Go tell the king what you have seen"; and the Cushite prostrated himself to Joab and ran off. [22]Ahimaaz son of Zadok continued to persist, and said to Joab, "Whatever happens—please let me also run after the Cushite." But Joab said, "Why should you run, my son? This news will not provide any [benefit] for you." [23]"Whatever happens—let me run!" So he said to him, "Run." Ahimaaz ran by the route of the plain and overtook the Cushite. [24]David was sitting between the two gates [of the city]. The *lookout* went up to the roof of the gate, to the wall; *he raised his eyes and looked*—and behold, a man running alone! [25]***The look out called out*** and told the king. The king said, "if he is alone, there is news in his mouth," and he kept drawing closer. [26]Then the lookout saw another man running; the lookout called out to the gatekeeper and said, "Behold, [another] man is running alone!" The king said, "This man is also ***a herald!***" [27]The lookout said, "I recognize ***the first one's stride as the stride*** of Ahimaaz son of Zadok." And the king said, "He is a good man; he is coming with ***good news***." [28]Ahimaaz called out and said to the king, "***Peace!***"... (II Samuel 18:19-28)

[7]How pleasant are the ***footsteps*** of the ***herald*** upon the mountains ***announcing peace, heralding good tidings (good news), announcing salvation***, saying unto Zion, 'Your God has reigned!' [8]***The voice of your lookouts, they raise their voice***, they sing glad song in unison; ***with their own eyes they will see*** that HASHEM returns to Zion. [9]Burst out, sing glad song in unison, O ruins of Jerusalem, for HASHEM will have comforted His people; He will have redeemed Jerusalem. [10]HASHEM has bared His holy arm before the eyes of all the nations; all ends of the earth will see the salvation of our God (Isaiah 52:7-10)!

- Isaiah 52:7 uses the phrase, "How pleasant are ***the footsteps*** of the herald." Thus, there is an emphasis upon the feet of someone bearing news. This is thematically connected to II Samuel 18:27a where David's watchman stated, "I recognize ***the first one's stride as the stride*** of Ahimaaz son of Zadok." Note how both passages place a special emphasis on the feet.
- Isaiah 52:7 states, "How pleasant are the footsteps of ***the herald*** upon the mountains…" This is thematically connected to II Samuel 18:26 where David's lookout stated, "The king said, "This man is also ***a herald!***"
- Isaiah 52:7 states that the herald is heralding ***good news***. II Samuel 18:19-32 uses the word *news* four times, two of which involve the phrase ***good news***.
- Isaiah 52:7 states that the herald is ***announcing, "Peace!"*** In II Samuel 18:28, ***Ahimaaz called out, "Peace!"*** Notice how the NKJV (as well as most other English translations) translate the Hebrew word שלום (peace) as *all is well*. Once again, we see that they are trying to help us with the translation. However, as I've stated before, the translators often obscure thematic connections to other passages when they try to "smooth out the Hebrew." It is the word *peace* in II Samuel 18:28 that caused me to connect it to the prophecy of Isaiah 52. If I had stayed with the English translations, I may not have seen the connection as readily.[56]

- Isaiah 52:8 states, "The voice of your *lookouts, they raise their voice...*" This is thematically connected to II Samuel 18:24-25 which involves *King David's lookout*. Notice how Isaiah 52:8 states that the lookouts *raise their voice*. This verse perfectly describes the actions of David's lookout in II Samuel 18:25-26 who **called out** concerning the runners as they approached.
- Lastly, notice how Isaiah 52:8 states that *"with their own eyes they [the lookouts] will see that HASHEM returns to Zion."* This is thematically connected to II Samuel 18:24 where it states that David's lookout, *"raised his eyes and looked."* Although he saw something different than the lookout of Isaiah 52:8, the connection is clear that the lookouts will see something with their eyes.

All of these thematic connections are intentional. It's not enough to find the thematic connections. We must ask why the connections exist and try to provide a sound answer for their occurrence. I believe these passages are thematically connected so extensively because Adonai eagerly wants us to see that the story in II Samuel 18:19-32 is a thematic fulfillment[57] of Isaiah 52:7-10!

Yeshua's Prophetic Fulfillment

Now, let's look into the prophetic significance of the events in II Samuel 18:19-32. In Chapter 6, we noted that the scripture will often hint at deeper truths. We saw this in the case of the phrase *good news*. We examined a few usages of this phrase and noted that the events were actually prophetic pictures concerning the work of the Messiah, although the immediate context indicated otherwise. II Samuel 18:19-32 mentions the phrase *good news* two times. Furthermore, we definitely know that both are references to the actual good news of the death, burial and resurrection of the Messiah, because (as we saw in Chapter 6), the events surrounding Absalom's death were a perfect shadow of what happened to Messiah Yeshua! In other words, II Samuel 18:1-18 was a wonderful thematic presentation of the death of Messiah Yeshua who 1) was lifted up on a tree, 2) hung between heaven and earth and 3) bore a crown of thorns.

At this point, I'd like to show you how the chiastic structure teaches this same point. In the chiastic structure of II Samuel 18:19-32, note how element B states that the king's son Absalom is dead. This passage is thematically connected to B', where it states that Absalom has been killed.

Element B—II Samuel 18:20b-21—"But today you shall take no **news, because the king's son is dead.**" Then Joab said to the Cushite, "**Go, tell the king what you have seen.**" So **the Cushite bowed himself to Joab and ran.**

Element B'—II Samuel 18:31—Just then the Cushite came, and the Cushite said, "**There is good news**, my lord the king! For **the LORD has avenged you this day of all those who rose against you.**"

The amazing thing about element B' is that *the Cushite explicitly equates the good news with Absalom's death* as stated in element B! The picture is clear. Absalom's death is the good news born by the Cushite! Since we know Absalom's death is actually a picture of Messiah Yeshua's death, we simply need to understand that the Holy One is using this chiastic structure to teach that the gospel/good news pertains to the death of the Messiah on our behalf. As you can see, the Tanakh devotes an extensive amount of teaching concerning the good news.

II Samuel 18:19-32 is definitely a prophetic/thematic fulfillment of Isaiah 52:7-10. But there is another profound truth lurking under this connection. Thematically, we know that II Samuel 18:19-32 pertains to announcing the good news of the death, burial and resurrection of the Messiah. However, our thematic connections show that it is also a thematic fulfillment of Isaiah 52:7-10, which is a prophecy of the second coming of the Messiah, not the first! So how can a scripture referring to the second coming of the Messiah (Isaiah 52:7-10) be applied to an event (the death, burial and resurrection of the Messiah) that occurred at His first coming? It's the nature of prophecy. This is one of the reasons why the Jewish people thought (and to this day many still believe this) that there would be two Messiahs. Many prophecies blur the distinction of two separate advents of the Messiah by mentioning aspects of both in the same prophecy! Note how the prophecy of Joel mentions aspects of Yeshua's first and second advents in the same breath.

> "And it shall come to pass afterward that *I will pour out My Spirit on all flesh; your sons and your daughters shall prophesy, your old men shall dream dreams, your young men shall see visions. And also on My menservants and on My maidservants I will pour out My Spirit in those days.* **And I will show wonders in the heavens and in the earth: blood and fire and pillars of smoke. The sun shall be turned into darkness, and the moon into blood, before the coming of the great and awesome day of the LORD.** And it shall come to pass that whoever calls on the name of the LORD shall be saved. **For in Mount Zion and in Jerusalem there shall be deliverance, as the LORD has said, among the remnant whom the LORD calls** (Joel 2:28-32).

Each portion of this passage in italics actually occurred at Yeshua's first coming.[58] Everything in bold will occur at His second coming. Joel's prophecy was partially fulfilled in Acts 2:16-21. Notice how Peter actually quotes this entire passage to explain the events associated with Shavuot (Pentecost), even though the part of the prophecy in bold won't occur until Yeshua's second advent! The prophecy of Joel obscures the fact that the portion of the prophecy in bold won't occur until 2,000 years later. Yet Joel mentions these events in the same breath! This is but one example of how events from the first and second coming of the Messiah are mixed together. This is one of the ways Adonai hid the facts concerning two separate advents of the Messiah because He wanted to reveal the fullness of these truths in His own timing. Failure to understand this nuance of Messianic prophecy is the reason why many Jewish people believe in two separate Messiahs instead of one who comes to His people two separate times.

Please take another look at Isaiah 52:7-10 and notice how it flows as if it were speaking of only one event in time. Thematically, we can break these verses into two portions. First of all, Isaiah 52:7-8a is a long section which essentially states the following: heralds on the mountains of Israel have begun to announce that the God of Israel has begun to reign.

> How beautiful upon the mountains are *the feet of him who brings good news,* who *proclaims peace, who brings glad tidings* of good things, *who proclaims salvation,*

The Scroll of the Gospel of David

who says to Zion, "Your God reigns!" *Your watchmen shall lift up their voices*, with their voices they shall sing together.

We've already seen how this portion of the prophecy of Isaiah is thematically linked with the announcement of the death, burial and resurrection of Yeshua. Furthermore, we will soon see an even stronger connection as we demonstrate its fulfillment based on the four Gospels. Now, note how Isaiah 52:8b-10 continues the prophecy, stating that the good news pertains to certain events:

- ♦ Adonai will bring back Zion
- ♦ Adonai will redeem Jerusalem
- ♦ Adonai will make bare His holy arm before the nations
- ♦ All the ends of the earth will see the salvation of the God of Israel

In case you haven't noticed, Isaiah 52:8b-10 is a prophecy of events that are to occur at the second advent of the Messiah! Let's put a New Testament definition onto each event prophesied in Isaiah 52:8b-10.

- ♦ Adonai will bring back Zion—This is a prophecy of the regathering of the whole House of Israel from the nations to Jerusalem by the hand of the Messiah.
- ♦ Adonai will redeem Jerusalem—This is a prophecy of the great deliverance of the city of Jerusalem—which will be under siege—by the Messiah when He returns.
- ♦ Adonai will make bare His holy arm before the nations—Again, this is a prophecy of the great deliverance for the people of Israel by the Messiah.
- ♦ All the ends of the earth will see the salvation of the God of Israel—This is yet another prophecy of the Messiah's deliverance of the nation of Israel at His return. Note how this passage is thematically connected to Revelation 1:7 which states, "… *every eye shall see Him*, even they who pierced Him. And all the tribes of the earth will mourn because of Him. Even so, Amen."

There it is again. One prophetic utterance that actually pertains to events separated by over 2,000 years! Since II Samuel 18:19-32 relates how Ahimaaz and the Cushite ran to bear the good news of Absalom's demise, we should expect that this is a prophetic picture of how the good news of Yeshua's death, burial and resurrection was proclaimed immediately after the said events.

In Chapter 6, we examined passages from the Gospels that described Yeshua's death. Now let's see what happened after He was in the grave for three days and three nights. These events are recorded for us in Matthew 28:1-20, Mark 16:1-8, Luke 24:1-11 and John 20:1-10. According to Matthew 28:5-7 and Mark and 16:6-7, angels met certain women who had come to anoint Yeshua's body with spices. They told the women, "go quickly and *tell His disciples that He is risen from the dead*…" Stated otherwise, the angels told the women to *go and bear the good news of Yeshua's death, burial and resurrection*. Notice how perfectly this matches the account in II Samuel 18:19-32.

Then Joab said to the Cushite, "*Go, tell* the king what you have seen." So *the Cushite* bowed himself to Joab and *ran* (II Samuel 18:21).

This passage relates how Joab sent the Cushite with the good news of Absalom's demise, which, as we have seen, is a thematic picture of Yeshua's death, burial and resurrection.[59] According to Matthew 28:8, "They [the women] *went out quickly* from the tomb with fear and great joy, and *ran to bring His disciples word* [the good news]."

In a strange twist of thematic significance, Matthew 28:9-10 records how Yeshua met the women on their way to tell the disciples the good news. According to Matthew 28:9, the women came, ". . . and *held Him by the feet* and worshipped Him." Do you remember the significance of the central axis of II Samuel 18:19b-32b? The central axis, II Samuel 18:27a, emphasized the feet of the runners. We have already seen how closely II Samuel 18:19-32 (especially II Samuel 18:27a) is thematically connected to Isaiah 52:7a, which states, "*How beautiful* upon the mountains *are the feet* of him who brings good news." Matthew 28:9 emphasizes Yeshua's feet! Truly, how beautiful were His feet in the sight of the women!

Although the Gospel passages we've quoted concerning the women are clearly thematically connected to II Samuel 18:19-32, there exists an even greater thematic connection! According to John 20:3-4, Peter and John both ran to the tomb.

Peter therefore went out, and the other disciple, and were going to the tomb. So they both ran together, *and the other disciple outran Peter and came to the tomb first* (John 20:3-4).

Notice that John outran Peter. This is thematically connected to Ahimaaz and the Cushite who both raced to bring the good news to King David. You may recall that Ahimaaz outran the Cushite! Furthermore, II Samuel 18:29-31 relates how Ahimaaz approached David. David questioned him concerning Absalom, and when he couldn't answer David's question, David asked him to step aside. This little prophetic side-step was replayed centuries later when, just as Ahimaaz outran the Cushite only to stand aside and wait until he came with the good news, John outran Peter to the tomb only to step aside until Peter came, entered the tomb, and saw proof of the resurrection of Messiah first.

A Father's Broken Heart

David's Prophetic Picture

II Samuel 18:33 records David's reaction to the news that Absalom had perished in the battle.

Then the king was deeply moved, and went up to the chamber over the gate, and wept. And as he went, he said thus: "O my son Absalom—my son, my son Absalom—if only I had died in your place! O Absalom my son, my son (II Samuel 18:33)!"

Struck with grief, David retreated to the chamber above the city gate and began to lament concerning his son Absalom. At this point, the plot makes a peculiar change. This is recorded for us in II Samuel 19:3-4:

> So the victory that day was turned into mourning for all the people. For the people heard it said that day, "The king is grieved for his son." And the people stole back into the city that day, as people who are ashamed steal away when they flee in battle.

This passage relates how David's servants reacted to His emotional outpouring over Absalom. The peculiar aspect of these events is that David's men had won the battle. They had defeated David's renegade son who had attempted to kill him and secure the throne. This should have been a time of rejoicing. The scripture is silent concerning how many—if any—of David's men lost their lives in the battle. Nonetheless, they had risked their lives for David. Upon seeing David weep so bitterly over Absalom's fate, their victory was turned into a time of shame. Instead of rejoicing and celebrating the victory, David's men were distraught, and ashamed to the point that they all stole back into the city ". . . as people who are ashamed steal away when they flee in battle." This paradox is captured in Joab's words to David, who rebuked him for causing the people to lose heart.

> Then Joab came into the house to the king, and said, *"Today you have disgraced all your servants who today have saved your life, the lives of your sons and daughters, the lives of your wives and the lives of your concubines, in that you love your enemies and hate your friends.* For you have declared today that you regard neither princes nor servants; for today I perceive that if Absalom had lived and all of us had died today, then it would have pleased you well. Now therefore, arise, *go out and speak comfort to your servants. For I swear by the LORD, if you do not go out, not one will stay with you this night. And that will be worse for you than all the evil that has befallen you from your youth until now* (II Samuel 19:5-8)."

Notice two things:

- Instead of rejoicing over the defeat of Absalom, David's men behaved as if they had lost the battle. They acted like those who are ashamed because they have fled from a battle. According to II Samuel 19:5-7, it appears that David's men had totally lost heart!
- David is hidden from the view of his servants. Except for Joab who went into the chamber to see David, none of his other servants see him. They have only heard that he is lamenting over his son Absalom.

Yeshua's Prophetic Fulfillment

Let's begin by looking at David's reaction to the news of Absalom's death. We have noted that David wept and grieved bitterly over Absalom, so much so that his servants' hearts were totally dismayed even after winning so great a victory over the king's enemies. Remember the interpretive technique called remez (רֶמֶז), or hint. Some Bible scholars believe the Hebrew word remez originated from the verbal root רמה (ramah) or רמם (ramam).[60] These words mean to raise something up or elevate higher. The idea here is that although something may look like one thing at eye level it looks like something else when you raise or elevate it. Scripturally speaking, a remez interpretation means that you are able to see something else being hinted at within the text other than the plain meaning. In modern Hebrew, remez is the basis for the idea of a traffic light! The idea is straightforward. The colors red, yellow and green are simply colors. However, once they are lifted up—within the context of a traffic light—they actually confer a meaning to the viewer. There is another message being told by the colors red, yellow and green when they are lifted up other than the plain sense of the colors. To those who understand the rules of driving, these colors tell them when to stop, slow down and/or go. To one who doesn't understand the purpose of a traffic light, they are simply colors. II Samuel 18:33 contains a hidden jewel that can only be discovered if we use the remez level of interpretation. We have already seen that Absalom's death foreshadows the death of the Messiah who was hung on a tree. However, David is a Messianic figure. II Samuel 18:33 is hinting to the fact that David is giving us a picture of the Messiah's heart for His people when He stated, "If only I had died in your place." David's statement is prophetic. This is Yeshua's heart for His people, for you and me. Furthermore, note Joab's response to David's lament in II Samuel 19:5-6.

> [5]Then Joab came into the house to the king, and said, "Today you have disgraced all your servants who today have saved your life, the lives of your sons and daughters, the lives of your wives and the lives of your concubines, [6]*in that you love your enemies* and hate your friends. For you have declared today that you regard neither princes nor servants; for today I perceive that if Absalom had lived and all of us had died today, then it would have pleased you well.

Notice how Joab stated that David loved his enemies. Is this not true of Yeshua? He loved those who executed Him and made intercession for them. This is yet another instance of a prophetic teaching hidden within the dialogue. This phenomenon is not unique. There are many times in scripture where the utterances and/or emotions of a Messianic figure are actually giving us prophetic glimpses into the mind of Messiah Yeshua! Take the two spies sent to Rahab as an example. In Chapter Five we noted the profound thematic connections between the two spies sent to Rahab by Joshua and Jonathan and Ahimaaz who were spies sent on David's behalf. At that time, I showed quite conclusively how Joshua's two spies helped connect Jonathan and Ahimaaz to Samson, one of the Tanakh's premiere Messianic figures. We did that as follows:

- ♦ The two young spies are thematically connected to Samson (A = B)
- ♦ Sampson is thematically connected to (or a picture of) Yeshua the Messiah (B = C)
- ♦ Therefore, the two young spies are thematically connected to (or a picture of)Yeshua the Messiah (A = C)

But . . .

- ♦ Jonathan and Ahimaaz are thematically connected (equivalent) to the two young spies (A = B)

- The two young spies are thematically connected to (or a picture of) Yeshua the Messiah (B = C)
- Therefore, Jonathan and Ahimaaz are thematically connected to (or a picture of) Yeshua the Messiah (A = C)

If   the two young spies = Samson

$$A = B$$

And   Samson = Yeshua

$$B = C$$

Then   the two young spies = Messiah Yeshua

$$A = C$$

But . . .

If   Jonathan and Ahimaaz = The Two Young Spies

$$A = B$$

And   The Two Young Spies = Yeshua

$$B = C$$

Then   Jonathan and Ahimaaz = Messiah Yeshua

$$A = C$$

The important point I want you to remember is that Joshua's two young spies are equivalent to Samson, i.e., they are also Messianic figures! And how do they teach us about the work of the Messiah? If you remember, the two spies made an oath to Rahab.

> So the men answered her, "*Our lives for yours*, if none of you tell this business of ours. And it shall be, when the LORD has given us the land, that we will deal kindly and truly with you (Joshua 2:14)."

Notice the content of their oath. They said they would die in her place! This is yet another remez level teaching that the Messiah will die on the behalf of others. It's a Messianic teaching embedded within the story of the spies' reconnaissance of Jericho. The only way you can know that this passage has Messianic significance is if you know they are Messianic figures. Thus, we have seen another example of the fact that the Messiah will die on the behalf of others. But there is still another more fascinating proof of His vicarious sacrifice.

The Scroll of the Gospel of David

Messianic teachings concerning the death, burial and resurrection of the Messiah literally overflow the pages of the Scriptures. In fact, sometimes Messianic prophecy unfolds in some of the most obscure places. Take, for instance, the book of Esther. As I prepared for a Purim message a few years ago, I happened upon a chiastic structure in this book. Esther 1:5 – 8:17 is one large chiastic structure with many, many thematic connections. It is listed below.

A) Es 1:5-7 — Seven-day feast; in Shushan; courtyard decorations of *white, turquoise and purple*; couches of *gold*

   B) Es 1:19, 21 — A royal *edict* from the *king; not to be revoked*; confer her *estate* to another; the *king did according to the word of Memucan*; *letters* sent to *all the kings provinces*; in its *own script* and *each people their own language*; each man *rule in his own home*; Vashti was *banished*;

      C) Es 2:1-23 —

- Es 2:1 — After a period of *time passed*, the king *remembered Vashti's offense*
- Es 2:2-4 — The king desired to *honor someone (a new queen)*
- Es 2:4, 9, 17 — *Cosmetics were put* on Esther; Esther was given 7 attendants and the *best quarters*; Esther reigned in Vashti's place and was *given the royal crown*
- Es 2:19-21 — *Mordecai was sitting at the king's gate*; King gave a banquet for Esther (*Esther's banquet*); the maidens were gathered a *second* time; Esther said nothing about her Jewish heritage; a *plot to kill the king*
- Es 2:22 — The plot to kill the king is revealed to Mordecai, who reveals it to Esther, who reveals it to the king
- Es 2:23 — The matter was *investigated by the king* and found to be true; *Bigthan and Teresh were hanged on gallows*

         D) Es 3:1 — Haman is *promoted and elevated*; his seat is *above all the officers*

            E) Es 3:2-5 — Servants *at the king's gate* would *bow before Haman*; Haman was *filled with wrath*

               F) Es 4:3 — In every province there was mourning, weeping, lament and *fasting* among the Jews

                  G) Es 4:5 — *Esther sent* Hathach to Mordecai to ask him *why everyone was fasting*

                     H) Es 4:8 — Mordecai told Esther to go to the *king to implore and plead with him on behalf of the Jews*

                        I) Es 4:9-10 — Esther was *given a message* from Mordecai and *she sent a reply* to him

                           J) *Es 4:11 — All the king's officials and the people of the royal provinces know that for any man or woman who approaches the king in the inner court without being summoned the king has but one law: that he be put to death. The only exception to this is for the king to extend the gold scepter to him and spare his life. But thirty days have passed since I was called to go to the king*

                        I) Es 4:12-13 — Mordecai was *given a message* from Esther and he *sent a reply* to her

                     H) Es 4:14 — Mordecai told Esther that if *she remained silent (didn't implore and plead with the king)* she would perish also

G) Es 4:15—*Esther sent* to Mordecai to *tell him why she wanted everyone to fast*

  F) Es 4:16—Gather all Jews in Shushan and we will all *fast* for three days and three nights

    E) Es 5:9—Mordecai *wouldn't bow before Haman at the king's gate*; Haman was *filled with wrath*

   D) Es 5:11 Haman recounts how the "king had *promoted him and elevated* him *above"* the other officials

  C) Esther 6:1-7:10—
- Es 6:1-2—After a period of *time passed*, the king was *reminded of Mordecai's good deed*
- Es 6:3, 6, 11—The king desired to *honor the man* who saved his life
- Es 6:7-11—Mordecai was *dressed in royal attire*; Mordecai was *given the royal horse*; Mordecai *wore the royal crown*
- Es 6:1-14, 7:2-4—*Mordecai* returned to the *city gate*; Haman was quickly escorted to *Esther's banquet*; the king asked Esther on the *second* day of the feast; Esther revealed her Jewish heritage; a *plot to kill the Jews*
- Es 7:4— The plot to kill the Jews is revealed to Mordecai, who reveals it to Esther, who reveals it to the king
- Es 7:5-10—*The king investigated Esther's words* questioning her as to the specifics; *Haman is hanged on gallows*

 B) Es 8:1-14—"For an *edict* which is written in the *king's* name . . . *may not be revoked"*; "I have given Haman's *estate* to Esther"; "you may *write in the name of the king"*; Mordecai's *letter* was *promulgated in every province*; each *people in its own language. . .* in *their own script and language*; permission for the *Jews to defend themselves*; Haman was *killed*

A) Es 8:15-17—A feast and a holiday; Mordecai's apparel was *white, turquoise and purple*; he wore a *gold* crown

The main point is the central axis. Remember, often the central axis is the most important point of the chiastic structure, but other times it is the turning point of the story. In the book of Esther, the central axis serves both purposes. Can you determine the Messianic significance of it? Remember, whenever you see someone who is supposed to die but they end up living, and the number three is present, you are into Messianic prophecy. This type of scenario is used by the Ruach (Spirit) to teach us (in a shadowy picture) about the death, burial and resurrection of the Messiah in three days. Remember, it's a shadow of the reality to come. This is the significance of the central axis of the major chiastic structure of the book of Esther! When Esther approached the king, she should have been condemned to death because she had not been summoned. However, the king extended mercy towards her in that he did not kill her even though she hadn't been summoned. Furthermore, she hadn't been summoned in *30* (see the number *THREE*!) days! This is the sign of resurrection, which is the Sign of the Messiah in Esther's life. And, it's just another example of a shadowy teaching of the death, burial and resurrection of the Messiah in three days, **<u>THE MOST PROPHESIED EVENT IN THE ENTIRE TANAKH</u>**. The paradox of our understanding is that apart from understanding the literary techniques of the Tanakh, this wisdom remains hidden. Now, we truly know why

Esther 4:11 is the central axis of the story. It's actually a Messianic prophecy of the death, burial and resurrection of the Messiah!

Now that we see the sign of the Messiah in Esther's life, we know that this particular story/scene will teach us something about the work of the Messiah. Although reluctant at first, Esther approached the king knowing that she could face death. But remember why she finally decided to approach the king. It was an attempt to SAVE HER PEOPLE from annihilation!!! A different thematic interpretation is that she was willing to lay down her life for her people, Israel! That is what Messiah Yeshua did. He was willing to give his life in order to save the lives of His entire people (see Luke 22:42)! This central axis in the book of Esther is actually a teaching on the death, burial and resurrection of the Messiah. It also teaches us He will lay down his life for His people. This is all pictured for us through Adonai's willing servant, Esther. Baruch HaShem!!! There's more in the Book of Esther of course, but that's a subject for another day. Let's return to the pictures that David's life paints for us.

Thus, David's lament to die on behalf of Absalom is actually the heart of the Messiah. We see this taught thematically here in II Samuel 18:33 as well as with other Messianic figures, including Joshua's two spies and Esther.

Earlier, I emphasized two main points concerning II Samuel 19:5-8. Instead of rejoicing over the defeat of Absalom, David's men were behaving as if they had lost the battle through cowardice. In actuality, they should have rejoiced in their great victory; however, information about David caused them to lose heart. The thematic parallel to the Gospel accounts is very straightforward. According to John 20:19 the disciples were hiding from the Jews because of fear!

> Then, the same day at evening, being the first day of the week, when *the doors were shut where the disciples were assembled, for fear of the Jews*, Jesus came and stood in the midst, and said to them, "Peace be with you."

How is this thematically connected to II Samuel 19:5-8? Yeshua had just won the greatest battle planet Earth has ever witnessed! According to Hebrews 2:14-15 and Colossians 2:14-15, Yeshua won a great victory by triumphing over hasatan through His death! In other words, just as in the battle with Absalom, so likewise with the battle against hasatan. Both David's men and the disciples should have been rejoicing in their respective victories. But, in both cases, the servants of the victor were actually ashamed even though a victory had been won. Why did David's men lose heart? Because of the report they heard about David. Similarly, Yeshua's disciples were downtrodden, as well, because of the report concerning Yeshua. They believed the report that He had died and was not resurrected. They lost hope thinking that theirs was a lost cause, and just like David's men, they were not able to rejoice in the great victory that had actually taken place.

The second point I made earlier is that both David and Yeshua are hidden from the view of their respective followers. David was in a chamber and out of view of his followers and Yeshua was not present with His disciples. What did Joab tell David he needed to do in order to restore the confidence of his followers? According to II Samuel 19:7-8, Joab told David that he needed to go and appear to his followers so that they could see him and not lose heart. So David went and sat in the gate.

Next, a dispute arose among the tribes of Israel (the ten northern tribes) concerning whether or not to support David as their king. But, in the end, they decided to receive him as their king. This put the tribes of Judah and Benjamin in a bad light since they had been reluctant in receiving David back. Remember, although some of those in the tribes of Judah/Benjamin supported David and left to be with him during the failed coup, many of them supported Absalom. In fact, Amasa, a relative of David, was the commander of Absalom's army! Thus, as David returned, it was noticed that not all of Judah/Benjamin had come to welcome him back. David, therefore, devised a plan to win their trust. This is recorded for us in II Samuel 19:11-14.

> [11]So King David sent to Zadok and Abiathar the priests, saying, "Speak to the elders of Judah, saying, 'Why are you the last to bring the king back to his house, since the words of all Israel have come to the king, to his very house? *[12]You are my brethren, you are my bone and my flesh. Why then are you the last to bring back the king?' [13]And say to Amasa, 'Are you not my bone and my flesh? God do so to me, and more also, if you are not commander of the army before me continually in place of Joab.'"* [14]So he swayed the hearts of all the men of Judah, just as the heart of one man, so that they sent this word to the king: "Return, you and all your servants (II Samuel 19:11-14)!"

David's plan was simple. He made an offer of reconciliation to Amasa, the military leader of the failed coup attempt. David figured that once those who had sided with Absalom heard of his kindness to Amasa they would return.

As with David, so with Yeshua. Yeshua needed to restore the confidence of His disciples who had totally lost heart, believing that He was dead. In order to do this, He appeared to them just as David made himself known to his followers by sitting in the city gate. This is recorded for us in Luke 24:36-39 and John 20:19-20.

> [36]Now as they said these things, Jesus Himself stood in the midst of them, and said to them, "Peace to you." [37]But they were terrified and frightened, and supposed they had seen a spirit. [38]And He said to them, "Why are you troubled? And why do doubts arise in your hearts? *[39]Behold My hands and My feet, that it is I Myself. Handle Me and see, for a spirit does not have flesh and bones as you see I have* (Luke 24:36-39)."

> [19]Then, the same day at evening, being the first day of the week, when the doors were shut where the disciples were assembled, for fear of the Jews, Jesus came and stood in the midst, and said to them, "Peace be with you." [20]When He had said this, *He showed them His hands and His side. Then the disciples were glad when they saw the Lord* (John 20:19-20).

When David made his offer of reconciliation to Amasa he used a particular phrase:

> [12]You are my brethren, you are *my bone and my flesh*. Why then are you the last to bring back the king?' [13]And say to Amasa, '*Are you not my bone and my flesh?* God do so to me, and more also, if you are not commander of the army before me continually in place of Joab (II Samuel 19:12-13).

Notice David's emphasis on the subject of *flesh and bone*! In a thematic parallel, Yeshua restored the confidence of His disciples by 1) appearing to them and 2) having them examine His *flesh and bones*! Moreover, Yeshua posed a question regarding *flesh and bones* just as David did! Baruch HaShem! Once again, we have another perfect thematic match at the right time. The next chapter will be our last. In it, we will see the conclusion of all that David's flight from Absalom has to offer us concerning our Messiah Yeshua.

Running Chart of the Thematic Connections Between II Samuel 15:10 – 20:2 and the Gospels

II Samuel	The Gospels
II Samuel 18:21—Joab told the Cushite to go tell the good news of Absalom's demise	**Matthew 28:6-7 and Mark 16:6-7**—Angels told the women to go tell the good news of Yeshua's resurrection
II Samuel 18:27a—The emphasis on the feet of Ahimaaz	**Matthew 28:9-10**—The women embraced Yeshua's feet
II Samuel 18:29-31—Ahimaaz outran the Cushite to David; Ahimaaz has to step aside and wait for the Cushite to arrive	**John 20:3-4**—John outran Peter to the tomb; John stepped aside and waited for Peter to arrive
II Samuel 19:3-4—David's men stole back into the city in shame as if they'd lost the battle even though they had won a great victory; David's men had lost heart because of David's lament over Absalom	**John 20:19**—Yeshua's disciples were hiding in a room for fear of the Jews, as if all hope was lost, when in reality, Yeshua had won the greatest victory; the disciples were heartbroken concerning Yeshua's death
II Samuel 19:5-8 and 11-14—Joab told David he needed to appear before his servants to turn their hearts back to him; David appealed to "flesh and blood" to win the trust of his servants	**Luke 24:36-39 and John 20:19-20**—Yeshua appeared to His disciples to turn their hearts from unbelief to faith; Yeshua appealed to "flesh and blood" to win the trust of His disciples

Chapter 8

The Complete Picture

Introduction

This is the last chapter of our journey through II Samuel 15:10 – 20:2. Throughout our study we have discovered how this passage thematically parallels the four gospels. The previous chapters gave us prophetic glimpses of events which transpired before Yeshua's final hours alive until after His resurrection. Chapter 7 focused mainly on a proper understanding of the gospel and those events that occurred immediately after the resurrection of Yeshua, including His attempts to convince the disciples He had truly risen from the dead. Therefore, we should expect that this last portion of David's prophetic picture will concentrate on other events recorded in the last sections of the gospels.

The Benefits of Yeshua's Sufferings

David's Prophetic Picture

Let's begin our study with a perusal of II Samuel 19:16-23, the story of Shimei's approach to David upon his return. In order to understand the significance of David's actions towards Shimei, you must recall what happened when David fled from Jerusalem. II Samuel 16:5-8 records this event for us in detail.

> ⁵Now when King David came to Bahurim, there was a man from the family of the house of Saul, whose name was Shimei the son of Gera, coming from there. *He came out, cursing continuously as he came.* ⁶*And he threw stones at David and at all the servants of King David.* And all the people and all the mighty men were on his right hand and on his left. ⁷Also *Shimei said thus when he cursed: "Come out! Come out! You bloodthirsty man, you rogue!* ⁸*The LORD has brought upon you all the blood of the house of Saul, in whose place you have reigned*; and the LORD has delivered the kingdom into the hand of Absalom your son. So now you are caught in your own evil, because you are a bloodthirsty man!"

As you can, see Shimei railed upon David and falsely accused him of being a bloodthirsty man! Notice his scathing rebuke of David. Obviously, he would never have said these things had not David been on the run. Well, the tide has turned, and as David returned to Jerusalem, Shimei was one of the first people to greet him. Now, with the reminder of how he treated David when he fled from Jerusalem, notice how Shimei approached David.

> Now Shimei the son of Gera fell down before the king when he had crossed the Jordan. ¹⁹ Then he said to the king, "***Do not let my lord impute iniquity to me, or remember what wrong your servant did*** on the day that my lord the king left Jerusalem, that the king should take *it* to heart. ²⁰ For I, your servant, know that ***I have sinned***. Therefore here I am, the first to come today of all the house of Joseph to go down to meet my lord the king (II Samuel 19:18b-20)."

Shimei approached David in repentance. Obviously, one should doubt the sincerity of his "repentance." After all, what was the basis for his change of heart? It was simply self-preservation. True repentance would have occurred had he approached David while he was still on the run. Instead, it was not until David was restored to authority and had the power of life or death over his soul that he "repented." My point is simple. *If there was anyone who deserved to die, it was Shimei.* His actions in II Samuel 16:5-8 demonstrated that he had clearly sided with Absalom in his rebellion. Truly, Shimei placed himself among the opposition. One of David's soldiers, Abishai, realized Shimei's hypocrisy and wanted to take his head off.

> ²¹ But Abishai the son of Zeruiah answered and said, "Shall not Shimei be put to death for this, because he cursed the LORD's anointed (II Samuel 19:21)?"

Also, please pay particular attention to the words used by Shimei when he approached David. "***Do not let my lord impute iniquity to me,*** or remember what wrong your servant did . . . For I, your servant, know that ***I have sinned*** (II Samuel 19:19-20). Even Shimei knew he had sinned and deserved to die! Although this should have been his fate, note how David responded to this situation.

> ²² And David said, "What have I to do with you, you sons of Zeruiah, that you should be adversaries to me today? ***Shall any man be put to death today in Israel***? For do I not know that today I *am* king over Israel?" ²³ Therefore the king said to Shimei, "***You shall not die.***" And the king swore to him (II Samuel 19:22-23).

Clearly, the predominant theme of this passage pertains to forgiveness from sin. It's not a coincidence that it occurs at this point in David's prophetic picture of the work of Yeshua our Messiah.

Yeshua's Prophetic Fulfillment

This story will help us understand *why* the Messiah had to die. In our studies we have seen many pictures of the death, burial and resurrection of the Messiah (the most prophesied event in the entirety of the Tanakh, I might add!). As one endeavors to explain any subject, an effort should be made to answer the following questions—who, what, when, where, why and how. I have endeavored to show how the Tanakh's prophetic pictures explain the who, what, when, where, why and how of Messianic prophecy. For example, previous chapters describe in detail how the story of Absalom's rebellion contained a picture of Yeshua's death on the tree. A few of the facts concerning the Messiah's work of salvation included answers to the following questions:

- WHO is this prophecy about? This passage pertains to the Messiah.
- WHAT will happen to the Messiah? He will die.
- WHEN will this event occur? This event will occur at His first advent.
- WHERE will these events occur? These events will occur in Jerusalem and be associated with the Mount of Olives.
- WHY will the Messiah need to die? The story of Esther taught us that He will die to save His people from death.
- HOW will the Messiah die? He will die (be hung on a tree to die, be buried and resurrected) within the context of betrayal by his trusted friends.

These are just a few of the things we've learned and they are by no means exhaustive. In this section, we will understand another teaching on *why* the Messiah died on our behalf.

First, let's put the story of Shimei in chronological and prophetic context. We have seen that Shimei's request for forgiveness occurred after David won his battle against Absalom and began his return to Jerusalem. We have also noted that David's victory over Absalom contained a picture of Yeshua's death, burial and resurrection. Thus, prophetically, we are now at a point after Yeshua's resurrection. It is important to know this because it helps put the story of Shimei's return in context. How? The story of Shimei's repentant approach to David is a teaching on the benefits of Yeshua's sufferings – the forgiveness of sins! In other words, it's only appropriate that a story about forgiveness should occur after the story of the death, burial and resurrection of Yeshua – which is the gospel, the very basis for the forgiveness of sins.

In the previous section, we saw that Shimei surely did not deserve to be forgiven. Yet, David forgave him. This is simply a picture of the goal of Yeshua's death. Through His death He secured forgiveness of sins for mankind. Furthermore, we can infer that Shimei's story teaches us that we receive forgiveness for even our rebellious sins! Earlier, I had you note Shimei's statement:

¹⁹ Then he said to the king, "***Do not let my lord impute iniquity to me, or remember what wrong your servant did*** on the day that my lord the king left Jerusalem, that the king should take *it* to heart (II Samuel 19:19)."

Look at the phrase, "Do not let my lord impute iniquity to me, or remember what wrong your servant did." Have you noticed the theological importance of the following two phrases uttered from Shimei?

- Do not let my lord impute iniquity to me.
- Do not remember what wrong your servant did.

These two phrases describe the work of the Messiah perfectly! The Tanakh itself uses these phrases to describe the work that God does in forgiving His children.

- ¹ Blessed is he whose transgression is forgiven, Whose sin is covered. ² ***Blessed is the man to whom the LORD does not impute iniquity***, And in whose spirit there is no deceit (Psalm 32:1-2).
- "I, even I, am He who blots out your transgressions for My own sake; And ***I will not remember your sins*** (Isaiah 43:25)."
- No more shall every man teach his neighbor, and every man his brother, saying, 'Know the LORD,' for they all shall know Me, from the least of them to the greatest of them, says the LORD. For I will forgive their iniquity, ***and their sin I will remember no more*** (Jeremiah 31:34)."

Shimei used the very phrases that Adonai inspired the prophets to use when describing His forgiveness of us! As we quote from references in the Tanakh we must be careful not to miss their Messianic importance. For example, one may be tempted to read the following narrow-minded view into the three verses listed above:

These verses don't have anything to do with the Messiah. They are simply verses stating that Adonai would forgive the penitent Israelite who made the proper sacrifices. These passages simply describe forgiveness for the Jew under the first covenant.

Such a view totally misses the point of the first covenant and the purpose of animal sacrifice in the Tanakh. Animal sacrifice was meant to teach about redemption and forgiveness of sins *through the Messiah*. The view that Israelites were forgiven based on "Old Testament" sacrifices is erroneous. The sins of the "Old Testament" saints were forgiven based on the eternal sacrifice of Yeshua - not the blood of bulls and goats.

- ¹ For the law, having a shadow of the good things to come, and not the very image of the things, can never with these same sacrifices, which they offer continually year by year, make those who approach perfect. ² For then would they not have ceased to be offered? For the worshipers, once purified, would have had no more consciousness of sins. ³ But in those sacrifices there is a reminder of sins every year. ⁴ ***For it is not possible that the blood of bulls and goats could take away sins . . .*** ¹¹***And every priest stands ministering daily and offering repeatedly the same sacrifices, which can never take away sins*** (Hebrews 10:1-4, 11).
- ¹¹ But Christ came as High Priest of the good things to come, with the greater and more perfect tabernacle not made with hands, that is, not of this creation. ¹² Not with the blood of goats and calves, but with His own blood He entered the Most Holy Place once for all, having obtained eternal redemption. ¹³ For if the blood of bulls and goats and the ashes of a heifer, sprinkling the unclean, sanctifies for the purifying of the flesh, ¹⁴ how much more shall the blood of Christ, who through the eternal Spirit offered Himself without spot to God, cleanse your conscience from dead works to serve the living God? ¹⁵ And for this reason He is the Mediator of the new covenant, ***by means of death, for***

- *²¹ But now the righteousness of God apart from the law is revealed, being witnessed by the Law and the Prophets, ²² even the righteousness of God, through faith in Jesus Christ, to all and on all who believe. For there is no difference; ²³ for all have sinned and fall short of the glory of God, ²⁴ being justified freely by His grace through the redemption that is in Christ Jesus, ²⁵ whom God set forth as a propitiation by His blood, through faith, to demonstrate His righteousness, because in His forbearance God had passed over the sins that were previously committed, ²⁶ to demonstrate at the present time His righteousness, that He might be just and the justifier of the one who has faith in Jesus (Romans 3:21-26).*

These three passages clearly teach the following:

- The sacrifices offered during first covenant never took away the sins of the penitent Israelite. Furthermore, that was not their purpose.
- Yeshua's death provided the atonement/remission of sins for those who transgressed under the first covenant as well as those of us who have transgressed under the second covenant.

Adonai's eternal purpose was always centered around the sacrificial death of Messiah Yeshua to provide remission of sins for every human being who put their trust in Him regardless of whether they sinned during the time period of the first or second covenant. The necessity of Yeshua's sacrifice and its focus as the goal of the sacrifices offered during the first covenant is beautifully demonstrated in Psalm 40:6-8, which is expounded upon by the writer of the letter to the Hebrews.

- *⁵ Therefore, when He came into the world, He said: "Sacrifice and offering You did not desire, but a body You have prepared for Me. ⁶ In burnt offerings and sacrifices for sin You had no pleasure. ⁷ Then I said, 'Behold, I have come—in the volume of the book it is written of Me—to do Your will, O God.'" ⁸ Previously saying, "Sacrifice and offering, burnt offerings, and offerings for sin You did not desire, nor had pleasure in them"* (which are offered according to the law), *⁹ then He said, "Behold, I have come to do Your will, O God." He takes away the first that He may establish the second. ¹⁰ By that will we have been sanctified through the offering of the body of Jesus Christ once for all. ¹¹ And every priest stands ministering daily and offering repeatedly the same sacrifices, which can never take away sins. ¹² But this Man, after He had offered one sacrifice for sins forever, sat down at the right hand of God, ¹³ from that time waiting till His enemies are made His footstool. ¹⁴ For by one offering He has perfected forever those who are being sanctified. ¹⁵ But the Holy Spirit also witnesses to us; for after He had said before, ¹⁶ "This is the covenant that I will make with them after those days, says the LORD: I will put My laws into their hearts, and in their minds I will write them," ¹⁷ then He adds, "Their sins and their lawless deeds I will remember no more." ¹⁸ Now where there is remission of these, there is no longer an offering for sin (Hebrews 10:5-18).*

Psalm 40:6-8 simply shows us that the blood sacrifices of the first covenant were not the ultimate goal of the Father. His goal was realized through the Son who came to do the Father's will by giving His life as a ransom-offering for our souls. Note how the writer of the book of Hebrews beautifully connects Isaiah 43:25 and Jeremiah 31:34 (Their sins and their lawless deeds I will remember no more) to the work of Yeshua referenced in Psalm 40:6-8. He knew that the basis for Adonai not remembering Israel's sins was found in the sacrifice of Yeshua who offered His body, the goal to which the Levitical sacrifices pointed.

Thus, Psalm 32:1-2 and Isaiah 43:25 clearly have the sacrificial work of Yeshua in mind as the basis for 1) the blessedness of the man to whom the Lord does not impute iniquity and 2) remembering their sins no more. As I stated earlier, it's amazing that Shimei's words to David contained the two statements concerning what Messiah Yeshua accomplished through His death, burial and resurrection!

[19] Then he said to the king, "*Do not let my lord impute iniquity to me, or remember what wrong your servant did* on the day that my lord the king left Jerusalem, that the king should take *it* to heart (II Samuel 19:19)."

The story of forgiveness secured by Shimei from David is a prophecy of the primary benefit of Yeshua's work of salvation! For even more evidence, consider how our key verses from the book of Psalms are used elsewhere in the New Testament writings.

[5] But to him who does not work but believes on Him who justifies the ungodly, his faith is accounted for righteousness, [6] just as *David also describes the blessedness of the man to whom God imputes righteousness apart from works*: [7] " Blessed are those whose lawless deeds are forgiven, And whose sins are covered; [8] *Blessed is the man to whom the LORD shall not impute sin* (Romans 4:5-8)."

Do you think it's a coincidence that Paul referenced Psalm 32:1-2 as an example of one who has received forgiveness from the Messiah? Is it a coincidence that Paul uses the phrase, "shall not impute sin?" When David penned Psalm 32, may he have thought of Shimei's words and how he had forgiven Shimei of his sins. Notice once more how Shimei's words (*Do not let my lord impute iniquity to me*) are used by Paul in II Corinthians to describe the forgiveness of sins we have obtained through Yeshua's sacrificial death!

[18] Now all things are of God, who has reconciled us to Himself through Jesus Christ, and has given us the ministry of reconciliation, [19] that is, that God was in Christ reconciling the world to Himself, *not imputing their trespasses to them*, and has committed to us the word of reconciliation. [20] Now then, we are ambassadors for Christ, as though God were pleading through us: we implore you on Christ's behalf, be reconciled to God. [21] For He made Him who knew no sin to be sin for us, that we might become the righteousness of God in Him (II Corinthians 5:18-21).

Truly, David's forgiveness of Shimei is a prophetic picture of the forgiveness we receive through Yeshua, and it is not without a parallel in the gospels.

²¹ So Jesus said to them again, "Peace to you! As the Father has sent Me, I also send you." ²² And when He had said this, He breathed on them, and said to them, "Receive the Holy Spirit. ²³ *If you forgive the sins of any, they are forgiven them; if you retain the sins of any, they are retained* (John 20:21-23)."

As you can see, John 20:21-23 is a story about forgiveness of sins obtained through the death, burial and resurrection of the Messiah. However, we have yet another thematic parallel in the gospels where Shimei's request for forgiveness seems to be a prophetic glimpse into future events. Luke 24:46-49 records some of Yeshua's last words before His ascension into heaven.

⁴⁶ Then He said to them, "Thus it is written, and thus it was necessary for the Christ to suffer and to rise from the dead the third day, ⁴⁷ *and that repentance and remission of sins should be preached in His name to all nations*, beginning at Jerusalem. ⁴⁸ And you are witnesses of these things. ⁴⁹ Behold, I send the Promise of My Father upon you; but tarry in the city of Jerusalem until you are endued with power from on high."

This passage echoes the theme of forgiveness of sin through the Messiah, which in case you haven't noticed, is the point being prophesied of through the story of Shimei's forgiveness. This message of remission of sins is the direct result of Yeshua's work of atonement. I can't help but notice how II Corinthians 5:18-21 (referenced above) contains verbiage that thematically connects II Samuel 19:19-20 to Luke 24:46-49. It's as if II Corinthians is a bridge thematically connecting these two passages.

- II Corinthians 5:19 states, "God was in Christ reconciling the world to Himself, *not imputing their trespasses to them*," whereas Shimei stated, *"Do not let my lord impute iniquity to me."*
- II Corinthians 5:20 states, *"Now then, we are ambassadors for Christ*, as though God were pleading through us: we implore you on Christ's behalf, be reconciled to God," whereas Luke 24:47-48 states, *"and that repentance and remission of sins should be preached in His name to all nations*, beginning at Jerusalem. And you are witnesses of these things." Clearly, the common connection is the sending forth of the disciples to preach repentance and remission of sins.

Concerning Shimei, Ziba and Mephibosheth

David's Prophetic Picture

The next portion of scripture I'd like to look at is II Samuel 19:15-39. Even though we've covered these verses in the previous section, it has more to reveal to us. First, let's start by breaking this passage into some more manageable thematic chunks. A quick glance over this passage reveals the following three major stories.

- The story of how Shimei approached David seeking forgiveness for his past sins
- The story of how Mephibosheth approached David and explained why he didn't join with David when he fled from Jerusalem
- The story of how Barzillai approached David and secured blessings for Chimham (who was probably Barzillai's son).

It is easy to group these three stories together because they share some common themes. For example, note how all three stories began.

- And Shimei the son of Gera, a Benjamite, who was from Bahurim, *hurried and came down* with the men of Judah *to meet King David* (II Samuel 19:16).
- Now Mephibosheth the son of Saul *came down to meet the king* (II Samuel 19:24a).
- And Barzillai the Gileadite came *down from Rogelim* and went across the Jordan with the king, *to escort him* across the Jordan (II Samuel 19:31).

Other themes clearly connecting these three stories include the fact that 1) each of these three individuals approached David, 2) they all wanted to help escort David back to Jerusalem and 3) each person who approached David walked away with a blessing of some sort. Surely, these three stories are related. At a literal level they represent blessings and gifts of grace bestowed by David. In fact, although all three individuals received blessings from David, they actually represent three distinct situations. Barzillai clearly deserved his blessing. He was faithful to the king from the beginning. You will recall that he brought the king provisions when he fled from Absalom. We learned earlier that Mephibosheth had remained faithful to David; however, he was framed by Ziba, and David wasn't sure whether or not Mephibosheth had betrayed him. Yet, he still obtained a blessing. Shimei is the one who outright rejected David and yet he received the blessing of forgiveness. So, as you can see, from David's perspective, each individual related to him based on a different level of faithfulness.

Of these three stories, we should guess that the stories of Shimei and Mephibosheth would be more closely related. Why? Because, in David's mind neither of them had been totally faithful to him by supporting him in his dark hour of testing.[61] In contrast, Barzillai was faithful from beginning to end.

Let's begin with the story of Shimei's approach to David. Notice that Ziba also came with Shimei (II Samuel 19:17). We already know that Shimei had rejected king David and was only approaching to save his hide. Therefore, I think it interesting that Ziba approached with Shimei. Why didn't Ziba stay with the king? He left with the king, so how did he wind up teaming with Shimei? I don't know. But I do know that Ziba was a thief! He slandered Mephibosheth so that he could get his property. His connection here with Shimei is just another piece of evidence pointing to his shady motives. You will recall from Chapter 3 that we thematically connected Ziba's actions to Hushai's actions of "betrayal."[62] Thus, in each direction we find thematic evidence pointing to Ziba's unwholesome character. How fitting that he appeared with Shimei.

Quite often we gain quite a bit of insight by stepping back and looking at the big picture in a passage. Let's do this with Shimei. Shimei appears twice in our foundational passage – once in II Samuel 16:5-13 and again in II Samuel 19:16-23. If we compare and contrast his two appearances we can see a stark contrast in behavior. In fact, we most certainly should compare his first and second appearances in this story because they are thematically connected through our major chiastic structure!

  B)

    C)

      D)

        E) II Samuel 16:5-13—*David came to Bahurim*; Shimei *came out to meet David*; *Abishai wanted to kill Shimei*; *David forgave Shimei*;

          E`) II Samuel 19:16-23—*Shimei was from Bahurim*; he *hastened to meet the king*; *Abishai wanted to kill Shimei*; Shimei *begged David for forgiveness*;

      D')

    C')

  B')

In previous chapters we've seen how a passage in one half of a chiastic structure helps shine light on its thematic equivalent in the other half. Applying this strategy here we can see the following contrast. Shimei's first appearance occurred when David was fleeing from Absalom. We are told that Shimei rejected David, cursing him as he and his men fled from Absalom. In his second appearance, Shimei is seen asking David for forgiveness and seeking to be restored back in good graces with King David.

The second story of interest is the story of Mephibosheth's approach toward David (II Samuel 19:24-30). The major theme of this story is the question of Mephibosheth's loyalty. When David fled, Mephibosheth did not join David and David wants to know why. As we learned in Chapter 3, Ziba slandered Mephibosheth who was lame and not able to catch up with David. What's most important though, is how David questioned Mephibosheth concerning his loyalty. Remember that II Samuel 19:24-30 is thematically connected to II Samuel 16:1-4 through our main chiastic structure. II Samuel 16:1-4 relates how Ziba showed false loyalty to David and accused Mephibosheth of being disloyal. This story took place within the context of other people who approached David to demonstrate their loyalty to him as he fled from Absalom. The dominant theme is loyalty to David. In the next section, let's see how these stories interact and support one another to complete a significant prophetic foreshadowing.

Yeshua's Prophetic Fulfillment

Throughout our study we have seen how various characters in II Samuel 15:10 – 20:2 cast shadows that represent some of the people we read about in the gospels. Beyond a shadow of doubt[63] Ahithophel is a portrait of Judas. Absalom's death is a picture of Yeshua's death and David's calamity is a picture of the Messiah's passion. But what about Shimei? Could he represent anyone? Let's see.

First, let's concentrate on the story of Shimei's approach to David. In the previous section, we just noted the two faces of Shimei, once during David's flight from Absalom and again during David's return. Perhaps if we put David's actions in prophetic perspective we will be able to see another aspect of Shimei's significance. David's flight from Absalom prophetically represents the beginning of Yeshua's betrayal. In Chapter 3, we saw how events in II Samuel 16 were thematically equivalent to the scenes sketched for us in the Garden of Gethsemane by the gospel writers. David's return to Jerusalem in II Samuel 19 is thematically equivalent to those events that occurred after Yeshua's resurrection. Now let's look at Shimei's actions through the prophetic lens. Can we think of someone who rejected Yeshua as he was led away to be executed, but later sought forgiveness after Yeshua's resurrection? Yes, we can. The evidence points to Peter. How can we be sure? Please note the following themes that connect Shimei and Peter.

- Shimei rejected David (II Samuel 16:5-13), whereas Peter rejected Yeshua (Matthew 26:34, Mark 14:66-72).
- Shimei cursed David as he fled from Jerusalem (II Samuel 16:5-8), whereas Peter began to curse and swear when he was accused of being associated with Yeshua (Matthew 26:74).

Do we have any other evidence that places Peter at this chronological point? Yes, we have also seen another allusion to him in II Samuel 16:5-14. Once again we can use elements E and E' of our major chiastic structure to provide more thematic evidence that there are allusions to Peter in II Samuel 19:15-23. If you recall, in Chapter 3 we connected Peter to Abishai! Remember, initially Peter wanted to use the sword to protect Yeshua just as Abishai wanted to take off Shimei's head. However, Yeshua rebuked Peter just as David rebuked Abishai, not wanting His disciples to kill those confronting Him. Thus, we have multiple evidences thematically pointing to Peter at this chronological point in our story.

Next, recall the story of Mephibosheth's approach to David. You will recall that the major topic associated with that passage was the question of Mephibosheth's loyalty to David, because he was under the impression that Mephibosheth had left him when he fled from Absalom. Certainly, you can see the parallel to Yeshua's questioning of Peter in John 21? Thus it seems that we have determined the prophetic reason why, as we discovered in the previous section, the stories of Shimei's and Mephibosheth's approach to David are so closely thematically connected. Taken together they sketch a portrait of the actions of Peter! It should not surprise us that two individuals from the Tanakh are used to paint the picture of one person in the gospels. We've seen this before. Remember the cupbearer and the baker, who together provided the shadowy image of Messiah Yeshua? In Chapter 5 we saw how both Jonathan and Ahimaaz were used to show us a picture of Yeshua's death and resurrection. There are many other examples, but that should suffice for now. Here is a list of thematic connections we can make to connect Peter to Shimei and Mephibosheth.

- When David fled from Absalom he was under the impression that Mephibosheth had forsaken him (II Samuel 16:1-4 and II Samuel 19:25), whereas Peter actually forsook Yeshua during His sufferings (Matthew 26:34 and Mark 14:66-72).
- David questioned Mephibosheth's loyalty (II Samuel 19:25), whereas Yeshua questioned Peter's loyalty (John 21:15-19).
- David forgave Mephibosheth for "forsaking him"[64] (II Samuel 19:29), whereas Yeshua forgave Peter (John 21:15-19).[65]

- Mephibosheth was frustrated that David questioned him so about his loyalty (II Samuel 19:27-28). The gospels state that Peter "was grieved" the third time Yeshua questioned him about his love for Him (John 21:17).

Barzillai, the Faithful Servant

David's Prophetic Picture

The last story concerning someone coming to escort king David across the Jordan pertains to a man named Barzillai. Unlike Shimei and Mephibosheth, Barzillai was one who had shown unswerving loyalty to David. His story is recorded in II Samuel 19:31-39. David gave Barzillai a personal invitation to come to Jerusalem where he would care for him.

And the king said to Barzillai, "*Come across with me*, and *I will provide for you* while you are with me in Jerusalem (II Samuel 19:33)."

What follows is a curious discussion concerning Barzillai's ability to be of use to David. Apparently, Barzillai had lived a long life (he was 80 years old) and many of his senses were on the wane. He complained that his sense of taste and hearing were of no use anymore. Furthermore, he confided that his sense of discernment wasn't so good. Based on these assessments he felt that he was of no use to David.

- ³⁴ But Barzillai said to the king, "How long have I to live, that I should go up with the king to Jerusalem? ³⁵ *I am today eighty years old. Can I discern between the good and bad? Can your servant taste what I eat or what I drink? Can I hear any longer the voice of singing men and singing women*? Why then should your servant be a further burden to my lord the king? ³⁶ Your servant will go a little way across the Jordan with the king. And why should the king repay me with such a reward (II Samuel 19:33-36)?

Based on his self-assessment, he felt it better to concern himself with preparations for his impending death and for David to show any kindness due him to his son[66] Chimham.

- ³⁷ Please *let your servant turn back again, that I may die in my own city, near the grave of my father and mother. But here is your servant Chimham; let him cross over with my lord the king, and do for him what seems good to you.*" ³⁸ And the king answered, "Chimham shall cross over with me, and I will do for him what seems good to you. Now whatever you request of me, I will do for you." ³⁹ Then all the people went over the Jordan. And when the king had crossed over, the king kissed Barzillai and blessed him, and he returned to his own place (II Samuel 19:37-39).

The curious points are as follows. It seems this story focuses on three main themes. First, Barzillai is concerned with his old age and imminent death. Secondly, at a time when one would expect Barzillai to be wise and full of discernment, he seemed to have strong reservations concerning his ability to perceive things correctly. Finally, this story focuses on how the blessing due Barzillai will be bestowed (at his request) to another.

Yeshua's Prophetic Fulfillment

We just learned that Barzillai's judgment wasn't so keen. He lacked the ability to make proper assessments of his situation. As we read through the gospels we are presented with a similar scenario concerning the sense of understanding of the disciples! Like Barzillai, they were veterans when it came to understanding the Messiah. They, like no other individuals had been with Yeshua throughout His ministry. Yeshua told His disciples many times that He would suffer, die, be buried and raised from the dead in three days. He did not hide this fact from them! He told them point blank that these events would occur. Yet, after His death and resurrection we read numerous times of the doubt and unbelief of the disciples. I'm suggesting that Barzillai is a picture of Yeshua's disciples. Just as Barzillai should have been at a point in his life to exercise good, wise judgment and discernment concerning the affairs of life, so likewise, the disciples should have been at a point in their lives where they could make proper judgments concerning the events Yeshua clearly spoke to them about.

He rebuked their unbelief and hardness of heart, because they did not believe those who had seen Him after He had risen.

- ⁹ Now when He rose early on the first day of the week, He appeared first to Mary Magdalene, out of whom He had cast seven demons. ¹⁰ She went and told those who had been with Him, as they mourned and wept. ¹¹ And when they heard that He was alive and had been seen by her, *they did not believe.* ¹² After that, He appeared in another form to two of them as they walked and went into the country. ¹³ And they went and told it to the rest, *but they did not believe them either.* ¹⁴ Later He appeared to the eleven as they sat at the table; and *He rebuked their unbelief and hardness of heart, because they did not believe those who had seen Him after He had risen* (Mark 16:9-14).
- ¹ Now on the first day of the week, very early in the morning, they, and certain other women with them, came to the tomb bringing the spices which they had prepared. ² But they found the stone rolled away from the tomb. ³ Then they went in and did not find the body of the Lord Jesus. ⁴ And it happened, as they were greatly perplexed about this, that behold, two men stood by them in shining garments. ⁵ Then, as they were afraid and bowed their faces to the earth, they said to them, "Why do you seek the living among the dead? ⁶ He is not here, but is risen! *Remember how He spoke to you when He was still in Galilee,* ⁷ *saying, 'The Son of Man must be delivered into the hands of sinful men, and be crucified, and the third day rise again.'"* ⁸ And they remembered His words. ⁹ Then they returned from the tomb and told all these things to the eleven and to all the rest. ¹⁰ It was Mary Magdalene, Joanna, Mary the mother of James, and the other women with them, who told these things to the apostles. ¹¹ *And their words seemed to them like idle tales, and they did not believe them* (Luke 24:1-11).
- Then He said to them, *"O foolish ones, and slow of heart to believe* in all that the prophets have spoken (Luke 24:25)!"

- But while *they still did not believe for joy*, and marveled, He said to them, "Have you any food here?" ⁴² So they gave Him a piece of a broiled fish and some honeycomb ⁴³ And He took it and ate in their presence (Luke 24:41-43).
- The other disciples therefore said to him, "We have seen the Lord." So he said to them, "*Unless I see in His hands the print of the nails, and put my finger into the print of the nails, and put my hand into His side, I will not believe* (John 20:25)."

As you can see, the unbelief of the disciples is a major theme found within the gospel accounts of events that occurred after Yeshua's resurrection. I believe the story of Barzillai's lack of discernment is a great shadow of the lack of discernment of the disciples who failed to "believe in all that the prophets have spoken," and especially of all that Yeshua had spoken.

The other peculiar aspect of Barzillai's statements concerned his thoughts about his death. Remember, Barzillai was an old man and was concerned about *the circumstances concerning his death*! He wanted to make proper arrangements so that his death and funeral arrangements would be taken care of. Amazingly enough, there seems to be a parallel found in the gospels!

- ¹⁸ Most assuredly, I say to you, when you were younger, you girded yourself and walked where you wished; *but when you are old, you will stretch out your hands, and another will gird you and carry you where you do not wish.*" ¹⁹ *This He spoke, signifying by what death he would glorify God.* And when He had spoken this, He said to him, "*Follow Me* (John 21:18-19)."

In this passage, Yeshua informed Peter of two facts that are thematically connected to Barzillai. First of all, both Barzillai and Peter would die when they were old. The second connection concerns where they would die. Barzillai would die where he wanted! Remember Barzillai's plans? He was making arrangements so that he could die in a particular place – "in my own city, near the grave of my father and mother." Furthermore, he had complete control over where he would die and be buried. Similarly, Yeshua made statements concerning where Peter would die. However, in stark contrast, Yeshua informed Peter he would not have any say in where he would die. It would be a decision for others to make.

Another beautiful connection concerns something Barzillai asked. In II Samuel 19:34 Barzillai asked David, "*How long have I to live*, that I should go up with the king to Jerusalem?" Amazingly enough, we can see a fulfillment of this theme in the gospels. Immediately after Yeshua informed Peter of the death by which he would glorify Him, the following conversation took place.

- ¹⁸ Most assuredly, I say to you, when you were younger, you girded yourself and walked where you wished; but when you are old, you will stretch out your hands, and another will gird you and carry you where you do not wish." ¹⁹ This He spoke, signifying by what death he would glorify God. And when He had spoken this, He said to him, "Follow Me." ²⁰ Then Peter, turning around, saw the disciple whom Jesus loved following, who also had leaned on His breast at the supper, and said, "Lord, who is the one who betrays You?" ²¹ Peter, seeing him, said to Jesus, "But Lord, what about this man?" ²² Jesus said to him, "*If I will that he remain till I come, what is that to you? You follow Me.*" ²³ *Then this saying went out among the brethren that this disciple would not die. Yet Jesus did not say to him that he would not die, but, "If I will that he remain till I come, what is that to you (John 21:18-23)?"*

A simple comparison of II Samuel 19:34 with John 21:22-23 reveals an amazing connection – how long Barzillai would live versus how long John would live!

Finally, let us take note of II Samuel 19:33.

- And the king said to Barzillai, "***Come across with me***, and I will provide for you while you are with me in Jerusalem."

Notice what David said to Barzillai – ***Come across with me***. Does this sound familiar? It should. Notice what Yeshua said to Peter in John 21:19 – "This He spoke, signifying by what death he would glorify God. And when He had spoken this, He said to him, '***Follow Me***.'" I believe the connection is self explanatory. On the one hand, I've stated that Barzillai's story is the story of the disciples in general; however, this statement by David is specifically connected to something Yeshua said to Peter!

The Restoration of the Kingdom

David's Prophetic Picture

In this last section I'd like to point out one last recurring theme that permeates the entire story of David's flight from Absalom. This prophetic story started with David as sovereign over Israel, reigning from Jerusalem. He was king in Israel, ruler of *the kingdom of Israel*. With the commencement of Absalom's attack and David's flight from Jerusalem, David's sovereignty over the kingdom was interrupted. The fact of the matter is that David relinquished control of Jerusalem and his kingship and fled into exile.

- Then the king said, "And where is your master's son?" And Ziba said to the king, "Indeed he is staying in Jerusalem, for he said, '***Today the house of Israel will restore the kingdom of my father to me*** (II Samuel 16:3).'"
- 25 Then the king said to Zadok, "Carry the ark of God back into the city. ***If I find favor in the eyes of the LORD, He will bring me back and show me both it and His dwelling place***. 26 But if He says thus: 'I have no delight in you,' here I am, let Him do to me as seems good to Him (II Samuel 15:25-26)."
- The LORD has brought upon you all the blood of the house of Saul, in whose place you have reigned; and ***the LORD has delivered the kingdom into the hand of Absalom your son***. So now you are caught in your own evil, because you are a bloodthirsty man (II Samuel 16:8)!"
- 9 Now all the people were in a dispute throughout all the tribes of Israel, saying, "The king saved us from the hand of our enemies, he delivered us from the hand of the Philistines, and ***now he has fled from the land because of Absalom***. 10 But Absalom, whom we anointed over us, has died in battle. Now therefore, why do you say nothing about ***bringing back the king*** (II Samuel 19:9-10)?"

♦ And David said, "What have I to do with you, you sons of Zeruiah, that you should be adversaries to me today? Shall any man be put to death today in Israel? *For do I not know that today I am king over Israel* (II Samuel 19:22)?"

It is interesting to review how the battle lines were drawn along particular tribal affiliations. Absalom's men were primarily from the ten tribes of Israel known later in history as Ephraim and/or the house of Israel. Although some from the men of Judah and Benjamin were part of the rebellion, most were from the men of Israel. II Samuel 19:9-10 records the discussions of those from the tribes of Israel (meaning the ten tribes or Ephraim) who had been part of Absalom's army. As they reflected on how David had saved them from their enemies, they became remorseful that they had sided with Absalom and debated about bringing the king back. Their final decision was that it would be better to go and bring David back.

In II Samuel 19:11-14, David verbally chided the men of Judah (the tribe to which he was related by blood) for not being the first to welcome him back! He recognized the fact that it was the *men of Israel* who had initially agreed to bring him back. After David skillfully regained the confidence of the men of Judah, they, along with only a few men from the tribes of Israel, went to escort the king across the Jordan back to Jerusalem. This brings us to II Samuel 19:40-43 where the scripture records, "Then behold! – All the men of Israel came to the king." At this point, there was a verbal confrontation between the men of Israel and the men of Judah over who should have the privilege of being David's primary escort back to Jerusalem. During the exchange, the men of Israel had this to say:

♦ And the men of Israel answered the men of Judah, and said, "*We have ten shares in the king*; therefore we also have more right to David than you. Why then do you despise us—were we not the first to advise bringing back our king (II Samuel 19:43)?"

Note how the men of Israel stated that they have "ten shares in the king." By this they implied that there were ten tribes of Israel versus only one tribe of Judah, and therefore they should escort the king back. Thus, we see that when David was restored as king over the nation, significant divisions along tribal lines existed.

The very last portion of our main passage, II Samuel 20:1-2, records how the tribal partisanship between the men of Israel and Judah played itself out after David had regained the kingdom. A base man by the name of Sheba took advantage of the schism regarding David's return and was able to persuade the men of Israel to rebel against David! Thus, our story ends on a bad note as the newly reunited nation found itself split again. The kingdom was divided.

Yeshua's Prophetic Fulfillment

In the last section, we noted how David had given up his kingship over Israel when he fled into exile. The last portions of the story of Absalom's rebellion are primarily concerned with the following two issues.

♦ Returning the kingship and authority to David
♦ Although the kingship had been returned to David, the kingdom of Israel remained divided and needed restoration

This last section, the story of David's return to sovereignty over Israel is a prophetic shadow of what we read in Matthew 28:18-20 and Mark 16:19-20.

- ⁱ⁸ And Jesus came and spoke to them, saying, "**All authority has been given to Me in heaven and on earth.** ¹⁹ Go therefore and make disciples of all the nations, baptizing them in the name of the Father and of the Son and of the Holy Spirit, ²⁰ teaching them to observe all things that I have commanded you; and lo, I am with you always, *even* to the end of the age." Amen (Matthew 28:18-20).
- ¹⁹ So then, after the Lord had spoken to them, He was received up into heaven, *and sat down at the right hand of God.* ²⁰ And they went out and preached everywhere, the Lord working with them and confirming the word through the accompanying signs. Amen (Mark 16:19-20).

How beautiful is the prophetic picture given to us by David. At the beginning of II Samuel 15, David reigned over Israel exercising all of his kingly authority over his subjects. With the onset of Absalom's rebellion, David temporarily lost the kingdom into the hands of his rebellious son who had convinced a large portion of the children of Israel to anoint him in place of his father. The story concludes with David receiving authority to rule over the kingdom of Israel. It's a prophetic picture. I'm not saying that Yeshua lost the kingdom! This last section of David's story is all about how authority was given to him to reign in Israel. And that is the parallel to Yeshua. All power and authority in heaven and on earth was given to Him as He sat at the right hand of the Father in heaven.

The last scripture I'd like to cover is not part of one of the gospel accounts; however, chronologically, the events it speaks of occurred during the time that Yeshua showed Himself alive to His disciples. Acts 1:1-11 is a record of events that occurred while Yeshua was still showing Himself alive to the disciples. Just before Yeshua ascended to heaven, the disciples had a pressing issue they wanted to question Him about. It is recorded for us in Acts 1:4-8.

⁴ And being assembled together with *them,* He commanded them not to depart from Jerusalem, but to wait for the Promise of the Father, "which," *He said,* "you have heard from Me; ⁵ for John truly baptized with water, but you shall be baptized with the Holy Spirit not many days from now." ⁶ ***Therefore, when they had come together, they asked Him, saying, "Lord, will You at this time restore the kingdom to Israel?"*** ⁷ And He said to them, "It is not for you to know times or seasons which the Father has put in His own authority. ⁸ But you shall receive power when the Holy Spirit has come upon you; and you shall be witnesses to Me in Jerusalem, and in all Judea and Samaria, and to the end of the earth."

Notice the issue they are concerned with – the kingdom of Israel! As I pointed out earlier, the kingdom of Israel succumbed to civil war soon after Solomon's death. At that time, the kingdom of Israel was divided into two separate warring kingdoms – the northern kingdom of Israel (also know as the House of Israel or the House of Ephraim) and the southern kingdom of Judah. Large portions of scripture record the tragic story of the division of the whole house of Israel into separate warring kingdoms. Equally important are the major portions of Messianic prophecy that promise the eventual reunification of the two houses of Israel into one nation.

This is a work of the Messiah as He alone will be able to accomplish such a task. The last story recorded for us in II Samuel 20:2, the fracturing of David's short-lived kingdom into opposing camps (men of Israel versus men of Judah), is simply the shadowy image of the necessity of the reunification of the kingdom of Israel, which is the subject of the disciples' question to Yeshua. Baruch HaShem!

Running Chart of the Thematic Connections Between II Samuel 15:10 – 20:2 and the Gospels
The Complete Picture

II Samuel	The Gospel
II Samuel 13-14—Amnon, under satanic influence from hasatan, raped Tamar, initiated events leading to David's flight from Absalom	Luke 22:1-6—Judas, under satanic influence from hasatan, agreed to betray the Messiah, thus initiating events leading to Yeshua's sufferings
II Samuel 15:13-14— David informed his servants of Absalom's evil intentions and the potential that they would suffer if he caught them	Matthew 26:20-25, Mark 14:17-21, Luke 22:21-23, John 13:21-35, John 15:18-27 and John 16:1-4—Yeshua informed His disciples of the evil intentions of the one who would betray him and of the coming persecution
II Samuel 15:15 and 19-21—II Samuel 19:40-44 is thematically connected to II Samuel 15:15 and 19-21 through the chiastic structure and shows us how the men of Judah and Israel argue over who is closest to King David. David's servants declare their loyalty to David and Ittai the Gittite declared his willingness to die for King David	Matthew 26:31-35, Mark 14:27-31, Luke 22:24-34 and John 13:36-38—The disciples argue over who will be greatest in the kingdom; then they declare their willingness to die for Yeshua; and Peter declared his loyalty to Yeshua and willingness to die for Him.
II Samuel 15:22-23—David crossed the Kidron Valley	John 18:1a—Yeshua crossed the Kidron Brook
II Samuel 15:32—David approached the summit of the Mount of Olives where he would prostrate himself as a matter of habit	Matthew 26:36-46, Mark 14:32-42, Luke 22:39-46 and John 18:1—Yeshua went to the Garden of Gethsemane on the Mount of Olives to pray as was His habit
II Samuel 15:30—David and his servants approached the Mount of Olives weeping, with their heads covered and barefoot (bearing signs of shame)	Matthew 26:36-46, Mark 14:32-42 and Luke 22:39-46—Yeshua agonized in prayer on the Mount of Olives as He contemplated His impending suffering and death, His source of shame

II Samuel 16:1-4—Ziba, Mephibosheth's servant, brought David provisions for physical strength	Luke 22:43—Yeshua was given spiritual strength by an angel
II Samuel 16:1-4—Greedy Ziba, who tricked David into giving him Mephibosheth's estate, approached David with insincere compliments (groveling, fawning, etc.) and ulterior motives; Ziba made David think that Mephibosheth had betrayed him	Matthew 26:47-50, Mark 14:43-46, Luke 22:47-48 and John 18:2-9—Judas, the greedy thief, approached Yeshua with an insincere kiss of betrayal
II Samuel 15:30-37 and 16:15-19—Ahithophel betrayed David and Hushai "betrayed" David	Matthew 26:47-50, Mark 14:43-46, Luke 22:47-48 and John 18:2-9—Judas betrayed the Messiah
II Samuel 16:5-14—David was confronted by Shimei who accused him of many wrongdoings; Abishai, David's servant, wanted to cut Shimei's head off; David submitted to Adonai's will even stating that Shimei was sent by Adonai to curse him; David informed Abishai not to harm Shimei by retaliation	Matthew 26:47-56, Mark 14:43-50, Luke 22:47-53 and John 18:2-11—Yeshua was confronted by His accusers, a multitude of people who came to arrest Him; Peter cut off the ear (on the head) of the high priest's servant; Yeshua submitted to His Father's will and didn't resist being arrested; informed His disciples not to retaliate
II Samuel 16:20-17:14—Ahithophel and Hushai gather to give Absalom counsel on how to kill David; Ahithophel promised to strike David and cause his followers to flee; Hushai wanted to bring a multitude to take David	Matthew 26:56-75, Mark 14:50-72, Luke 22:54-71 and John 18:12-23—The chief priests and elders gathered together to take counsel on how to put Yeshua to death; in direct fulfillment of Zechariah 13:7 and Ahithophel's advice, Yeshua's disciples all forsook Him; a multitude came to arrest Yeshua
II Samuel 17:14 and 23—Ahithophel committed suicide by hanging himself; details concerning Ahithophel's burial	Matthew 27:3-10—Judas hanged himself; details concerning Judas' burial place

II Samuel 17:15-24—Jonathan and Ahimaaz eluded capture by descending into a well; David eluded capture by crossing the Jordan	*The thematic significance of these prophecies in II Samuel 17:15-24 (The death, burial and resurrection of the Messiah) are out of chronological order when compared to the Gospel accounts.*	*Prophetic pictures of the death, burial and resurrection of the Messiah*

II Samuel 17:27-29—Three men brought David and his servants all sorts of provisions because they were hungry, exhausted and thirsty in the desert, needing physical help	Matthew 27:32 and Mark 15:21—Simon the Cyrenian was compelled to help Yeshua carry the cross-bar, thus helping Him at a time He needed physical help

II Samuel 18:9—Absalom was caught by his hair in an elm tree	Matthew 27:29, Mark 15:17 and John 19:2,5—Yeshua had a crown of thorns upon his head
II Samuel 18:9—Absalom was hanging from a tree between heaven and earth	Matthew 27:35, 40; Mark 15:25, 30 and 32; Luke 24:20; and John 19:17, 23—Yeshua was executed by being hung from a tree
II Samuel 18:14-18—Absalom was pierced with three spears through the heart; Absalom was killed, buried in a pit and stones were placed over the mouth of the pit	John 19:34; Matthew 27:59-66, 28:1-8; Mark 15:46, 16:1-8; Luke 23:53, 24:1-7; and John 20:1-2—Yeshua was pierced with a sword; Yeshua was killed, buried in a sepulcher and a large stone was placed over the mouth of the sepulcher
II Samuel 18:21—Joab told the Cushite to go tell the good news of Absalom's demise	Matthew 28:6-7 and Mark 16:6-7—Angels told the women to go tell the good news of Yeshua's resurrection
II Samuel 18:27a—The emphasis on the feet of Ahimaaz	Matthew 28:9-10—The women embraced Yeshua's feet
II Samuel 18:29-31—Ahimaaz outran the Cushite to David; Ahimaaz has to step aside and wait for the Cushite to arrive	John 20:3-4—John outran Peter to the tomb; John stepped aside and waited for Peter to arrive
II Samuel 19:3-4—David's men stole back into the city in shame as if they'd lost the battle even though they had won a great victory; David's men had lost heart because of David's lament over Absalom	John 20:19—Yeshua's disciples were hiding in a room for fear of the Jews, as if all hope was lost, when in reality, Yeshua had won the greatest victory; the disciples were heartbroken concerning Yeshua's death
II Samuel 19:5-8 and 11-14—Joab told David he needed to appear before his servants to turn their hearts back to him; David appealed to "flesh and blood" to win the trust of his servants	Luke 24:36-39 and John 20:19-20—Yeshua appeared to His disciples to turn their hearts from unbelief to faith; Yeshua appealed to "flesh and blood" to win the trust of His disciples
II Samuel 19:16-23—David offered forgiveness to Shimei for his sins even though he didn't deserve it	John 20:21-23 and Luke 24:46-49—Yeshua empowered His disciples to forgive sins and commissioned them to preach the forgiveness of sins
II Samuel 19:15-30—Shemei, who had rejected David was later forgiven by David; Mephibosheth's loyalty was questioned by David who thought Mephibosheth had betrayed him; Mephibosheth is distressed that his loyalty is questioned	John 21:15-19—Peter, who had rejected Yeshua, was later forgiven by Yeshua; Peter's loyalty was questioned by Yeshua because Peter had actually betrayed Him; Peter was grieved that his love for Yeshua was being questioned

II Samuel 19:31-39—Barzillai lacked discernment; Barzillai would die an old man and would be able to choose where he would die and be buried; David said to Barzillai, "Come across with me."	**Mark 16:9-14, Luke 24:1-11, 25, 41-43, John 20:25, 21:18-19 and 21:22-23**—Yeshua's disciples lacked discernment, refusing to believe all that He had told them about His resurrection; Peter would die an old man but would not be able to choose where he would die and be buried; Yeshua told Peter, "Follow me."
II Samuel 19:9-10, 22, and 43—Authority to rule the kingdom of Israel was restored to David	**Matthew 28:18-20 and Mark 16:19-20**—All authority in heaven and on earth given to Yeshua
II Samuel 20:1-2—David's newly reestablished kingdom is quickly divided	**Acts 1:4-8**—The disciples question Yeshua about the restoration of the kingdom

Our Last Thematic Moment

The basis of this book is the chiastic structure of II Samuel 15:10 – 20:2. We have seen how the themes of the first half of this chiastic structure are repeated in the second half in reverse order. Furthermore, these literary jewels seem to surface throughout the pages of the Scriptures. Their ubiquitous nature has naturally led me to wonder, if, when the prophets of old penned Scripture, they were aware of the literary style they employed. In other words, did they write in chiastic patterns effortlessly/unconsciously as they were borne along by the Ruach HaKodesh (Holy Spirit), or did they have to sit down and plan each paragraph and sentence?

Although I can't answer this question with certainty, this last excursion into thematic profundity will certainly highlight the question above. II Samuel 19:24-30 records Mephibosheth's approach toward David at his return from exile. You would do well to remember the context. David, acting upon Joab's advice, was able to win the hearts of the men of Judah. As he returned to Jerusalem he stopped at the Jordan River (II Samuel 19:14-15). At this point, the Scripture states that the men of Judah went out to meet King David *at the Jordan River*. Along with them went Shimei and Ziba, Mephibosheth's servant. II Samuel 19:16-23 records Shimei's advance to David and his successful attempt at reconciliation. The next story pertains to Mephibosheth's approach to the king. Finally, II Samuel 19:31-40 records how Barzillai came to escort David *across the Jordan*. Thus, the Scripture has clearly developed the context of Mephibosheth's approach. Before Mephibosheth met King David, the men of Judah, Shimei and Ziba went to see him. Afterwards, Barzillai went to greet the king. The approach by the men of Judah, Shimei, Ziba and Barzillai all occurred *at the Jordan River*.

A closer examination of Mephibosheth's encounter with David is very telling. Please note how the Scripture introduces his approach:

> 24 Now Mephibosheth the son of Saul *came down to meet the king*. And he had not cared for his feet, nor trimmed his mustache, nor washed his clothes, from the day the king departed until the day he returned in peace (II Samuel 19:24).

Considering the context, when the Scripture states how Mephibosheth, "... came down to meet the king," where do you think this event occurred? I would venture to say, "At the Jordan of course. He's coming to meet King David just like the groups of people before and after him." Although that may seem to be the case, please note what is recorded in II Samuel 19:25.

²⁵ So it was, *when he had <u>come to Jerusalem</u> to meet the king* that the king said to him, "Why did you not go with me, Mephibosheth?"

Notice that Mephibosheth approached David, "... when he (Mephibosheth) had come to Jerusalem"! Please, note the phrase, "had come *to* Jerusalem." It appears that Mephibosheth came to see David *in Jerusalem*, not at the Jordan! The placement of II Samuel 19:24-30 (an event that occurred in Jerusalem) between two events that occurred *at the Jordan River* is peculiar indeed, as the following diagram illustrates.

II Samuel 19:15b – 23
The men of Judah, Shimei and Ziba approached David

At the Jordan

II Samuel 19:24 - 30
Mephibosheth approached David

In Jerusalem

II Samuel 19:31-40
Barzillai approached David

At the Jordan

Amazingly, not every translator translates II Samuel 19:25 in the same manner. Here are a few different translations of this passage.

- So it was, when he had *come <u>to</u> Jerusalem* to meet the king that the king said to him, "Why did you not go with me, Mephibosheth?" (New King James Version)
- And when he *came <u>to</u> Jerusalem* to meet the king, David said to him, "Why did you not go with me, Mephibosheth?" (Amplified Version)
- And when he *came <u>to</u> Jerusalem* to meet the king, the king said to him, "Why did you not go with me, Mephibosheth?" (English Standard Version)
- It was when he *came <u>from</u> Jerusalem* to meet the king that the king said to him, "Why did you not go with me, Mephibosheth?" (New American Standard Bible)
- It was when he *came <u>from</u> Jerusalem* to meet the king, that the king said to him, "Why did you not go with me, Mephibosheth?" (New American Standard Version)

- When he **came _from_ Jerusalem** to meet the king, the king asked him, "Why didn't you go with me, Mephibosheth?" (New International Version)
- Next Mephibosheth grandson of Saul **arrived _from_ Jerusalem** to welcome the king. He hadn't combed his hair or trimmed his beard or washed his clothes from the day the king left until the day he returned safe and sound. The king said, "And why didn't you come with me, Mephibosheth?"[67]
- Now Mephibosheth, Saul's grandson, **came down from Jerusalem** to meet the king. He had not cared for his feet, trimmed his beard, or washed his clothes since the day the king left Jerusalem. "Why didn't you come with me, Mephibosheth?" the king asked him.[68]

As you can see, some versions use the preposition, *from* whereas, others use the preposition, *to*. Does it really make a difference which one we use? Yes, it does. If Mephibosheth is coming *from* Jerusalem, it means he may have approached David at the Jordan *after* having left from Jerusalem. On the other hand, if Mephibosheth is coming *to* Jerusalem, it means that David has already crossed the Jordan and returned to Jerusalem. In other words, Mephibosheth is visiting David *after* his return to Jerusalem, not *at the Jordan* during his initial return.

The Hebrew word translated, *come* is בָא, the Qal stem perfect, third person masculine singular form of the root word, בוא, which means to go in, enter or come.[69] The sense of this word is almost always to go or come *into* something as opposed to going or coming *from* somewhere. For example, different stems and conjugations of this verb, בוא are used throughout II Samuel 19. Please note how in each instance the sense is to go or come *into* a place as opposed to *from* a place. All quotes are from the NKJV.

- II Samuel 19:3 – And the people stole back (לָבוֹא) *into* the city that day . . .
- II Samuel 19:5 – Then Joab *came into* (וַיָּבֹא) the house to the king . . .
- II Samuel 19:15 – And Judah *came to* (בָא) Gilgal . . .
- II Samuel 19:25 – So it was, when he had *come to* (בָא) Jerusalem . . .

As you can see, translating בָא as, *come to* (instead of come *from*) in II Samuel 19:25 is consistent with the translation of other forms of the verb בוא throughout II Samuel 19. Furthermore, the Etymological Dictionary of Biblical Hebrew states that the fundamental meaning of the verbal root בוא means to *come to an attractive place*.[70] This should make one wonder why some translators translate בָא as come *from* instead of come *to*.

I believe the answer is simple. Many translators try to smooth out the Hebrew based on their *interpretation* of the text. Because the Hebrew seems to be awkward at times, translators will abandon the normal meaning of the Hebrew and try to "help" us understand the text by translating it in a manner inconsistent with the literal translation. As stated earlier, the context of the verses immediately before and after the story of Mephibosheth's approach to David is clearly *at the Jordan River*. Knowing this, some translators are uncomfortable translating בָא as *come to*, because such a translation is not "consistent" with the immediate context. However, the Hebrew word means to come *into* not *from*; therefore it is best to translate the primary meaning and find another explanation for the apparent deviation from context.

An examination of the last two translations reveals that not only is the word, *from* substituted for the word, *to*, the basic meaning of the verb בוא, meaning *coming*, is changed (*arrived from* and *came from*) to convey the meaning that Mephibosheth traveled *from Jerusalem to the Jordan* to meet the king. The Message translators chose to translate the Hebrew word בוא as *arrived from*, whereas, the New Living Translation chose to translate it as *came down from*. These two translations, along with the New International version make extensive use of a translation technique called dynamic equivalence, which attempts to convey the thought expressed in a source text at the expense of literalness, word order, and grammatical voice if necessary. In other words, their main concern is making a story understandable in the language it's being translated into, not preserving word-for-word translation. Another approach to Scripture translation, formal equivalence, endeavors to preserve word-for-word translation even at the expense of natural expression in the target language. As you can imagine, as we compare the translations above, The Message and New Living Translation are translations that use dynamic equivalence, whereas the New King James Version and the English Standard Version utilize formal equivalence. The New American Standard Bible also uses formal equivalence; however, in this instance I think they fell short by translating בוא as came from. Ostensibly, the New International Version tries to strike a balance between the two techniques. In my estimation the NIV uses more dynamic equivalence than it should.

So what has happened here? Well, if it is true that Mephibosheth *came to Jerusalem* to meet King then he obviously did not approach David *at the Jordan* with the men of Judah, Shimei, Ziba and Barzillai! Therefore we must question why the story of Mephibosheth is recorded in II Samuel 19:24-30. Chronologically, it should not appear until after David reaches Jerusalem since that's where their encounter took place.

The answer to this conundrum is similar to why we saw a picture of the death, burial and resurrection of the Messiah in the first half of our chiastic structure, whereas these pictures shouldn't occur until the second half of the chiastic structure (in its proper chronological location). The story of Mephibosheth's approach to David (II Samuel 19:24-30) is added within the context of II Samuel 19:15b-40 (even though it is chronologically out of context) because it is meant to balance the chiastic presentation of the story of David's flight from Absalom! A portion of our main chiastic structure is shown below. Except for points A and A' the other elements of the chiastic structure share the dominant theme of how people have either come to show support for David or receive mercy from him. Note how element D', the story of Mephibosheth's rendezvous with David (in Jerusalem, not at the Jordan) has been added so as to balance element D where Mephibosheth is the subject.

A) II Samuel 15:10-12—Absalom *rebelled against the king*; "When you hear the *sound of the shofar*"; Absalom *stole the hearts of the men of Israel*; "There's *no one before the king to understand you*"

   B) II Samuel 15:13-24—The kings servants said, "Whatever my lord the king decides, *your servants are ready*"; Ittai said, "In whatever place my lord the king will be – *whether for death or life – there your servant will be*;" David and his servants *pass through the Kidron valley*

      C) II Samuel 15:32-37—Hushai *came to meet the king*; the king stated "*You will be a burden to me*"; "You will *defeat Ahithophel's council* for me; *stay behind*"

         D) II Samuel 16:1-4—Ziba *came to meet the king*; the king *asked a question about Mephibosheth*; the king *gave Mephibosheth's property to Ziba*

The Scroll of the Gospel of David

    E) II Samuel 16:5-13—*David came to Bahurim*; Shimei *came out to meet David*; *Abishai wanted to kill Shimei*; *David forgave Shimei*
    E`) II Samuel 19:16-23—*Shimei was from Bahurim*; he *hastened to meet the king*; *Abishai wanted to kill Shimei*; Shimei *begged David for forgiveness*
    D`) II Samuel 19:24-30—Mephibosheth *came to meet the king*; the king *asked Mephibosheth a question*; *Mephibosheth and Ziba must divide the property*
    C`) II Samuel 19:31-39—Barzillai *came to meet the king*; "*I will be a burden to you*"; Barzillai states that he has no discernment; Let me *stay back*
    B`) II Samuel 19:40-43—The men of Israel and Judah argue over who is *more loyal to the king*; David and his servants *pass over the Jordan*
A`) II Samuel 20:1-2—*Sheba rebelled against the king*; he *sounded the shofars*; the men of *Israel followed Sheba*; "*we have no part in David*"

Thus, to reiterate, Mephibosheth met David *in Jerusalem*, not at the Jordan. However, the writer of II Samuel inserted that story within the context of others who met David *at the Jordan*. This is a classic example where thematic considerations outweigh chronological considerations in the determination of where facts are placed within a story. The story of Mephibosheth's meeting with David (in Jerusalem) should not occur chronologically until after II Samuel 19:43 between elements A' and B'. From this last example, do you think the writer of II Samuel wrote this story effortlessly as he was borne along by the Ruach HaKodesh or did he sit down and plan his presentation of the story chiastically, inserting stories here and there to make this work of art fit like a well-made puzzle? Well, I can't answer that question for sure. But I do know this – Adonai has spoken clearly through the text and it is my desire that others would see things I've seen, hear what I've heard and understand what I've understood. This has been a very intense study; however, the message is simple:

The Messiah would come, suffer, die, be buried for three days and three nights, raise from the dead and repentance from sins would be preached in His name throughout the nations.

This, my friends, is the most prophesied event in the entirety of your Bible!

Endnotes

Intoduction Endnotes

¹ Patai, Raphael, The Messiah Texts, Avon Books, © 1979, p. vii.

² The meanings of chiastic structures and parallelisms will be covered in the main text.

Text Endnotes

¹ Adonai is the Hebrew word meaning *my Lord*.

² Yeshua is the Hebrew name for Jesus.

³ Tanakh is a Hebrew acronym for the three divisions of the Old Testament – the Torah (first five books of Moses), Neviim (the Prophets) and Khetuvim (Writings).

⁴ This phrase concerning death being swallowed up in victory is a quote of Isaiah 25:8. It was used by Paul (II Corinthians 15:54) when speaking of the resurrection of believers and our ultimate victory over death!

⁵ Genesis 3-4 is almost exactly connected to II Samuel 13-14 and only partially connected to II Samuel 11-12. These passages were added just to show how extensively passages are thematically connected in the scriptures. It also demonstrates that passages have multiple thematic connections. Since our primary aim is to show how Genesis 3-4 is thematically connected to II Samuel 13-14, I won't comment much on the connection between Genesis 3-4 and II Samuel 11-12 other than to whet your appetite for thematic study by saying that this connection is a powerful one used to show how Adonai performs character development thematically. As you can see, ***Absalom is clearly thematically connected to Cain***. And I'm sure that doesn't surprise you at all.

⁶ Note that the curse against Chavah involved a curse on her and childbirth. In II Samuel 12, the baby born to Bathsheba and David died.

⁷ The main theme connecting this section of the table pertains to separation. Chavah was separated from the Tree of Life and Tamar was banished from Amnon's house. The wording of David's response to the child's death hints at separation—"But now he is dead; why should I fast? Can I bring him back again? I shall go to him, but he shall not return to me (II Samuel 12:23)."

⁸ When you read II Samuel 14, which is the story of the woman who went before David with a story concerning her two sons, note that the story is about how one son murdered his brother in the field! This story is meant to parallel the story of Absalom and Amnon, and, as we now see, the story of Cain and Abel.

⁹ The Tanakh. The Artscroll Series, Stone Edition. Brooklyn: Mesorah Publications Ltd., 1996, p. 763.

¹⁰ Parallelisms are similar to chiastic structures except that the themes of the second half of the story are presented in the same order as in the first half.

¹¹ Remember Absalom's hair in the tree, not falling to the earth when he died.

¹² Why do I state that Adonai has shown us this through His infinite wisdom? Because He is the one Who inspired the chiastic structure. We, as humans, have nothing to do with their existence. We can only find them. The beauty of studying thematically is that we simply allow Him to point these things out to us. Finding the chiastic structures He has placed in His word is our blessed task. But always remember, He placed them there. They did not originate in the heart of man. Therefore, when you find them, you have found a treasure, placed there by your heavenly Father.

¹³ Remember that a seer is another name for a prophet. A prophet is simply *someone who speaks God's words*! Therefore, it is easy to see how this passage is thematically connected to II Samuel 16:23, which states that the words of Ahithophel were like the *oracles of God*!

¹⁴ Remember what we learned in Chapter 2. The covering of the head and going about barefoot are outward signs of shame! Remember how Tamar put her hands on her head expressing shame after Amnon raped her? Do you think it's a coincidence that the passage relating how Absalom had relations with his father's concubines is thematically connected to David showing outward signs of shame through our chiastic structure? Only Adonai could make this literary masterpiece work out.

¹⁵ This is also confirmed in Acts 1:18-21 — ¹⁸Now this man *purchased a field with the wages of iniquity*; and falling headlong, he burst open in the middle and all his entrails gushed out. ¹⁹ And it became known to all those dwelling in Jerusalem; so that field is called in their own language, *Akel Dama, that is, Field of Blood*.²⁰ "For it is written in the Book of Psalms: 'Let his dwelling place be desolate, And let no one live in it'; and, 'Let another take his office.'

¹⁶ Remember, in the Thematic Moments section of Chapter 2, Absalom was thematically connected to Cain, Esau, Adonijah and hasatan. Now, he's thematically connected to Ahithophel, the one who casts the shadow of Judas, who betrayed Yeshua. As you can see, Adonai is "piling on" to make sure we understand that Absalom's character is, well . . . let's just say not so wholesome.

¹⁷ This excludes II Samuel 17:14 and 24-25, which we've already discussed.

¹⁸ I haven't told you the Messianic significance of most of II Samuel 17:14-23 yet because we must cover more background material to make it understandable. However, once we understand the Messianic significance of these verses you will clearly see that it does not match the chronological order of the Gospels.

¹⁹ The verses of this chiastic structure are based on the numberings found in The Tanakh. The Artscroll Series, Stone Edition. Brooklyn: Mesorah Publications Ltd., 1996, p. 1373-1675.

²⁰ And Nicodemus, who at first came to Jesus by night, also came, bringing a mixture of **myrrh** and aloes, about a hundred pounds (John 19:39).

The Scroll of the Gospel of David

---

²¹ Many Messianic prophesies pertain to the suffering, death, burial and resurrection of the Messiah. Each prophecy is like a snapshot of various stages of Messianic prophecy. There is no single prophecy that contains every element of the Messiah's life and mission. For example, even though II Samuel 15:10 – 20:2 and Daniel 6:1-23 are both pictures of the suffering of the Messiah, II Samuel 15:10 – 20:2 does not contain all of the Messianic information contained in Daniel 6:1-23 as you shall soon see.

²² The verses of this chiastic structure are based on the numberings found in The Tanakh. The Artscroll Series, Stone Edition. Brooklyn: Mesorah Publications Ltd., 1996, p. 1793.

²³ The Tanakh. The Artscroll Series, Stone Edition. Brooklyn: Mesorah Publications Ltd., 1996, p. 531.

²⁴ This is usually done through the Sign of the Messiah (see chapter two).

²⁵ Whenever a chiastic structure is separated by lots of text – as in the present example – there is no central axis. As you can see, the two halves of this chiastic structure are in two separate books!

²⁶ Some form of the number three (3, 30, 300, 3,000) appears eleven times within Judges 13-16? Remember, Adonai uses repetition. You can barely read more than two paragraphs without running into a three in Judges 13-16. Perhaps Adonai is trying to tell us something about Samson?

²⁷ Do you remember another person whose birth was announced by an angel? That's right, Messiah Yeshua.

²⁸ Judges 16:30b — So the dead that he killed at his **death** were more than he had killed in his **life**.

²⁹ I Peter 5:8 — Be sober, be vigilant; because your adversary *the devil, as a roaring lion*, walketh about, seeking whom he may devour.

³⁰ Please be aware that this is only the Torah's foundational definition of salvation. Salvation actually does include forgiveness, wholeness, restoration, the resurrection, etc. However, you must remember that the Torah is only giving you the foundational definition of salvation as seen in Exodus 14. The rest of the teaching on salvation is developed throughout the Tanakh and New Testament.

³¹ According to II Samuel 18:1, David has thousands with him.

³² The Tanakh. The Artscroll Series, Stone Edition. Brooklyn: Mesorah Publications Ltd., 1996, p. 769.

³³ Remember, some references in this book are listed according to the Artscroll Tanakh. In most English versions this verse will be II Samuel 19:2.

³⁴ Most English translations, translate the Hebrew word הַתְּשֻׁעָה as victory. Although it is true that this word can be translated victory, salvation or deliverance, in this instance, I believe it is best translated as salvation. Why do I say this? Am I stating this based on my linguistic knowledge? No! I'm stating this because we know the Torah's foundational definition of salvation. And as we have seen, this story is literally pregnant with allusions to the splitting of the Red Sea, the foundational teaching on salvation.

³⁵ See the Running Chart of the Thematic Connections Between II Samuel 15:10 – 20:2 and the Gospels for the complete set of connections to the Gospel accounts.

³⁶ This translation is from the Artscroll Stone Edition of The Tanakh. The Artscroll Series, Stone Edition. Brooklyn: Mesorah Publications Ltd., 1996, p. 625.

³⁷ As you begin to study thematically, you will notice that outlining is an invaluable tool.

[38] The Tanakh. The Artscroll Series, Stone Edition. Brooklyn: Mesorah Publications Ltd., 1996, p. 799 states, "The ground [*virtually*] burst from their noise."

[39] The Tanakh. The Artscroll Series, Stone Edition. Brooklyn: Mesorah Publications Ltd., 1996, p. 771.

[40] The Crosswalk online Hebrew Lexicon can be found at http://bible.crosswalk.com/Lexicons/Hebrew/.

[41] As you begin to learn about Messianic prophecy, it is easy to assume that the pictures of the Messiah will always be in the lives of the actual Messianic figures. This is what I thought initially. I didn't understand why I could see the sign of the Messiah (i.e., the sign of resurrection) and pictures of Messianic prophecy in the lives of people other than the ones I knew to be Messianic figures. It's a mistake to only look to the lives of the main Messianic figures to see Messianic prophecy. The example of the cup bearer and the baker should make this abundantly clear.

[42] Other connections between David and Absalom are the fact that both of them had sexual relations with someone else's wife and 2) both of them ordered someone else's death.

[43] More New Testament references to the execution, burial and resurrection of the Messiah will be noted later.

[44] The Greek word translated as cross was actually a vertical wooden stake with a crossbar shaped more like a T than the cross popularized by Christianity.

[45] It is also easy to thematically connect Absalom to the baker since both died by being hung on a tree and both had vegetation associated with their heads.

[46] Hailstones are simply solidified water. Thus, the Egyptians were drowned by having water poured upon them, whereas the five Amorite kings were bludgeoned by having solidified water pelt them. In both stories, Adonai used a form of water to destroy Am Yisrael's enemies! That's a thematic connection if I've ever seen one!

[47] "We," meaning modern folks trained in linear, Greek-Roman thinking patterns.

[48] A brief perusal of Psalm 110:1-7 will clearly reveal itself as Messianic. Furthermore, the writer of the book of Hebrews applies the prophecy of Psalm 110 to the Messiah Yeshua (Hebrews 5, 6 and 7).

[49] I will use these two terms interchangeably.

[50] Remember, Besor is the Hebrew word for good news!

[51] These passages are thematically connected to those in Category I through similar words or themes.

[52] Actually, I believe this verse has a remez (hint) teaching concerning the good news, just like verses in Category IV. I just haven't discovered it yet. Do you see the connection?

[53] Although it would be nice to think that there is a clear time separation between the fulfillments of these two streams of prophecy, we will soon see that there is actually some overlap. In other words, a certain aspect of the good news—the aspect dealing with the reign of Adonai on the earth—actually occurs during the first and second advents!

[54] Remember, this passage is a Category I scripture which will be fulfilled at Yeshua's Second Advent.

[55] The Tanakh. The Artscroll Series, Stone Edition. Brooklyn: Mesorah Publications Ltd., 1996, p. 771.

[56] If you are going to study the Scriptures thematically (which I think is the way Adonai intended) then you should always look at a Jewish translation alongside a non-Jewish transla-

tion. In many instances, the Jewish translation will help you see connections better. However, Jewish translations aren't perfect either, so use both when you can.

[57] I will discuss why II Samuel 18:19-32 only partially fulfills Isaiah 52:7-10 in the next section pertaining to the Messianic significance of these verses.

[58] Although Yeshua had already ascended to heaven, this event occurred on Shavuot immediately after the death, burial and resurrection of Yeshua at His first coming.

[59] Remember, the story of Absalom's demise includes the details of his death, burial in the pit and the monument he had built. In Chapter 6, we connected these three events to Yeshua's death, burial and resurrection.

[60] Words Mean Things Series II, by Bradford Scott, The Wildbranch Ministry.

[61] See Chapter 3 where we show quite conclusively that although Mephibosheth was truly faithful to David, he did not know whether to believe Mephibosheth or not.

[62] Remember that Hushai didn't actually betray David. David had asked Hushai to return to Jerusalem and be his spy, passing on secret information to David. Hushai only appeared to betray David in the eyes of Absalom.

[63] Pun intended.

[64] As we saw, Mephibosheth had remained true to David, but David did not understand this. Thus, David forgave Mephibosheth based on what he understood.

[65] You will recall that Peter denied Yeshua three times. It is significant that Yeshua questioned Peter's loyalty three times by asking Peter if he loved Him. Obviously, this gave Peter the chance to repent for those three denials.

[66] There is no direct reference to the relationship between Barzillai and Chimham. Thus, I assume Chimham was Barzillai's son.

[67] The Message – II Samuel 19:24-25 is listed.

[68] New Living Translation – II Samuel 19:24-25 is listed.

[69] Basics of Biblical Hebrew by Gary D. Pratico and Miles V. Van Pelt, Zondervan, 2001, p. 449.

[70] Etymological Dictionary of Biblical Hebrew by Samson Raphael Hirsch, Clark, 1999, p. 22.

LaVergne, TN USA
28 August 2009
156283LV00003B/1/P